Altruism
and Helping Behavior

Social Psychological Studies of
Some Antecedents and Consequences

Contributors

JUSTIN ARONFREED

LEONARD BERKOWITZ

ELLEN BERSCHEID

JAMES H. BRYAN

JOHN M. DARLEY

CARL H. FELLNER

JONATHAN L. FREEDMAN

HARVEY A. HORNSTEIN

HARRY KAUFMANN

BIBB LATANÉ

MELVIN J. LERNER

PERRY LONDON

JACQUELINE R. MACAULAY

JOHN R. MARSHALL

EDNA I. RAWLINGS

DAVID ROSENHAN

JOHN SCHOPLER

SHALOM H. SCHWARTZ

ELAINE WALSTER

G. WILLIAM WALSTER

ALTRUISM
AND HELPING BEHAVIOR

Social Psychological Studies
of Some Antecedents and Consequences

EDITED BY

J. Macaulay
and
L. Berkowitz

Department of Psychology
University of Wisconsin
Madison, Wisconsin

ACADEMIC PRESS   New York and London   1970

ACADEMIC PRESS, INC.
111 Fifth Avenue, New York, New York 10003

United Kingdom Edition published by
ACADEMIC PRESS, INC. (LONDON) LTD.
Berkeley Square House, London W1X 6BA

LIBRARY OF CONGRESS CATALOG CARD NUMBER: 74-86370

PRINTED IN THE UNITED STATES OF AMERICA

List of Contributors

Numbers in parentheses indicate the pages on which the authors' contributions begin.

Justin Aronfreed (103), *Department of Psychology, University of Pennsylvania, Philadelphia, Pennsylvania*

Leonard Berkowitz (1, 143), *Department of Psychology, University of Wisconsin, Madison, Wisconsin*

Ellen Berscheid (179), *Department of Psychology, University of Minnesota, Minneapolis, Minnesota*

James H. Bryan (61), *Department of Psychology, Northwestern University, Evanston, Illinois*

John M. Darley (13, 83), *Department of Psychology, Princeton University, Princeton, New Jersey*

Carl H. Fellner (269), *Department of Psychiatry, University of Wisconsin Medical School, Madison, Wisconsin*

Jonathan L. Freedman (155), *Department of Psychology, Columbia University, New York, New York*

Harvey A. Hornstein (29), *Department of Psychology, Teachers College, Columbia University, New York, New York*

Harry Kaufmann (77), *Department of Psychology, Hunter College, New York, New York*

Bibb Latané (13, 83), *The Ohio State University, Columbus, Ohio*

Melvin J. Lerner (205), *Department of Behavioral Science, University of Kentucky, Lexington, Kentucky*

Perry London (241), *Department of Psychology, University of Southern California, Los Angeles, California*

Jacqueline R. Macaulay (1, 43), *Department of Psychology, University of Wisconsin, Madison, Wisconsin*

John R. Marshall (269), *Department of Psychiatry, University of Wisconsin Medical School, Madison, Wisconsin*

Edna I. Rawlings (163), *Department of Psychiatry, University of Iowa, Iowa City, Iowa*

David Rosenhan (251), *Department of Psychology, Swarthmore College, Swarthmore, Pennsylvania*

John Schopler (231), *Department of Psychology, University of North Carolina, Chapel Hill, North Carolina*

Shalom H. Schwartz (127), *Department of Sociology, University of Wisconsin, Madison, Wisconsin*

Elaine Walster (179), *Department of Sociology, University of Wisconsin, Madison, Wisconsin*

G. William Walster (179), *Department of Educational Psychology, University of Wisconsin, Madison, Wisconsin*

Preface

This volume represents a progress report on research in the area of altruism and helping. It is directed, as our subtitle indicates, toward social psychologists. Its concerns are chiefly those of the theorist and researcher in this field, not those of the practitioner or the philosopher. Nonetheless, much in this volume should be of interest to any practitioner or philosopher — or social critic or plain "people-watcher" — who is interested in the origins of altruism, in behavior in public places, and in social interaction generally. One impetus to this research has been a series of newspaper stories in the past few years describing the apparent callousness of people in the face of unusual demands for help. The studies and theoretical discussions collected here can help us understand such incidents. By identifying important conditions governing reactions to people in need, these papers are the initial steps in the development of systematic ideas about help-giving and altruism.

The present collection is also significant because of the varied methodology described in these papers. Some of the research reported here was carried out in carefully controlled and complex laboratory situations, using students of various ages as subjects. Other research was conducted "in the field." This field research has involved not only the traditional interviewing and observing of selected samples, but also the transplantation of controlled experimental designs to the thoroughfares and gathering places of our communities, with "subjects" consisting of nonstudent adults engaged in their usual pursuits.

As editors, we found our contributors' work to be thoroughly interesting. Our only regret is that we could not include papers by all those researchers whose work we know to be relevant and valuable to our purposes. The usual pressures of time and scheduling must be blamed for our omissions. Even with omissions, however, this volume covers a wide range of work in the field of altruism and helping. We are hopeful that the result of collecting it into one volume will stimulate further research to deepen our understanding of prosocial behavior.

Contents

Altruism
and Helping Behavior

Social Psychological Studies of
Some Antecedents and Consequences

OVERVIEW

Jacqueline R. Macaulay and Leonard Berkowitz

This book is an outgrowth of a conference held at the University of Wisconsin in June, 1968, dealing with research on helping and altruism. The topics, while not new to social science generally, were relatively novel for experimental social psychology, and the present collection is representative of the current state of research in this area. We see here diverse exploratory approaches to the study of altruism and still-developing theoretical conceptions. We also see a desire to grapple with important social problems, an inclination to study behavior involving questions of moral conduct and conscience, and a willingness to carry out experiments in nonlaboratory settings—situations less limited in stimuli and behavior alternatives than the laboratory.

When we came to organize these papers, we found several possible schemes for doing so. The material could be arranged in terms of specific conceptual themes such as social influence, equity and cost–benefit considerations, social norms and ideals of social responsibility, empathy, guilt, and so on. However, since most papers touched on more than one concept, this sort of organization was very difficult to arrange. Our organizational decisions were somewhat arbitrary, then, and hinged on similarities which may be more apparent to the editors than to the readers. In this overview we will briefly describe the papers in terms of some of the concepts which we feel are most central to the collection as a whole.

1

WHAT IS ALTRUISM?

There are several definitional problems that are yet to be solved. We will begin by trying to dispose of (or evade) one of them: What is "altruism?" For Darley and Latane, the researchable question really is "What determines, in a particular situation, whether or not one person helps another in distress?" By impli-·cation in this definition, any behavior which benefits another in need, regardless of the helper's motives, is altruistic. A very different kind of answer to this question is given by Aronfreed. He identifies a basic motive for altruism and confines usage of the term to behavior which meets this motivational standard. For Aronfreed, altruism is a dispositional component (not a specific form) of behavior which is controlled by anticipation of its consequences for another individual. He regards empathy as essential for altruism. Unless the actor responds empathically to social cues conveying another's experience (or to cognitive representation of another's experience), the behavior cannot be called altruistic. External outcomes to the actor are irrelevant, according to this definition. Behavior controlled by expectation of increased self-esteem is also said to be nonaltruistic. The actor must experience empathic or vicarious pleasure, or relief of distress, as a result of behaving in a way that has consequences for another.

Whether or not empathy is essential to altruism is probably a definitional matter which the reader will have to decide for himself. However, Aronfreed makes a valuable point in questioning very broad usages of the term "altruism." Many different motives may impel one individual to benefit another. Helpful behavior may stem from social pressures or expectations that all costs incurred in giving aid will be repaid, perhaps with interest, one way or another. It would be stretching the common meaning of altruism to include such acts.

While the Darley and Latane conception of altruism seems too general, Aronfreed's may be too narrow. For one thing, several kinds of empathic reactions may influence helping. In addition to experiencing vicariously the relief felt by the person whose need has been met, we might also experience vicariously the helper's satisfaction and be motivated to experience such satisfaction directly. In a study referred to by Berkowitz in this volume, empathy with a helpful and rewarded model presumably led subjects to assist someone else similarly. Conversely, empathic experience of the distress (or guilt) felt by someone who had caused another person to suffer might conceivably lead people to avoid feeling guilty themselves by alleviating others' suffering.

It seems somewhat arbitrary, then, to confine usage of the term "altruism" to behavior motivated by empathic experience of another's satisfaction or need. The origins of altruism can be very complex, as London's paper vividly shows.

We prefer to define altruism more generally, as behavior carried out to benefit another without anticipation of rewards from external sources. This definition is similar to Rosenhan's "socially autonomous altruism." Of course, it would be difficult to be sure in any given study that a particular act meets this definition of altruism, but we can lessen the possibility that our subjects are anticipating rewards by using various experimental controls.

SITUATIONAL DETERMINANTS OF HELPING

The first section of this volume concerns·situational determinants of helpfulness. The papers here deal with conditions external to the actor which affect his behavior. The explanation of the effects of these conditions, however, can largely be given in terms of the diverse theoretical factors more explicitly dealt with in subsequent sections of the book.

Latané and Darley studied situational variations which affect people's readiness to help out in emergencies. Their subjects were put in novel, stressful situations which seemed to call for immediate action. When the subjects were alone, they were likely to respond with help fairly quickly. If they were with several strangers, however, they were much slower to give aid, and often no action at all was forthcoming. Latané and Darley explain these findings in terms of diffusion of responsibility. They noted in one study particularly that their unhelpful subjects were not apathetic or indifferent to the emergency, but instead seemed anxious and distressed. Thus the explanation for their results does not lie in the subjects's callous rejection of social responsibility. Instead, Latané and Darley propose, when others are present two things may happen. First, each individual's feelings of personal responsibility for helping are weaker and so the various costs which may result from offering help loom relatively large. Second, the apparent lack of concern of the others present (who actually may just be trying to look calm while they figure things out) leads all of those present to interpret the situation as not very serious.

Hornstein studied another kind of situational factor: information about a helping model's reactions to his own helpfulness. Models similar to the observer who expressed positive feelings as a result of their decision to be helpful were more likely to be emulated than were dissimilar models expressing the same feelings or similar models showing annoyance as a result of their helpfulness. Hornstein discusses his results in terms of information about the rewards and costs of being helpful. An explanation in terms of empathy might also be advanced.

In a second study, Hornstein found that when the helpful model made a personal decision to be helpful, contrary to the normative advice of friends or contrary to previous negative experience with others, he was relatively likely to be emulated by observers. That is, if the model's assistance appeared to be a response to external pressures (which would not be operative for the observer), the observer was less likely to be helpful in a similar way. Hornstein sees his results as supportive of the hypothesis that attribution processes affect behavior: The observers attribute motives of idealism (e.g., adherence to internalized norms) to a model who acts contrary to external pressures.

Macaulay demonstrated that not only generosity but also selfishness on the part of a model increased charity by others when the social standards calling for such charity were relatively clear. She also found some indirect evidence of guilt feelings on the part of people not making a donation: Those who did not donate themselves after seeing the model donate tended to downgrade the charity. These results can be explained in terms of norm salience, whether the model adheres to charitable ideals or flaunts them.

Bryan found that generous models increased generosity and selfish models increased selfishness. Unlike Macaulay's results, however, these results would not seem well served by a normative interpretation. Bryan's models did some preaching, as well as acting, in an effort to make norms salient. The preaching did affect the child-observers' judgment of the model, but neither preaching nor inconsistency between preaching and the model's behavior influenced observer behavior. Bryan suggests that the effect of the model's actions may be best understood in terms of disinhibition of action through provision of information about permissible behavior in the situation. Only action, perhaps, can do this for children; awareness of norms will not serve as a disinhibitor.

SOCIAL NORMS AND THE SOCIALIZATION OF ALTRUISM

Kaufmann's study provides an interesting note in juxtaposition with the results of preaching by Bryan's models. A person who was said to allow harm to happen to another—who did not intervene to help out in an emergency—was less disapproved of by Kaufmann's subjects if the law was said not to require him to help and if the potential victim did not come to harm than if the reverse was the case. On the basis of Bryan's and Kaufmann's studies we can conclude that the preaching implicit in legal sanction and the actual preaching of people like Bryan's models do affect moral judgment. However, Bryan's results also suggest that, at least among children, the relationship between norms and behavior may be very weak and perhaps even nonexistent at times.

Darley and Latané make another point which weakens the normative theory of altruism: While we can invoke norms to explain everything, there is no really good evidence that we do think about norms in the heat of the moment. Rather, we may be well trained to give post hoc normative explanations of our behavior, often in order to justify our actions. Furthermore, some situations are complex enough to elicit contradictory standards of conduct.

Darley and Latané describe several investigations of behavior in public settings where normative considerations would seem to be relevant. However, a normative theory of altruism does not seem to offer the most satisfactory interpretation of their results. In the first series of studies they found that compliance with a request was high when compliance was not costly or if some information was offered with the request. The more familiar the environment in another pair of studies, the more help was given to someone in need. In a further investigation of help giving in public places they found that people in a subway were most reluctant to correct someone who had given erroneous information in answer to a question when the misinformer seemed belligerent or when the question had been directed solely to the misinformer. When the requester had just shown himself to be a helpful person or looked to be from out of town, observers were relatively likely to offer help. However, the effect was not great enough to reach significance. Finally, Darley and Latané describe a study of contagion of playfulness: A disapproving onlooker in a Grand Central Station waiting room decreased the number of people who would join in an apparently spontaneous frisbee game, but only for as long as she remained in the situation. Darley and Latané feel that these results are explained more satisfactorily in terms of the observers' expectations of rewards and costs for certain actions than in terms of a normative model.

Aronfreed offers an analysis of the socialization of altruism which may also explain altruistic behavior better than the concept of internalized norms. In the experiments described by Aronfreed, subjects experienced pleasure or distress concomitant with cues indicating that another was also experiencing pleasure of distress. The subjects learned through experience or observation how the other's pleasure or relief from distress was produced. When they later were placed in a situation where they could give this pleasure or relief of distress to another, and the appropriate cues for such behavior were present, they tended to act for the benefit of the other person without apparent benefit to themselves. Aronfreed maintains that only when children learn to experience another's feelings empathically or vicariously (when there is "coupling of potentially rein-forcing changes of affectivity to social cues . . . about the experience of others") will they behave in a truly altruistic fashion.

Schwartz offers an analysis of the factors hypothesized to produce altruism at the adult level. This analysis includes the concept of norms as determinants of the direction that certain cognitive processes relevant to altruism will take. In order for altruistic action to occur, Schwartz maintains that there must be aware-ness that one's behavior has consequences for others. The second essential factor in altruism is ascription to one's self of some personal responsibility for another's fate. Norms enter this theoretical model once the actor becomes aware that his behavior has consequences for others: Altruistic norms are the social rules specifying when one should ascribe responsibility to the self for what happens to another. Situational and personality factors enter into this; awareness of consequences, ascription of responsibility, and the intervening internalized norms are more characteristic of some people than of others. Schwartz describes a study in which paper-and-pencil test assessments of these personality character-istics were compared with the subject's reputation for responsible behavior with his peers. Those subjects who scored high on both awareness of consequences and ascription of responsibility were rated as more responsible, but the two charac-teristics were not related to each other.

Berkowitz suggests that self-concern dampens altruism and his paper in this volume presents evidence to support this hypothesis. To the extent that we are self-concerned, we are not likely to recognize the consequences of our behavior for others, to empathize with others, to be aware of norms dictating responsibility for others, and perhaps are concerned with equity considerations at the expense of others' needs, etc. The research Berkowitz describes indi-cates that variation in the individual's internal state—in the degree of self-preoccupation—is at least a partial determinant of whether cues for prosocial behavior will be effective.

GUILT, EQUITY, JUSTICE, AND RECIPROCATION

In the third section of this volume are five papers which have in common themes involving equalization of rewards and costs among various participants in situations where norms of altruism, restitution, or reciprocation would seem to apply. Freedman deals with the desire to expiate guilt (to pay off, in one way or another, debts incurred through action which harms another) as a motive for helpful acts. In the research he summarizes, people induced to feel guilty (or assumed to feel guilty by the experimenter) showed a high degree of yielding to requests for help. Expiation of guilt, he indicates, can take several forms. For example, in addition to reparation, one can help someone other than the victim. Even confession seems to relieve guilt somewhat. Freedman notes that the vagueness of the guilt concept is a problem, but argues convincingly that some such aversive reaction to the transgression must be postulated in order to deal with the harm–doers' responses to their own behavior.

Rawlings adds the notion of anticipatory guilt to the traditional concept of reactive guilt. She found that female subjects most often reduced the pain inflicted on a peer at the cost of some pain to themselves if they had just hurt another (reactive guilt) or merely observed someone else being hurt. The subjects in this latter condition (presumably now well aware of an ideal that other people should not be hurt) could have felt guilty as a consequence of their temptation not to aid the second person—or they may have been sensitized to sympathy with this girl. Altruism in this condition was also related to the subjects' self-report of having experienced childhood socialization techniques likely to lead to internalization of norms. Thus, the altruists in this condition could have been responding to norms.

Walster, Berscheid, and Walster discuss the consequences of having transgressed in the larger context of equity theory. They point out that guilt is not the only kind of distress that a harm doer might feel when he sees he has harmed another; the harm doer may also fear retaliation. Their basic hypotheses are that a harm doer will feel distress of one sort or another after harming someone (intentionally or unintentionally) and that he will try to reduce this distress by restoring equity. Equity can be achieved either psychologically through cognitive change (justification) or through actual restitution. Walster *et al.* present an outline of the various means available to alleviate the distress of the harm doer, and they cite experimental evidence to back up each point. They postulate that, other things being equal, the harm doer will choose the most adequate way of restoring equity and will prefer the technique yielding the highest outcome/input ratio. For example, if overcompensation would result from any effort to restore actual equity, the harm doer may ignore the chance to make restitution in favor of justifying the hurt he has inflicted.

Lerner also deals with reactions to inequity—reactions stemming from the general knowledge that inequity exists in a supposedly just world. When there was some way to restore actual equity in the experiments he describes, his subjects indicated a willingness to do so (for example, by voting to remove another from a painful experimental condition). However, they responded to the knowledge of inequity by distortion or denial if they could not right the balance (and if distortion was, in fact, possible). Lerner contrasts the respect we supposedly have in our culture for martyrs with his subjects' apparent willingness to devalue a martyr they had just observed.

Schopler describes how another form of inequity can arise and, most importantly, discusses the kind of situation in which actual inequity might seem to have been created but where little effort to change the balance of rewards occurs. That is, we may confer benefits on someone without his believing that a social debt has been incurred and that he should reciprocate. For example, if we are guilty of something, the same cultural view of equity that allows us to expiate guilt by a good deed for a third party would prevent this third party from feeling indebted to us. Schopler argues that people tend to see nonaltruistic motives behind certain apparently altruistic acts, and consequently do not feel obliged to reciprocate. To illustrate, a very large favor is suspicious; possibly we feel that no rational person would give so much without expecting a return. If he does expect something other than repayment, then the beneficiary is not obligated to pay him back since he (the benefactor) thinks he will gain in some other way for his generosity.

NATURALISTIC STUDIES OF ALTRUISM

The last section of the book consists of three papers describing people who have done relatively unusual good deeds and who probably would be viewed as altruists by many. They risked their lives or careers or gave up much for the sake of others. How do they stack up alongside the descriptions of altruists developed in experimental studies?

Rosenhan studied civil rights activists and found that he had three groups of would-be altruists. There were those who were financial supporters, who had not really invested much, relative to their resources, in the civil rights movement. Then there were those who had gone on a single freedom ride or participated only briefly in the movement. These latter people seem to be guilt-ridden or neurotic types who might have engaged in civil rights work for reasons of personal distress as much as through empathy with the distress of others. Finally, those who devoted a year or more to civil rights work Rosenhan calls the "fully committed" people. These latter civil rights workers would seem to have had the socialization experiences held necessary for true altruism in Aronfreed's and Schwartz's analyses or in a normative theory of altruism. Equity considerations would be hard to establish as motives for the fully committed workers, unless one allows a motive to establish equity in the world at large as part of the traditional equity concept. While they may have been rewarded by self-approval or others' admiration, the potential costs when they undertook the work were great.

London's paper describes some Christians who rescued Jews from the Nazis in World War II. His subjects also would seem to have had the socialization experiences held necessary for altruism by several theorists since they tended to have strong relationships with an idealistic parent. On the other hand, they were somewhat marginal people and while they may have adopted their parents' values, they probably cannot be described as conformists to the values of society at large. Whether empathy was involved in their decision to help others would be hard to decide; certainly some of these rescuers had no great love for their clients. Further, while some rescuers were paid for their work, the possible cost involved (death) could have outweighed these monetary rewards. Their motives remain an intriguing mystery. Whatever drove them, many of them had a spirit of adventure and access to resources to do their work, and these factors also seem to be essential parts of their story.

Fellner and Marshall studied kidney donors, persons who had an unusual chance to benefit another. These people were not looking for this particular opportunity to do a good deed, but when it did come, they did not avoid it. In all but one of the 20 cases investigated, the donors seem to have made their decision to donate a kidney without much reflection on possible consequences. Their faith in the medical profession may have been very strong, but they undoubtedly knew that the operation to remove a kidney is a serious and possibly dangerous affair. It is difficult to explain their action in terms of external rewards, and we cannot say for sure that they anticipated receiving benefits from others. They might have found rewards in their greatly increased self-esteem, but as the investigators suggest, this heightened pride could have been the consequence of their behavior rather than the incentive for it.

This summary, of course, cannot hope to do complete justice to the papers included in this volume. Our overview has not adequately represented the range of questions asked by the investigators, the often ingenious procedures employed in seeking answers, or the many interesting and even intriguing findings they obtained. Having shown that no single, simple explanatory scheme can satisfactorily account for all of these instances of helpfulness, we can only suggest to the reader that he investigate the papers in this book and formulate his own questions and answers.

SITUATIONAL DETERMINANTS OF HELPING

SOCIAL DETERMINANTS OF BYSTANDER
INTERVENTION IN EMERGENCIES [1]

Bibb Latané and John M. Darley

Almost 100 years ago, Charles Darwin wrote: "As man is a social animal, it is almost certain that he would . . . from an inherited tendency be willing to defend, in concert with others, his fellow-men; and be ready to aid them in any way, which did not too greatly interfere with his own welfare or his own strong desires" (*The Descent of Man*). Today, although many psychologists would quarrel with Darwin's assertion that altruism is inherited, most would agree that men will go to the aid of others even when there is no visible gain for themselves. At least, most would have agreed until a March night in 1964. That night, Kitty Genovese was set upon by a maniac as she returned home from work at 3:00 AM. Thirty-eight of her neighbors in Kew Gardens came to their windows when she cried out in terror; but none came to her assistance, even though her stalker took over half an hour to murder her. No one even so much as called the police.

Since we started our research on bystander response to emergencies, we have heard about dozens of such incidents. We have also heard many explanations: "I would assign this to the effect of the megalopolis in which we live, which makes closeness very difficult and leads to the alienation of the individual

[1]The research reported in this paper was supported by National Science Foundation Grants GS1238, GS1239, GS2292, and GS2293, and was conducted at Columbia University and New York University.

from the group," contributed a psychoanalyst. "A disaster syndrome," explained a sociologist, "that shook the sense of safety and sureness of the individuals involved and caused psychological withdrawal from the event by ignoring it." "Apathy," others claim. "Indifference." "The gratification of unconscious sadistic impulses." "Lack of concern for our fellow men." "The Cold Society." These explanations and many more have been applied to the surprising failure of bystanders to intervene in emergencies—failures which suggest that we no longer care about the fate of our neighbors.

But can this be so? We think not. Although it is unquestionably true that the witnesses in the incidents above did nothing to save the victim, "apathy," "indifference," and "unconcern" are not entirely accurate descriptions of their reactions. The 38 witnesses of Kitty Genovese's murder did not merely look at the scene once and then ignore it. Instead they continued to stare out of their windows at what was going on. Caught, fascinated, distressed, unwilling to act but unable to turn away, their behavior was neither helpful nor heroic; but it was not indifferent or apathetic either.

Actually, it was like crowd behavior in many other emergency situations; car accidents, drownings, fires, and attempted suicides all attract substantial numbers of people who watch the drama in helpless fascination without getting directly involved in the action. Are these people alienated and indifferent? Are the rest of us? Obviously not. It seems only yesterday we were being called overconforming. But why, then, do we not act?

Paradoxically, the key to understanding these failures of intervention may be found exactly in the fact that so surprises us about them: so many bystanders fail to intervene. If we think of 38, or 11, or 100 individuals, each looking at an emergency and callously deciding to pass by, we are horrified. But if we realize that each bystander is picking up cues about what is happening and how to re-act to it from the other bystanders, understanding begins to emerge. There are several ways in which a crowd of onlookers can make each individual member of that crowd less likely to act.

DEFINING THE SITUATION

Most emergencies are, or at least begin as, ambiguous events. A quarrel in the street may erupt into violence or it may be simply a family argument. A man staggering about may be suffering a coronary, or an onset of diabetes, or he simply may be drunk. Smoke pouring from a building may signal a fire, but on the other hand, it may be simply steam or airconditioner vapor. Before a bystander is likely to take action in such ambiguous situations, he must first define the event as an emergency and decide that intervention is the proper course of action.

In the course of making these decisions, it is likely that an individual bystander will be considerably influenced by the decisions he perceives other bystanders to be taking. If everyone else in a group of onlookers seems to regard an event as nonserious and the proper course of action as nonintervention, this consensus may strongly affect the perceptions of any single individual and inhibit his potential intervention.

The definitions that other people held may be discovered by discussing the situation with them, but they may also be inferred from their facial expressions or behavior. A whistling man with his hands in his pockets obviously does not believe he is in the midst of a crisis. A bystander who does not respond to smoke obviously does not attribute it to fire. An individual, seeing the inaction of others, will judge the situation as less serious then he would if alone.

But why should the others be inactive? Probably because they are aware that other people are also watching them. The others are an audience to their own reactions. Among American males, it is considered desirable to appear poised and collected in times of stress. Being exposed to the public view may constrain the actions and expressions of emotion of any individual as he tries to avoid possible ridicule and embarrassment. Even though he may be truly concerned and upset about the plight of a victim, until he decides what to do, he may maintain a calm demeanor.

If each member of a group is, at the same time, trying to appear calm and also looking around at the other members to gauge their reactions, all members may be led (or misled) by each other to define the situation as less critical than they would if alone. Until someone acts, each person sees only other nonresponding bystanders and is likely to be influenced not to act himself. A state of "pluralistic ignorance" may develop.

It has often been recognized that a crowd can cause contagion of panic, leading each person in the crowd to overreact to an emergency to the detriment of everyone's welfare. What we suggest here is that a crowd can also force inaction on its members. It can suggest by its passive behavior that an event is not to be reacted to as an emergency, and it can make any individual uncomfortably aware of what a fool he will look for behaving as if it is.

Where There's Smoke, There's (Sometimes) Fire[2]

In this experiment we presented an emergency to individuals either alone or in groups of three. It was our expectation that the constraints on behavior in public combined with social influence processes would lessen the likelihood that members of three-person groups would act to cope with the emergency.

College students were invited to an interview to discuss "some of the problems involved in life at an urban university." As they sat in a small room waiting to be called for the interview and filling out a preliminary questionnaire, they faced an ambiguous but potentially dangerous situation. A stream of smoke began to puff into the room through a wall vent.

Some subjects were exposed to this potentially critical situation while alone. In a second condition, three naive subjects were tested together. Since subjects arrived at slightly different times, and since they each had individual questionnaires to work on, they did not introduce themselves to each other or attempt anything but the most rudimentary conversation.

As soon as the subjects had completed two pages of their questionnaires, the experimenter began to introduce the smoke through a small vent in the wall. The "smoke," copied from the famous Camel cigarette sign in Times Square, formed a moderately fine-textured but clearly visible stream of whitish smoke. It continued to jet into the room in irregular puffs, and by the end of the experimental period, it obscured vision.

All behavior and conversation were observed and coded from behind a one-way window (largely disguised on the subject's side by a large sign giving preliminary instructions). When and if the subject left the experimental room and reported the smoke, he was told that the situation "would be taken care of." If the subject had not reported the smoke within 6 minutes from the time he first noticed it, the experiment was terminated.

The typical subject, when tested alone, behaved very reasonably. Usually, shortly after the smoke appeared, he would glance up from his questionnaire, notice the smoke, show a slight but distinct startle reaction, and then undergo a brief period of indecision, perhaps returning briefly to his questionnaire before again staring at the smoke. Soon, most subjects would get up from their chairs,

[2]A more complete account of this experiment is provided in Latané and Darley (1968). Keith Gerritz and Lee Ross provided thoughful assistance in running the study.

walk over to the vent and investigate it closely, sniffing the smoke, waving their hands in it, feeling its temperature, etc. The usual Alone subject would hesitate again, but finally would walk out of the room, look around outside, and, finding somebody there, calmly report the presence of the smoke. No subject showed any sign of panic, most simply said: "There's something strange going on in there, there seems to be some sort of smoke coming through the wall . . . ." The median subject in the Alone condition had reported the smoke within 2 minutes of first noticing it. Three-quarters of the 24 people run in this condition reported the smoke before the experimental period was terminated.

Because there are three subjects present and available to report the smoke in the Three Naive Bystanders condition as compared to only one subject at a time in the Alone condition, a simple comparison between the two conditions is not appropriate. We cannot compare speeds in the Alone condition with the average speed of the three subjects in a group because, once one subject in a group had reported the smoke, the pressures on the other two disappeared. They could feel legitimately that the emergency had been handled and that any action on their part would be redundant and potentially confusing. Therefore, we used the speed of the first subject in a group to report the smoke as our dependent variable. However, since there were three times as many people available to respond in this condition as in the Alone condition, we would expect an increased likelihood that at least one person would report the smoke by chance alone. Therefore, we mathematically created "groups" of three scores from the Alone condition to serve as a baseline.[3]

In contrast to the complexity of this procedure, the results were quite simple. Subjects in the three-person-group condition were markedly inhibited from reporting the smoke. Since 75% of the Alone subjects reported the smoke, we would expect over 98% of the three-person groups to include at least one reporter. In fact, in only 38% of the eight groups in this condition did even one person report ($p < .01$). Of the 24 people run in these eight groups, only one person reported the smoke within the first 4 minutes before the room got noticeably unpleasant. Only three people reported the smoke within the entire experimental period. Social inhibition of reporting was so strong that the smoke was reported faster when only one person saw it than when groups of three were present ($p < .01$).

[3]The formula for calculating the expected proportion of groups in which at least one person will have acted by a given time is $1-(1-p)^n$ where p is the proportion of single individuals who acted by that time and n is the number of persons in the group.

Subjects who had reported the smoke were relatively consistent in later describing their reactions to it. They thought the smoke looked somewhat "strange." They were not sure exactly what it was or whether it was dangerous, but they felt it was unusual enough to justify some examination. "I wasn't sure whether it was a fire, but it looked like something was wrong." "I thought it might be steam, but it seemed like a good idea to check it out."

Subjects who had not reported the smoke were also unsure about exactly what it was, but they uniformly said that they had rejected the idea that it was a fire. Instead, they hit upon an astonishing variety of alternative explanations, all sharing the common characteristic of interpreting the smoke as a nondangerous event. Many thought the smoke was either steam or airconditioning vapors, several thought it was smog, purposely introduced to simulate an urban environment, and two actually suggested that the smoke was a "truth gas" filtered into the room to induce them to answer the questionnaire accurately! Predictably, some decided that "it must be some sort of experiment" and stoically endured the discomfort of the room rather than overreact.

The results of this study clearly support the prediction. Groups of three naive subjects were less likely to report the smoke than solitary bystanders. Our predictions were confirmed—but this does not necessarily mean that our explanation of these results is the correct one. As a matter of fact, several alternative explanations center around the fact that the smoke represented a possible danger to the subject himself as well as to others in the building. For instance, it is possible that the subjects in groups saw themselves as engaged in a game of "chicken" in which the first person to report would admit his cowardliness. Or it may have been that the presence of others made subjects feel safer, and thus reduced their need to report.

To rule out such explanations, a second experiment was designed to see whether similar group inhibition effects could be observed in situations where there is no danger to the individual himself for not acting. In this study, male Columbia University undergraduates waited either alone or with a stranger to participate in a market research study. As they waited they heard a woman fall and apparently injure herself in the room next door. Whether they tried to help and how long they took to do so were the main dependent variables of the study.

The Fallen Woman[4]

Subjects were telephoned and offered $2 to participate in a survey of game and puzzle preferences conducted at Columbia by the Consumer Testing Bureau (CTB), a market research organization. When they arrived, they were met at the door by an attractive young woman and taken to the testing room. On the way, they passed the CTB office, and through its open door they were able to see a desk and bookcase piled high with papers and filing cabinets. They entered the adjacent testing room, which contained a table and chairs and a variety of games, and they were given questionnaires to fill out. The representative told subjects that she would be working next door in her office for about 10 minutes while they were completing the questionnaire and left by opening the collapsible curtain which divided the two rooms. She made sure that subjects were aware that the curtain was unlocked and easily opened and that it provided a means of entry to her office. The representative stayed in her office, shuffling papers, opening drawers, and making enough noise to remind the subjects of her presence. Four minutes after leaving the testing area, she turned on a high fidelity stereophonic tape recorder.

The Emergency

If the subject listened carefully, he heard the representative climb up on a chair to reach for a stack of papers on the bookcase. Even if he were not listening carefully, he heard a loud crash and a scream as the chair collapsed and she fell to the floor. "Oh, my God, my foot . . . I . . . I . . . can't move . . . it. Oh . . . my ankle," the representative moaned. "I . . . can't get this . . . thing . . . off me." She cried and moaned for about a minute longer, but the cries gradually got more subdued and controlled. Finally she muttered something about getting outside, knocked over the chair as she pulled herself up and thumped to the door, closing it behind her as she left. The entire incident took 130 seconds.

The main dependent variable of the study, of course, was whether the subjects took action to help the victim and how long it took them to do so. There were actually several modes of intervention possible: a subject could open the screen dividing the two rooms, leave the testing room and enter the CTB office by the door, find someone else, or most simply, call out to see if the representative needed help. In one condition, each subject was in the testing room alone while he filled out the questionnaire and heard the fall. In the second condition, strangers were placed in the testing room in pairs. Each subject in the pair was unacquainted with the other before entering the room and they were not introduced.

[4]This experiment is more fully described in Latané and Rodin (1969).

Across all experimental groups, the majority of subjects who intervened did so by pulling back the room divider and coming into the CTB office (61%). Few subjects came the round-about way through the door to offer their assistance (14%), and a surprisingly small number (24%) chose the easy solution of calling out to offer help. No one tried to find someone else to whom to report the accident.

Since 70% of Alone subjects intervened, we should expect that at least one person in 91% of all two-person groups would offer help if members of a pair had no influence upon each other. In fact, members did influence each other. In only 40% of the groups did even one person offer help to the injured woman. Only eight subjects of the 40 who were run in this condition intervened. This response rate is significantly below the hypothetical baseline ($p < .001$). Social inhibition of helping was so strong that the victim was actually helped more quickly when only one person heard her distress than when two did ($p < .01$).

When we talked to subjects after the experiment, those who intervened usually claimed that they did so either because the fall sounded very serious or because they were uncertain what had occurred and felt they should investigate. Many talked about intervention as the "right thing to do" and asserted they would help again in any situation.

Many of the noninterveners also claimed that they were unsure what had happened (59%), but had decided that it was not too serious (46%). A number of subjects reported that they thought other people would or could help (25%), and three said they refrained out of concern for the victim—they did not want to embarrass her. Whether to accept these explanations as reasons or rationalizations is moot—they certainly do not explain the differences among conditions. The important thing to note is that noninterveners did not seem to feel that they had behaved callously or immorally. Their behavior was generally consistent with their interpretation of the situation. Subjects almost uniformly claimed that in a "real" emergency they would be among the first to help the victim.

These results strongly replicate the findings of the Smoke study. In both experiments, subjects were less likely to take action if they were in the presence of others than if they were alone. This congruence of findings from different experimental settings supports the validity and generality of the phenomenon; it also helps rule out a variety of alternative explanations suitable to either situation alone. For example, the possibility that smoke may have represented a threat to the subject's personal safety and that subjects in groups may have had a greater concern to appear "brave" than single subjects does not apply to the present experiment. In the present experiment, nonintervention cannot signify bravery. Comparison of the two experiments also suggests that the absolute number of nonresponsive bystanders may not be a critical factor in producing social inhibition of intervention; pairs of strangers in the present study inhibited each other as much as did trios in the former study.

Other studies we have done show that group inhibition effects hold in real life as well as in the laboratory, and for members of the general population as well as college students. The results of these experiments clearly support the line of theoretical argument advanced earlier. When bystanders to an emergency can see the reactions of other people, and when other people can see their own reactions, each individual may, through a process of social influence, be led to interpret the situation as less serious than he would if he were alone, and consequently be less likely to take action.

These studies, however, tell us little about the case that stimulated our interest in bystander intervention: the Kitty Genovese murder. Although the 38 witnesses to that event were aware, through seeing lights and silhouettes in other windows, that others watched, they could not see what others were doing and thus be influenced by their reactions. In the privacy of their own apartments, they could not be clearly seen by others, and thus inhibited by their presence. The social influence process we have described above could not operate. Nevertheless, we think that the presence of other bystanders may still have affected each individual's reponse.

DIFFUSION OF RESPONSIBILITY

In addition to affecting the interpretations that he places on a situation, the presence of other people can also alter the rewards and costs facing an individual bystander. Perhaps most importantly, the presence of other people can reduce the cost of not acting. If only one bystander is present at an emergency, he carries all of the responsibility for dealing with it; he will feel all of the guilt for not acting; he will bear all of any blame others may level for nonintervention. If others are present, the onus of responsibility is diffused, and the individual may be more likely to resolve his conflict between intervening and not intervening in favor of the latter alternative.

When only one bystander is present at an emergency, if help is to come it must be from him. Although he may choose to ignore them out of concern for his personal safety, or desire "not to get involved," any pressures to intervene focus uniquely on him. When there are several observers present, however, the pressures to intervene do not focus on any one of the observers; instead, the responsibility for intervention is shared among all the onlookers and is not unique to any one. As a result, each may be less likely to help.

Potential blame may also be diffused. However much we wish to think that an individual's moral behavior is divorced from considerations of personal punishment or reward, there is both theory and evidence to the contrary. It is perfectly reasonable to assume that under circumstances of group responsibility for a punishable act, the punishment or blame that accrues to any one individual is often slight or nonexistent.

Finally, if others are known to be present, but their behavior cannot be closely observed, any one bystander may assume that one of the other observers is already taking action to end the emergency. If so, his own intervention would only be redundant—perhaps harmfully or confusingly so. Thus, given the presence of other onlookers whose behavior cannot be observed, any given bystander can rationalize his own inaction by convincing himself that "somebody else must be doing something."

These considerations suggest that even when bystanders to an emergency cannot see or be influenced by each other, the more bystanders who are present, the less likely any one bystander would be to intervene and provide aid. To test this suggestion, it would be necessary to create an emergency situation in which each subject is blocked from communicating with others to prevent his getting information about their behavior during the emergency.

A Fit to be Tried[5]

A college student arrived in the laboratory, and was ushered into an individual room from which a communication system would enable him to talk to other participants (who were actually figments of the tape recorder). Over the intercom, the subject was told that the experimenter was concerned with the kinds of personal problems faced by normal college students in a high-pressure, urban environment, and that he would be asked to participate in a discussion about these problems. To avoid embarrassment about discussing personal problems with strangers, the experimenter said, several precautions would be taken. First, subjects would remain anonymous, which was why they had been placed in individual rooms rather than face-to-face. Second, the experimenter would not listen to the initial discussion himself, but would only get the subject's reactions later by questionnaire.

[5]Further details of this experiment can be found in Darley and Latané (1968).

The plan for the discussion was that each person would talk in turn for 2 minutes, presenting his problems to the group. Next, each person in turn would comment on what others had said, and finally there would be a free discussion. A mechanical switching device regulated the discussion, switching on only one microphone at a time.

The Emergency

The discussion started with the future victim speaking first. He said he found it difficult to get adjusted to New York and to his studies. Very hesitantly and with obvious embarrassment, he mentioned that he was prone to seizures, particularly when studying hard or taking exams. The other people, including the one real subject, took their turns and discussed similar problems (minus the proneness to seizures). The naive subject talked last in the series, after the last prerecorded voice.

When it was again the victim's turn to talk, he made a few relatively calm comments, and then, growing increasingly loud and incoherent, he continued:

> I er I think I I need er if if could er er somebody er er er er er er er give me a little er give me a little help here because I er I'm er er h-h-having a a a a real problem er right now and I er if somebody could help me out it would er er s-s-sure be sure be good . . . because er there er er a cause I er I uh I've got a a one of the er sie . . . er er things coming on and and and I could really er use some help so if somebody would er give me a little h-help uh er-er-er-er-er c-could somebody er er help er uh uh uh (chocking sounds) . . . . I'm gonna die er er I'm . . . gonna die er help er er seizure (chokes, then quiet).

The major independent variable of the study was the number of people the subject believed also heard the fit. The subject was led to believe that the discussion group was one of three sizes: a two-person group consisting of himself and the victim; a three-person group consisting of himself, the victim and the other person; or a six-person group consisting of himself, the victim, and four other persons.

The major dependent variable of the experiment was the time elapsed from the start of the victim's seizure until the subject left his experimental cubicle. When the subject left his room, he saw the experimental assistant seated at the end of the hall, and invariably went to the assistant to report the seizure. If 5 minutes elapsed without the subject's having emerged from his room, the experiment was terminated.

Ninety-five percent of all the subjects who ever responded did so within the first half of the time available to them. No subject who had not reported within 3 minutes after the fit ever did so. This suggests that even had the experiment been allowed to run for a considerably longer period of time, few additional subjects would have responded.

Eighty-five percent of the subjects who thought they alone knew of the victim's plight reported the seizure before the victim was cut off; only 31% of those who thought four other bystanders were present did so. Everyone of the subjects in the two-person condition, but only 62% of the subjects in the six-person condition ever reported the emergency. To do a more detailed analysis of the results, each subject's time score was transformed into a "speed" score by taking the reciprocal of the response time in seconds and multiplying by 100. Analysis of variance of these speed scores indicates that the effect of group size was highly significant ($p < .01$), and all three groups differed significantly one from another ($p < .05$).

Subjects, whether or not they intervened, believed the fit to be genuine and serious. "My God, he's having a fit," many subjects said to themselves (and we overheard via their microphones). Others gasped or simply said, "Oh." Several of the male subjects swore. One subject said to herself, "It's just my kind of luck, something has to happen to me!" Several subjects spoke aloud of their confusion about what course of action to take: "Oh, God, what should I do?"

When those subjects who intervened stepped out of their rooms, they found the experimental assistant down the hall. With some uncertainty but without panic, they reported the situation. "Hey, I think Number 1 is very sick. He's having a fit or something." After ostensibly checking on the situation, the experimenter returned to report that "everything is under control." The subjects accepted these assurances with obvious relief.

Subjects who failed to report the emergency showed few signs of the apathy and indifference thought to characterize "unresponsive bystanders." When the experimenter entered her room to terminate the situation, the subject often asked if the victim was all right. "Is he being taken care of?" "He's all right, isn't he?" Many of these subjects showed physical signs of nervousness; they often had trembling hands and sweating palms. If anything, they seemed more emotionally aroused than did the subjects who reported the emergency.

Why, then, didn't they respond? It is not our impression that they had decided not to respond. Rather, they were still in a state of indecision and conflict concerning whether to respond or not. The emotional behavior of these nonresponding subjects was a sign of their continuing conflict, a conflict that other subjects resolved by responding.

The fit created a conflict situation of the avoidance–avoidance type. On the one hand, subjects worried about the guilt and shame they would feel if they did not help the person in distress. On the other hand, they were concerned not to make fools of themselves by overreacting, not to ruin the ongoing experiment by leaving their intercoms, and not to destroy the anonymous nature of the situation, which the experimenter had earlier stressed as important. For subjects in the two-person condition, the obvious distress of the victim and his need for help were so important that their conflict was easily resolved. For the subjects who knew that there were other bystanders present, the cost of not helping was reduced and the conflict they were in was more acute. Caught between the two negative alternatives of letting the victim continue to suffer or rushing, perhaps foolishly, to help, the nonresponding bystanders vacillated between them rather than choosing not to respond. This distinction may be academic for the victim, since he got no help in either case, but it is an extremely important one for understanding the causes of bystanders' failures to help.

Although subjects experienced stress and conflict during the emergency, their general reactions to it were highly positive. On a questionnaire administered after the experimenter had discussed the nature and purpose of the experiment, every single subject found the experiment either "interesting" or "very interesting" and was willing to participate in similar experiments in the future. All subjects felt that they understood what the experiment was all about and indicated that they thought the deceptions were necessary and justified. All but one felt they were better informed about the nature of psychological research in general.

CONCLUSION

We have suggested two distinct processes which might lead people to be less likely to intervene in an emergency if there are other people present than if they are alone. On the one hand, we suggested that the presence of other people may affect the interpretations each bystander puts on an ambiguous emergency situation. If other people are present at an emergency, each bystander will be guided by their apparent reactions in formulating his own impressions. Unfortunately, their apparent reactions may not be a good indication of their true feelings. It is possible for a state of "pluralistic ignorance" to develop, in which each bystander is led by the apparent lack of concern of the others to interpret the situation as being less serious than he would if alone. To the extent that he does not feel the situation is an emergency, he will be unlikely to take any helpful action.

Even if an individual does decide that an emergency is actually in process and that something ought to be done, he still is faced with the choice of whether he himself will intervene. Here again, the presence of other people may influence him—by reducing the costs associated with nonintervention. If a number of people witness the same event, the responsibility for action is diffused, and each may feel less necessity to help.

"There's safety in numbers," according to an old adage, and modern city dwellers seem to believe it. They shun deserted streets, empty subway cars, and lonely dark walks in dark parks, preferring instead to go where others are or to stay at home. When faced with stress, most individuals seem less afraid when they are in the presence of others than when they are alone.

A feeling so widely shared should have some basis in reality. Is there safety in number? If so, why? Two reasons are often suggested: individuals are less likely to find themselves in trouble if there are others about, and even if they do find themselves in trouble, others are likely to help them deal with it. While it is certainly true that a victim is unlikely to receive help if nobody knows of his plight, the experiments above cast doubt on the suggestion that he will be more likely to receive help if more people are present. In fact, the opposite seems to be true. A victim may be more likely to get help, or an emergency be reported, the fewer the people who are available to take action.

Although the results of these studies may shake our faith in "safety in numbers," they also may help us begin to understand a number of frightening incidents where crowds have heard but not answered a call for help. Newspapers have tagged these incidents with the label, "apathy." We have become indifferent, they say, callous to the fate of suffering of others. Our society has become "dehumanized" as it has become urbanized. These glib phrases may contain some truth, since startling cases such as the Genovese murder often seem to occur in our large cities, but such terms may also be misleading. Our studies suggest a different conclusion. They suggest that situational factors, specifically factors involving the immediate social environment, may be of greater importance in determining an individual's reaction to an emergency than such vague cultural or personality concepts as "apathy" or "alienation due to urbanization." They suggest that the failure to intervene may be better understood by knowing the relationship among bystanders rather than that between a bystander and the victim.

REFERENCES

Darley, J.M., and Latané, B. Bystander intervention in emergencies: Diffusion of responsibility. *Journal of Personality and Social Psychology,* 1968, 8, 377–383.

Latané, B., and Darley, J.M. Group inhibition of bystander intervention. *Journal of Personality and Social Psychology,* 1968, **10,** 215–221.

Latané, B., and Rodin, J. A lady in distress: Inhibiting effects of friends and strangers on bystander intervention. *Journal of Experimental Social Psychology,* 1969, 5, 189-202.

THE INFLUENCE OF SOCIAL MODELS
ON HELPING

Harvey A. Hornstein[1]

Along with other researchers, I assume the existence of a social responsibility norm (Berkowitz & Daniels, 1963, 1964); but I further assume that norms do not apply invariantly to all social situations. In any given situation it is incumbent upon the person involved to determine whether the particular situation is one in which he, especially, should assume responsibility for another person's welfare. He seeks to answer the question: "Under these conditions, what do people like me do?" On the basis of past research (Asch, 1956; Bandura & Walters, 1963) we can be reasonably certain that the resolution of this question is sometimes influenced by observing the activities of relevant social models.

Social learning theorists have employed the notion of vicarious reinforcement to explain social modeling and other imitative processes. Indeed, there is considerable evidence to suggest that observer behavior changes as a consequence of witnessing the reward–cost contingencies associated with a performer's behavior (Bandura, 1965a, b). Without denying the importance of observing

[1]This study was supported by National Science Foundation Grant GS1715, "Experiments in the social psychology of pro-social behavior," whose principal investigator is Harvey A. Hornstein. The author is sincerely grateful to Dr. Marion G. Hornstein and Dr. Peter Gumpert for the ideas and other assistance that they provided during the preparation of this paper. Appreciation is also expressed to Elisha Fisch and Michael Holmes who assisted in conducting many of the studies that are discussed.

29

reward–cost contingencies, these behavioral changes can be interpreted in alternative ways. Bandura (1968), a leading advocate of the vicarious reinforcement explanation, has himself said:

> . . . reinforcement stimuli presented to the model may therefore serve to facilitate or inhibit emulative behavior through their discriminative or informative function. Knowledge gained from witnessing the outcomes experienced by models would be particularly influential in regulating behavior under conditions where considerable ambiguity exists about what constitutes permissible or punishable actions, and where the observer believes that the model's contingencies apply to himself as well.

Taking this reasoning one step further, I would contend that as a general rule people seek information about the behavioral demands of their immediate social environment. When the demands are clear because of social proscription or physical constraint, the behavior of others is less relevant and therefore less influential in determining observer behavior. When the demands are less clear, observing others' behavior often provides information which then serves to regulate an observer's own behavior.

More specifically, observation of the helpfulness of relevant social models has at least three possible effects on the observer's own behavior. First, what a model does may increase the observer's awareness of certain alternatives. Data collected by various researchers (Bryan & Test, 1967; Rosenbaum & Blake, 1955; Rosenhan & White, 1967) adequately document the contention that observation of a helping model increases the likelihood of similar behavior from others.

Second, the consequences to the model for his behavior provide observers with evidence about reward–cost contingencies which can be associated with this behavior. If the observer anticipates similar experiences with the same behavior, negative consequences to the model will lead to less emulation of his behavior than positive consequences. Bandura (1965b) has demonstrated that observation of externally imposed reward or punishment to a filmed model will, respectively, increase and decrease imitative behavior. In Bandura's study, the subjects observed the model's outcomes, not how he felt about these outcomes. In the first study, described below, observers were given information not only about the model's helpful act but also about his feelings concerning this act.

Third, the motives that an observer attributes to a model for helping mediate his determination of how people like the observer are expected to behave. On entering social situations (particularly unfamiliar ones), people often try to determine what social expectations exist for their behavior. These expectations may not be the same for all types of people in the situation. For example, men may be expected to behave differently from women in a situation involving someone in need of help. If, in observing another's behavior, the observer believes that the model's behavior is influenced by factors which have no relevance for the observer, and if he believes that the model would not have behaved as he did in the absence of these factors, then the likelihood of behavior similar to the model's is lessened. In the second study described below, experimental conditions were varied in order to produce changes in the motivation that an observer–subject attributed to the behavior of a helping model.

CONSEQUENCES TO A HELPING MODEL AS A
DETERMINANT OF OBSERVER HELPING BEHAVIOR

The first test of these contentions involved a naturalistic field experiment conducted by myself, E. Fisch, and M. Holmes (Hornstein *et al.,* 1968).[2] In this study, the observer learned of an absent model's helpful act and read the model's report to the helped person of his feelings about this act. These feelings were either positive or negative, reflecting the extent to which he experienced helping another as pleasant or unpleasant. Our prediction was that when an observer believed that the model's experiences were valid predictors of his own future experiences, observation of positive feelings would increase the likelihood of imitative acts and observation of negative feelings would have the opposite effect. In situations in which the observer perceived himself to be dissimilar to the model, the model's experiences would not be seen as valid predictors of his own experiences and observation of his outcomes would have relatively little effect on the observer's behavior.

Method

To investigate these notions, data were gathered unobtrusively from passersby at two locations, three blocks apart, in a business and shopping area in midtown Manhattan. The basic procedure was to deposit an envelope on the

[2]For the complete report of this experiment, see Hornstein, Fisch, and Holmes (1968).

ground at a pedestrian thoroughfare. Protruding from the envelope was a man's wallet. Wrapped around the wallet was a typewritten letter which led the finder to believe that the wallet was lost not once, but twice. On the first occasion, it was found by the person who addressed the envelope to the wallet's owner and wrote a letter describing his feelings about returning the wallet. This well-intentioned person then lost the wallet himself, along with the envelope and his letter. Our subject had to decide whether to emulate the previous finder's behavior by returning the wallet or to keep it for himself.

The Wallet

The lost object was a black, split-cowhide man's wallet, worth about $2. The wallet's contents were selected to construct an object which would, in the absence of any experimental conditions, produce a 50% return rate. The wallet's contents were as follows: $2 in cash, a $26.30 check to the "E.M.H. Co.," a receipt for a rented tuxedo, a scrap of paper containing initials and a fictitious telephone number, and an identification card with the name, address, and telephone number of the wallet's owner. In addition, there were three 6 cent stamps, membership cards for a consumer's co-op and an athletic association (both fictitious), a blood donor's card, and appointment and calling cards from a podiatrist and a florist. The owner's name, Michael Erwin, was fictitious. It was chosen to avoid any unequivocal ethnic or religious group identification.

The Letter: Similar Model Conditions

The letter was typed on a 6 × 9 inch piece of white stationery with no identifying marks. The envelope was plain, white, and unstamped. It was properly addressed to the wallet's owner, but had no return address.

In all conditions the letter began in the same manner:

Dear Mr. Erwin

I found your wallet which I am returning. Everything is here just as I found it.

In the neutral condition, the letter said no more. In the positive and negative conditions, however, the letter continued by discussing the previous finder's feeling about returning the wallet.

In the positive condition the letter added:

. . . I must say that it has been a great pleasure to be able to help somebody in the small things that make life nicer. Its really been no problem at all and I'm glad to be able to help.

In the negative condition it said:

... I must say that taking the responsibility for the wallet and having to
return it has been a great inconvenience. I was quite annoyed at having to
bother with the whole problem of returning it. I hope you appreciate the
efforts that I have gone through.

The Letter: Dissimilar Model Conditions

The procedure used in the dissimilar model conditions was similar to the
one just described, except for the character of the social model. Since our
population was heterogeneous, we needed a model who would be perceived as
dissimilar by a wide variety of people.

In all dissimilar conditions, the letter began by saying:

Dear Mr. Erwin

I am visit your country finding your ways not familiar and strange. But I find
your wallet which I here return. Everythings is here just as I find it.

The neutral letter said no more. In the positive condition the letter
continued:

It great pleasure to help somebody with tiny things which make life nicer. It is
not problem at all and I glad to be able to help.

In the negative condition the letter continued:

To take responsibility for wallet and necessity to return it is great inconvenience. Is annoyance to bother with whole problem of return and hope you
appreciate effort I went to.

Except for the identification of the writer as a foreigner whose command of
English was not perfect, the information in this letter paralleled that provided
in the similar model letter.[3]

Procedure

One person surreptitiously dropped the envelope containing the wallet
and the letter. At the same time, two unobtrusively located observers verified
its recovery by a subject and recorded a number of the subjects's characteristics

---

[3]A group of independent judges was asked to identify the country of origin of the
letter's author. A great number of countries were identified and no biases were evident. Moreover, there was no statistically significant differences in the judges' liking for the similar and
dissimilar letter writers within each condition.

on a standard observation form.[4] In the first phase of this research, we were interested in the effect of expression of positive, neutral, and negative feelings by a similar model. In the second phase, we turned to the effects of the expression of such feelings by a dissimilar model. Similar model wallets were dropped on January 31st, February 1st, February 13th, and February 15th (all weekdays) in 1968. Dissimilar model wallets were dropped on March 12th, 14th, and 19th of 1968, again all weekdays.[5] In an effort to avoid any systematic biasing, we alternated dropping the various types of letters within the similar and dissimilar model conditions.

Results

Of the 105 wallets dropped, 40% were returned intact. A return was considered intact only if the wallet contained the money, i.e., some people returned the wallet with the cards but kept the money.

The data from the six conditions were analyzed using a simultaneous interval technique analogous to Scheffé's (1953) procedure for use with the analysis of variance (Miller, 1966). This technique allowed us to test our hypothesis by examining a number of specific contrasts among these six populations, while maintaining the simultaneous (or joint) confidence interval for all contrasts at .95.

The findings are shown in Table 1. Positive and neutral letters from a similar model produced more returns than negative letters ($p < .05$), but these two conditions were not significantly different from one another. Contrasts among the three dissimilar model conditions produced no statistically significant

---

[4]At the time of writing, we have observed some 500 subjects in ten different experimental conditions. We have recorded such things as race, sex, and apparent age, factors associated with socioeconomic status, as well as a number of social conditions concurrent with subjects finding the wallet, e.g., crowd size. The relationship between these factors and return rate will be reported in a separate paper. Suffice it to say that in this study there was no disproportionate representation of any of these observational categories in our experimental conditions.

[5]The return rates for the first 4 days (the similar model) and for the last 3 days (dissimilar model) are perfectly consistent with experimental data gathered prior to and since this study was completed: there are no differences either within the two groups of days or between them. Although the sample is too small to analyze the data for a days x condition interaction, an examination of these data show no consistent differences between days within each condition. Barring major social events (e.g., a blackout, riot or assassination), these data argue convincingly that we are dealing with a stationary stochastic process.

TABLE I

Return Rates for Neutral, Positive, and Negative
Letter Conditions for Similar and Dissimilar Models

Condition	Returns		No returns			
			Total		Number returned but not intact	Number not returned
	Number	Percentage	Number	Percentage		
Similar model						
Neutral	12	60	8	40	1	7
Positive	14	70	6	30	2	4
Negative	2	10	18	90	6	12
Dissimilar model						
Neutral	4	27	11	73	5	6
Positive	5	33	10	67	5	5
Negative	6	40	9	60	5	4

differences, nor were the return rates produced by these conditions different from the return rate obtained with a similar model sending a negative letter. However, positive and neutral letters from similar models produced more returns than positive and neutral letters from dissimilar models ($p < .05$).

To summarize: a letter from a similar model reporting positive or no experience produced more returns than a letter reporting negative experiences, whereas the experience (positive, negative or neutral) reported by a dissimilar model had no effect on the return rate.

The contentions expressed earlier are clearly supported by the data reported here. Social models are not simply influential by virtue of what they are doing. When the model is observed to experience negative feelings about his behavior, there is evidence that observers are deterred from behaving in the same fashion, assuming that the model is perceived as similar and thus as a relevant comparison person. When the model is perceived as dissimilar, however, his experiences have no differential effect on observer helping. We can assume that under dissimilar conditions, an observer attributes the model's experience to unique personal or social conditions that have little relevance to him, or, more specifically, to the reward–cost contingencies that he can anticipate for helping. The role of observer attribution and the conditions that affect it will be considered further in the next section.

THE ATTRIBUTION OF MOTIVE TO A MODEL
AS A DETERMINANT OF OBSERVER HELPING BEHAVIOR

Following Heider's (1958) work, there has been increased interest in the investigation of the determinants of causal attribution in person–perception (Jones & Davis, 1965; Kelley, 1967; Schopler, this volume). The basic paradigm in these studies is a two-person situation in which one person is an actor and the other a perceiver who is also the receiver of an act. In this section, I will extend attribution analysis to a three-person situation in which an observer (the subject) and an actor have the opportunity to help a third party, the recipient of the act. In this situation, the actor's opportunity to help precedes the observer's; consequently, the observer has an opportunity to see the actor's behavior and to attribute motive to his choice.

In a paper in this volume, Schopler presents a construct which is useful for the present discussion. In examining attribution processes in two-person situations, he distinguishes between donor-instigated and recipient-instigated attribution processes. He argues that recipients of benefits are less likely to reciprocate if the donor's behavior is attributed to a desire to satisfy his own needs or wishes (donor-instigated behavior) and more likely to reciprocate if the donor's behavior is attributed to recipient need (recipient-instigated behavior). I would add to Schopler's two categories a third, situation-instigated attribution processes, which includes attributions that place the cause of an act in impersonal supra-individual situational requirements (cf. Heider's chapter on "Oughts and Values," in Heider, 1958).

For the purpose of this paper, I would extend Schopler's hypotheses to include modeling effects as well as reciprocation by the recipient of a benefit. That is, I define "Donor-Instigated attribution processes" here as involving attributing motivation for a helpful act to compelling personal or social conditions *that are associated only with the actor and are not relevant for the observer.* Observers will be inclined to emulate the model only if they attribute the actor's helpfulness to the recipient-need (recipient instigated) or to situational conditions that are generally true and therefore relevant for them (situation instigated).

One compelling situation in which observers are likely to produce attributions of situation or recipient instigation involves an actor's behavior which is contrary to pressures from personal and social sources. I recently conducted a study using such situations. In this study, one group of actors indicated that they were helping and were under social pressure to do so, while another group indicated that they were helping but were under social pressure to do otherwise. In a second pair of conditions, one group indicated that they were helping despite a personal history of not being helped while others said that they were helping because they had been helped in the past. I expected relatively fewer helping acts from observers who were confronted with models whose helping was associated with social pressure to help or a "binding" personal history of being helped. That is, I assumed that when a model suggested that his helping was contingent on the existence of personal or social pressures peculiar to the model, observers would be less inclined to interpret the situation as one in which people like them are really expected to help. In contrast, when the model helps despite contrary personal or social reasons for not doing so, observers will infer that his behavior was motivated by reasons that are relevant to people like them (either recipient need or model-supported social norms and values). In fact, in these circumstances, the act of helping despite countervailing pressures serves as testimony to the importance of helping; hence observers will be more likely to help.

Method

Procedure

Data were gathered from 98 passersby using the same procedure described earlier. The letter that was found with the wallet contained our experimental manipulation. The neutral condition was identical to the similar model condition used before and did not identify the model's motive for helping. As before, the two sentences in the neutral letter constitute the beginning of the other letters. In one set of conditions, the model said his helping was either contrary to or consistent with social pressure from friends. The second and third sentences of the social pressure-contrary condition were:

> ... When I found it everyone who was around (including my best friends) said I should keep it and I was stupid if I returned it. I disagreed with them so here it is.

In the social pressure-consistent letter, the third and fourth sentences were:

> ... When I found it everyone who was around (including my best friends) said I should return it and I was stupid if I kept it. I agreed with them and here it is.

In a second set of conditions, the model said his helping was either contrary to or consistent with his own experiences in similar situations. In the personal experience-contrary conditions, the third and fourth sentences were:

... I want you to know that I have lost my wallet twice and no one ever sent mine back to me. That's why I'm sending yours back.

In the personal experience-consistent condition, the third and fourth sentences were:

... I want you to know that I lost my wallet twice and both times someone simply mailed it back to me. That's why I'm sending yours back.

Results

The results of this research appear in Table 2. The simultaneous interval technique described above was again employed with a joint confidence interval of .95. The data for the "social pressure" conditions were collected over the course of 2 weekdays in early spring, one week before we collected data in the "experience" conditions. Wallets in the neutral condition were dropped in random order with the other wallets in both time periods.

TABLE 2
Return Rates for Social Pressure,
Past Experience, and Neutral Conditions

	Returns		No returns			
			Total		Number returned but not intact	Number not returned
Condition	Number	Percentage	Number	Percentage		
Neutral	11	61	7	39	5	2
Past experience						
Contrary	8	53	7	47	3	4
Consistent	3	20	12	80	6	6
Social pressure						
Contrary	9	60	6	40	3	3
Consistent	3	20	12	80	7	5

These data clearly confirm the predictions. The likelihood of an observer's decision to help another person is influenced by a model's attempt to help that person. However, an observer is not influenced simply by what the model did; rather, influence stems from motives attributed to the model's behavior ($p < .05$ for the contrary-consistent condition comparisons). If these motives stem from factors such as situational characteristics or recipient need which would be as relevant for the observer as for the model to heed, then the observer is quite likely to emulate the model. When the attribution of motives defines the causative factor in the model's behavior as yielding to immediate external social pressures, or personal need to reciprocate indirectly past favors (e.g., donor-instigated behavior), then the model's influence declines.

Comparing the neutral condition to the experience- and social pressure-consistent conditions ($p < .05$) suggests that the neutral condition is not neutral at all. Subjects undoubtedly attribute motives to a model who has not only returned the wallet, without giving his own name and address, but has also taken the time to write a brief note. Possibly subjects infer that the neutral model is helping because of his concern for recipient needs or abstract social norms and values in the absence of social pressures to be helpful.

Although the return rates we obtained are consistent with our predictions, they appear to be inconsistent with some of the information contained in the experimental letters. In the experience- and social pressure-contrary conditions, for example, subjects were prone to help despite indications that others (people other than the helping model) think that wallets should not be returned. Similarly, in the experience- and social pressure-consistent conditions, subjects failed to help despite indications that others think wallets should be returned.

The judgments expressed by others cannot be interpreted independently of the model's behavior, or vice versa. When the model's helping is linked to the presence of personal or social pressures to help, observers presumably infer that the behavior was obligatory or compelled. That others have not helped, or say one should not help, may highlight the model's helping behavior because of the contrast it provides. The revelation of counter pressures to helping stands as testimony to the importance, in the observer's eyes, of helping in this situation. The model is setting higher standards for behavior than others might endorse, but the letter implies that these others who do not return wallets or who urge keeping a lost wallet should not be emulated. In a sense, this interpretation may explain the feelings that people have about heroes and the reasons that heroes are emulated. Often, heroes are those individuals who take an unpopular stand or attempt to perform feats that are out of keeping with concurrent physical constraints. Their contrary-to-the-crowd behavior, whether condemning an unjust war or rushing into a burning building, may heighten the perceived importance and desirability of such behavior.

One alternative interpretation of the data is to view the model's letter as a persuasive communication. From this perspective, the message in the two "consistent" conditions are seen as a one-sided argument, i.e., both the model and others agree about returning the wallet; whereas, in the "contrary" conditions, the message is a two-sided argument, and the model's behavior serves to refute the argument against returning the wallet. McGuire (1964) has indicated that refutational messages (i.e., messages which attack a person's beliefs, then refute the attack) are more likely to induce resistance to persuasion than supportive messages (i.e., messages which present information consistent with a person's beliefs). This interpretation assumes that subjects recognized that, ideally, one ought to return the wallet; at the same time, they were tempted to do otherwise. Given these assumptions, this interpretation suggests that messages which state and then refute (through action) counter-normative arguments are more likely to induce resistance to temptation than messages which only provide support for a norm.

Another interpretation concerns the role of choice. Observers may be more inclined to help when they observe models whose behavior is attributed to choice, unconstrained by role obligation, and, conversely, less inclined to help when they attribute the model's behavior to special role responsibilities. In this regard, Steiner and Field (1960) report that subjects who were in favor of racial integration were more influenced by prosegregation remarks when they believed that the speaker chose the prosegregation role than when they believed the role was assigned to him. This was true despite their greater liking for the speaker when his role was assigned and, thus, his behavior was a response to special responsibilities.

In summary, these experiments support our initial supposition that a social model is not influential simply by virtue of what he is doing. When a model is observed to experience negative feelings about his behavior, there is evidence that observers are deterred from imitating him, assuming that the model is perceived as similar and thus a relevant comparison person. Relevance is also critical in determining the consequences of attribution of motive to a model's behavior. If conditions are such that an observer attributes to the model motives that have relevance for him, he is more likely to define the situation as one in which people like him help than if he attributes to the model motives that have no relevance for him.

REFERENCES

Asch, S.E. Studies of independence and conformity: I. A minority of one against a unanimous majority. *Psychological Monographs,* 1956, **70** (9, Whole No. 416).

Bandura, A. Vicarious processes: A case of no-trial learning. In L. Berkowitz (Ed.), *Advances in experimental social psychology.* Vol. 2. New York: Academic Press 1965. (a)

Bandura, A. Influence of a model's reinforcement contingencies on the acquisition of imitative responses. *Journal of Personality and Social Psychology,* 1965, **1**, 589–595. (b)

Bandura, A. Social-learning theory of identificatory processes. In D.A. Goslin (Ed.), *Handbook of socialization theory and research.* Chicago: Rand McNally, 1968.

Bandura, A., & Walters, R.H. *Social learning and personality development.* New York: Holt, Rinehart & Winston, 1963.

Berkowitz, L., & Daniels, L.R. Responsibility and dependency. *Journal of Abnormal and Social Psychology,* 1963, **66**, 429–436.

Berkowitz, L., & Daniels, L.R. Affecting the salience of the social responsibility norm: Effects of past help on the responses to dependency relationships. *Journal of Abnormal and Social Psychology,* 1964, **66**, 275–281.

Bryan, J.H., & Test, M.A. Models and helping: Naturalistic studies in aiding behavior. *Journal of Personality and Social Psychology,* 1967, **6**, 400–407.

Heider, F. *The psychology of interpersonal relations.* New York: Wiley, 1958.

Hornstein, H.A., Fisch, E., & Holmes, M. Influence of a model's feelings about his behavior and his relevance as a comparison on other observers' helping behavior. *Journal of Personality and Social Psychology,* 1968, **10**, 222–226

Jones, E.E., & Davis, K.E. From acts to dispositions: The attribution process in person perception. In L. Berkowitz (Ed.), *Advances in experimental social psychology.* Vol. 2. New York: Academic Press, 1965.

Kelley, H.H. Attribution theory in social psychology. In D. Levine (Ed.), *Nebraska symposium on motivation.* Lincoln: University of Nebraska Press, 1967.

McGuire, W.J. Inducing resistance to persuasion. In L. Berkowitz (Ed.), *Advances in Experimental and social psychology.* Vol. 1. New York: Academic Press, 1964.

Miller, R.G., Jr. *Simultaneous statistical inference.* New York: McGraw–Hill, 1966, pp. 218–219.

Rosenbaum, M., & Blake, R. Volunteering as a function of field structure. *Journal of Abnormal and Social Psychology,* 1955, **50**, 193–196.

Rosenhan, D., & White, G.M. Observation and rehearsal as determinants of prosocial behavior. *Journal of Personality and Social Psychology,* 1967, **5**, 424–431.

Scheffé, H. A method for judging all contrasts in the analysis of variance. *Biometrika,* 1953, **40**, 87–104.

Steiner, I.D., & Field, W.L. Role assigmnent and interpersonal influence. *Journal of Abnormal and Social Psychology,* 1960, **61**, 239–246.

A SHILL FOR CHARITY[1]

Jacqueline R. Macaulay

As any gambler and fund raiser knows, the use of a shill increases the take. If one reasonably attractive person puts out his money, others are likely to do the same. There is empirical support for this belief. Bryan and Test (1967) demonstrated that a donating model increases the rate of donation to a Salvation Army bell ringer during the Christmas season. Blake, Mouton, and Hain (1956) and Helson, Mouton, and Blake (1958) found that a confederate's compliance with a request to sign either popular or unpopular petitions increased the number of onlookers who were also willing to sign. Rosenbaum and Blake (1955) and Rosenbaum (1956) found that a model who volunteers for an experiment increased volunteering among those who saw the model.

What is it that the model does that has such a reliable effect? The model may define what is allowable or best to do in the situation, or he may only remind the onlooker of what he himself thinks is proper in the situation. Either way, the model may indicate what behavior is likely to be rewarded by the approval of others, by self-approval, or by both. In addition, the model may lessen restraints against certain actions by showing that it is possible to behave in a given manner without being punished by an onlooker's disapproval. That is, he shows what norms are not relevant as well as what norms are relevant to the

[1]This research was supported by Grant GS1728 from the National Science Foundation, Division of Social Science, to Leonard Berkowitz. I wish to thank Dr. Berkowitz for editorial assistance in preparing this report.

situation. When it comes to charity, there may be competing norms: "Don't be a sucker; don't fall for a sob story," versus "It's good to give." The first kind of norm may restrain prosocial action. Several studies have shown that a model's actions can lower experimentally induced or naturally occurring restraints on certain public actions. These include volunteering in class for a psychology experiment (Schachter & Hall, 1952), jaywalking (Lefkowitz, Blake, & Mouton, 1955), and violating rules designed to keep subjects from doing what they wanted to do (Freed, Chandler, Mouton, & Blake, 1955; Kimbrell & Blake, 1958; Stein, 1967). Finally, results from a study by Blake, Rosenbaum, and Duryea (1955) indicate that people will take a model's cue as to how much they should give when asked for a donation, as if they were uncertain whether norms of generosity or prudent stinginess applied to the situation.

What happens then if the model actively refuses to accede to a public request for a helpful action? Studies by Blake *et al,* (1956), Helson *et al,* (1958), Rosenbaum and Blake (1955), and Rosenbaum (1956) show that a refusing model tends to decrease the incidence of the actions called for in comparison with the No-Model control condition. On the basis of these results, one could hypothesize that a refusing model in the Bryan and Test situation would lower donations to the bell ringer's pot. However, as suggested above, the donating model's action could remind the passerby of an obligation rather than simply defining what is proper behavior; a refusing model could serve as a reminder as well as an acquiescent model. A boomerang effect from a model's refusal would be particularly strong if the behavior called for was commonly regarded as laudatory—for example, alms-giving at Christmas time. In the four studies mentioned above, the behaviors requested of the refusing model probably were not widely regarded as morally obligatory. There undoubtedly was no clear-cut social consensus in these cases that students ought to sign a particular petition or volunteer for an experiment. In contrast, in the Bryan and Test situation, it seems much more likely that most onlookers would expect both increased self-approval and approval from others if they responded positively to the bell ringer's appeal. Thus the effect of a refusing model should be to increase the donation rate over that of No-Model control periods. Two experiments which test this hypothesis will be reported here.

EXPERIMENT 1

Procedure

The first experiment was run during the second week before Christmas, 1967, for periods of about 2 hours (plus breaks to keep the experimenters alert) during two late afternoons and two evenings when stores were open. Two chimneylike boxes with signs saying "Give to needy children" had been placed on the sidewalks of the downtown shopping area in Madison, Wisconsin, by the Volunteers of America. In the past, bell-ringing Santa Clauses had been stationed at each box, and although in recent years both boxes were not always manned during shopping hours, most shoppers were probably familiar with the bell-ringing Santa and his sidewalk chimney.

The experiment took place at only one of the boxes. (The other box was manned by a Santa only during the last day of the experiment.) The experimenter's Santa was instructed to give a neutral nod to any donations and to the model's speeches. He did, however, have to respond to small children and wise-cracking teenagers, but by and large, his only reward for donors and nondonors alike was a dose of nonspecific Christmas spirit.

The model M was a middleaged, middle-class woman similar in dress and appearance to many shoppers. In the Donation condition, she came along the other side of the sidewalk from Santa, crossed over when close to him, put down her large shopping bag and prepared to get her wallet out. As she did this she silently appeared to read the sign and then said, "Well, I guess I can give something," (with a smile) and dropped a coin in the box. In the Refusal condition, she appeared to read the sign, but before her wallet was in sight said, "No, I don't want to give anything here," shook her head disapprovingly, picked up her bag, and walked on. She alternated donations and refusals as well as direction of approach to Santa. The pairing of direction and action was switched every half hour. The time between each appearance of the model was determined by the walking speed and circuit which seemed natural under the circumstances. She walked at about the same speed as other shoppers, and rather than abruptly turning around after completing a trip past Santa, she did some window shopping at one or another store and then reversed directions in a manner which would appear natural for a shopper.

An observer O counted donors for 20 seconds from the time M spoke to Santa. Then O waited 20 seconds and counted donors for a control period of 20 seconds. The model usually reappeared about 30–40 seconds after the control period. Thus there were four conditions: Donation, Postdonation Control, Refusal, and Postrefusal Control. (The two control periods were introduced to regularize O's routine.) The donors were recorded by O, noting sex and approximate age (by decade).

An interviewer was stationed on the other side of the wide sidewalk from Santa. As M put down her bag, the interviewer counted off the first three people, teenaged or older, coming toward her and M. She approached the third one after he or she had passed Santa (and thus had a chance to donate). If this third person could not be approached for some reason, the interviewer was instructed to turn to the next person on her left. She was very successful at stopping the third person and very few respondents (Rs) refused to be interviewed or were substitutes. Most Rs were alone when interviewed. Those who were not alone were omitted from the interview analysis because a companion usually helped answer the questions. The interview was very short, consisting only of questions as to whether R had seen the model and could identify her action and what R thought of giving to the Volunteers of America.

Results

Effect of Santa Claus

At the end of the days during which no Santa Claus was present, only \$1 to \$3 was found in the box along with such things as cigarette butts and chewed chewing gum. In contrast, at the end of the 4 days when Santa had been present— for only 2 hours—there was from \$16 to \$25 in the box (model's donations not included). Evidently the presence of a Santa Claus was necessary to draw attention to the charity and, perhaps, to translate the ideal into action for most people.

Number of Donations

As Table 1 shows, the number of observation periods in which there was a donation was greater for the experimental than for the following control periods. However, there was apparent not only a difference in the number of donations between the two experimental conditions, but also between the two control conditions. Since donors during the experimental observation period could have been models for people passing by during the control observation periods, all observation periods following periods during which there had been a donation were dropped and the data reexamined. The difference between control periods was still apparent, calling into question the assumption that control periods

TABLE 1
Proportions of Observation Periods
during which Donations Occurred (Santa Study)

	Model donated		Model refused	
	Experimental	Control	Experimental	Control
Total no. of periods	92	92	92	92
Periods with male or female dona- tion (%)	34	26	26	17
Eliminating periods following a period during which a donation was recorded:				
Reduced no. of periods	75	61	68	68
Periods with male or female donation[a] (%)	32	28	28	17
Periods with dona- tion by male (%)	16	13	12	12
Periods with dona- tion by female[b] (%)	27	16	18	7

[a]The figures for male and female donations added together may be greater than the total given because in some observation periods donations by both sexes occurred.

[b]χ^2 analysis of donations by females in reduced sample of observation periods (n.s. = Not significant):

Source	df	χ^2	p
Expt'l. *vs.* control	1	5.35	.05
Donation *vs.* refusal	1	4.34	.05
Interaction	1	.73	n.s.
	3	10.42	.05

would be free of model influence. These control condition differences indicate that the true control rate (Santa present but no model) is lower than the rates seen in Table 1. In view of these differences, the initial analysis plan of combining control periods was discarded in favor of analyzing them as two conditions.

In this reduced sample of observation periods, the proportion of periods during which there were donations from *men* did not differ significantly from condition to condition. There was, however, a significant variation between conditions in the proportions of observation periods with a female donor. Analysis of the components of the χ^2 for the reduced sample of observation periods counting only female donors,[2] shows that the difference between experimental and control conditions (with Donation and Refusal combined) is significant, as is the difference between Donation and Refusal (experimental and the following control periods combined).[3] The interaction term is far from significant.

Number of Donors among Interview Respondents

As Table 2 indicates, the interviewer's count of the donors in her sample yields the same experimental—control finding as the tally of observation periods: those who saw the model were more likely to make a donation than those who did not see the model or could not identify her action. However, no difference between type of model action (Donation *vs.* Refusal) appears in the interviewer data.

---

[2] Since some observation periods had both male and female donors, combining male and female data would involve counting some periods twice. Therefore, male and female data must be analyzed separately. The difference in number of male and female donations in each condition probably reflects the difference in numbers of men and women shoppers—the latter are undoubtedly more numerous at any time in a shopping center.

[3] It can be argued that the relatively high number of donors in the Refusal condition only shows a diminishing effect of the earlier donation rather than an effect of the refusal. Also, it should be noted that the observer was not blind as to what data the experimenter wanted in the Donation condition and may himself have expected a boomerang effect in the Refusal condition. However, confidence in the interpretation offered for the results is increased by several observations. (1) Our study of pedestrian traffic indicates that it was unlikely that there were donors in the Refusal period who had seen the model donating 90 seconds or more earlier. (2) Dropping Refusal periods following control periods with donations did not lower the proportion of donations in the remaining Refusal periods. (3) Interview data (Table 2) also show donation rates to be increased by both model actions. (4) Interview data show an effect of the Refusal action on attitudes which would not seem to support an explanation of Refusal results in terms of diminishing effect of the earlier donation or in terms of observer bias. (5) Each of three observers produced the same pattern of results, including control period differences which presumably would run counter to observer bias. (Although there were different observers at various times, the same model and interviewer served at all times.)

TABLE 2A
Proportion of Donors among
Interview Respondents (Santa Study)

Type of model action	R saw model action	R did not see model action
Model donated		
% Donors	15	4
Total n	13	55
Model refused		
% Donors	20	7
Total n	15	44

TABLE 2B
χ^2 *Analysis*

Source	df	χ^2	p^a
Perception of model	1	4.63	.05
Donation *vs.* refusal	1	.80	n.s.
Interaction	1	.69	n.s.
	3	6.12	n.s.

[a]n.s. = Not significant.

Age of Donors

There was a tendency for the experimental conditions to have a greater proportion of female donors under the age of 40 than were seen in the control conditions. However, this experimental–control age difference for females is significant at only the .09 level ($\chi^2 = 2.39, df = 1$).

Awareness of the Model

Respondents were divided into those who said they saw the model and correctly identified her action, those who saw the model but could not say what she had done, and those who said they did not see the model. These categories were subdivided by the type of model action which Rs might have witnessed just before they were interviewed. Nineteen percent of passersby stopped by an interviewer after the model donated said they had seen what she did. A somewhat higher proportion, 24% of passersby stopped after the model refused to donate reported seeing what she did. This difference is not significant by χ^2 test. That about one in five shoppers would notice another shopper's actions during the Christmas shopping season seems about what could be expected.

Attitude toward Donating

Responses to the question, "What do you think of giving to the Volunteers of America?" were read independently by two coders. Their categorization schemes were very similar. The comparison yielded a χ^2 of 199.63, $df = 12$, $p < .001$. Since scaling these responses was a post hoc procedure, and since there was some uncertainty about the ordering of categories (particularly for "don't know" answers), a relatively conservative χ^2 analysis was made of the data. Responses were divided into only two attitude categories: enthusiastic, and not very enthusiastic or unfamiliar with the organization. (The combination of unenthusiastic responses with "don't know" responses was dictated by low expected cell frequencies.) Examples of responses in the first category are "Fine"; "I think it's wonderful if you have the money"; "A worthwhile organization." Examples of responses in the second category are, "It's all right"; "It's okay"; "It's good for the children to do"; "Well, I'm undecided"; "I don't know anything about it"; "I'm against it."

As expected, most Rs had a positive attitude toward donating to the Volunteers of America. This supports the assumption that there is a widespread consensus supporting giving to the charity. Only eight of 127 Rs expressed a negative opinion and only two of these were firmly negative. Sixteen Rs were unfamiliar with the organization. None of the latter saw what the model did. All those who were seen donating by the interviewer expressed a very positive opinion of the charity with the exception of one young man who said he gave not because he liked the organization but because he "dug" the bells and Santa.

Table 3 shows the results of the analysis of attitude data. When male and female attitudes toward donating were examined separately, no significant differences appeared. Percentage of each sex within the initial categories established by the coders were very similar.

A significant χ^2 for model action among those who saw the model's action shows that what she did affected both male and female Rs' opinions of giving to the charity. The model appears to have had a greater effect on women than on men, but sex differences within conditions are not significant. In general, if a passerby saw the model donate, he was less approving of the charity than Rs who did not see the model at all and than Rs who saw the model donate and then themselves contributed. The reverse is true of Rs who saw the model refuse to donate; they tended to voice the most enthusiastic opinions of donating to the Volunteers of America.

Discussion

In the Donation condition, the model served to increase donations even more than the Bryan and Test model had done. However, those who saw the model donate showed less enthusiasm for the charity than those who did not see a donating model — these Rs were mainly nondonors. The model apparently provoked some defensiveness or conflict on the part of those who saw her donate but did not give money themselves. The interviewer reported an anecdote which supports this interpretation. As the model began her act, one respondent took out her wallet, but as she heard the model's refusal, she returned her own wallet to her purse and in the interview said she had not seen the model. Possibly conformity with the model's negative action (or nonconformity with her positive action) led to uneasiness which was expressed by some in denial of awareness of the model. These results suggest the interpretation of the model's effect as that of reminding people of an obligation. Aware of the ideal, they evidently sought to justify their failure to comply with it by downgrading the ideal. One respondent made some comments which illustrate this hypothesized conflict: "Actually, giving at Christmas, I don't object. I wonder if the money is used properly. My first impulse when I saw her set her bag down was to donate, but I passed by."

In the Refusal condition, the model also served to increase donations but here she increased approval of the charity rather than decreasing it as in the Donation condition. The interview data suggest that part of the nondonating

TABLE 3A
Attitudes toward Donating (Santa Study)

	Model donated			Model refused		
Enthusiastic responses	R saw model action	R saw model, not action	R did not see model	R saw model action	R saw model, not action	R did not see model
Males						
% Enthusiastic	40	56	47	60	43	33
Total n	5	9	19	5	7	6
Females						
% Enthusiastic	0	50	56	100	63	27
Total n	7	8	18	8	15	15

TABLE 3B
χ^2 *Analysis of Attitudes*

Source	df	χ^2	p^a
Perception of model[b]	2	2.35	n.s.
Saw model: Donated *vs.* refused	1	9.90	.01
Saw model, not action: Donated *vs.* refused	1	.44	n.s.
Did not see model: Donated *vs.* refused	1	2.78	n.s.
Sex differences within each Perception–Model cell	6	7.45	n.s.
	11	22.93	.02

[a]n.s. = Not significant.

[b]Since there is a significant interaction of perception with model action, the 11 *df* for the total table were divided to allow a test of model action within each perception condition (Bresnahan & Shapiro, 1966). None of the sex differences within each perception-model cell was significant, so the combined χ^2 for these differences is reported.

model's effect may be that she made nongiving in this situation clearly improper or even unpleasant. On one hand, by acting in an improper and almost hostile manner, she not only served to remind passersby of their obligation, but if they agreed with her and derogated the charity themselves, they might appear too similar to this Scrooge-like person. Thus, she may have prevented some passersby from justifying their own nondonating behavior by downgrading the charity. On the other hand, the nondonors were, perhaps, in the rewarding position of being morally superior to the Scrooge-like model, at least in attitude if not in behavior. This factor might have decreased the salience of the fact of their own nonconformity to the ideal of Christmas giving, and thus decreased guilt feelings.

However, in spite of the greater approval of the charity in the Refusal condition, the donation rate was significantly lower than the rate in the Donation condition. This finding indicates that the nondonating model did not reduce restraints against public giving as much as the donating model—or perhaps the nondonating model increased restraints. Her behavior may have been disapproved of by most passersby, but she also may have suggested to a few that it might be foolish to put money in the box. One respondent's comments illustrate this type of interpretation: "I've passed them (the boxes) a couple of times shopping. Giving to children is a good thing. Santa makes a difference. I (didn't) give to the box that didn't have a Santa because no one else was. Perhaps I was embarrassed."

While the model is effective in raising the donation rate, both when she donates and refuses to donate, the data regarding the sex of donors suggest some general limitations on her effectiveness. Her behavior-induced definition of the situation may have had somewhat the same effect on the opinions of nondonor women, but she apparently did not influence many men to contribute to the charity. As a middle-aged woman, her influence may not have been potent enough to govern their behavior. Possibly only a male model of appropriate age would raise donation rates among men.

EXPERIMENT 2

In the first experiment the assumption was made, but not tested directly, that the perceived legitimacy of a charitable appeal is an important factor in determining the effect of a model who refuses to donate. When she violates a relatively clear-cut social ideal, she is likely to produce a boomerang effect. However, if the charity is not obviously legitimate, the negative model should have the effect observed by other experimenters: her refusal to donate should lower the donation rate over a No-Model control condition. In a second experiment, I attempted to vary the legitimacy of the charity. Although the attempt failed, the experiment yielded an interesting replication of the findings of the first study.

Procedure

University of Wisconsin students had formed a committee to collect money for the relief of starving Biafrans and had been very successful in the Student Union with a collection table surrounded by pictures of starving children. Passing students were very generous; well over $100 a day has been collected this way, including dollar bills, which are seldom found in the collection pot of the Santa on the downtown streets. I had the opportunity to take over this table for one full day. It was the last day of school before Christmas vacation and although both employees and passersby were scarce, they were plentiful enough to run the experiment.

Legitimate Appeal

In one condition, the table was surrounded by horrifying pictures of starvation. People coming from either direction could not miss these pictures, and few people can see them the first time without a strong reaction of some sort. On top of a stand next to the table which held two of these pictures was a hand-lettered sign in red which said, "Stop! Hunger and Starvation. Biafra–Nigeria Relief Committee."

The table was set up along the major traffic route through the Union. On it were a large coffee can for donations to "Biafran Relief" (a hard-to-read sign on the can), a pile of mimeographed material which was partly informational and partly political, a can containing out-of-date buttons for a earlier 1-day campaign titled "Lifeline for Biafra," and some miscellaneous bits of informational material which few people noticed. Note cards which could be used as Christmas cards were also for sale at five for $2—expensive enough so that a purchase would be considered partly charity.

Questionable Appeal

In the second condition it was hoped that the charitable appeal was less clearly legitimate. The pictures of the starving children and the sign were taken down and the mimeographed material was tacked up in their place. A hand-lettered sign above these sheets read simply "Biafra–Nigeria Committee." The pictures which had been taped to the side of the table were removed, but the material (listed above) on top of the table was not changed. The intended effect was that of a political organization's setup for dispensing information and soliciting funds. There presumably is no clear social ideal prescribing aid to a committee with political purposes such as there is to a committee collecting money for starving children.

These two conditions were alternated about every 90 minutes. The results do not vary between time blocks.

Model and Control Conditions

In the positive model condition, the model walked up to the table, picked up a leaflet, and said in a voice that carried quite well, "Well, I think it's a good cause. I'm glad someone's doing something for them." She then put some money in the can and walked on.

In the negative model condition, after looking at the leaflet she said, "Are you taking donations?" (Pause) "No, I don't think so. I just don't think it's worth it." or "No, I don't want to waste my money." She then walked off without making a donation.

After she made her speech, an observer recorded activity at the table for 60 seconds. He waited another 60 seconds and then recorded activity for 60 seconds again. The latter periods constitute the control condition. Occasionally someone would be present at the table throughout the experimental and control periods, but there was seldom anyone present in the hallway or at the table during both negative and positive model periods. The experiment was explained to those few people who saw the model twice.

Personnel

The model was a young women who appeared to be a senior or graduate student, somewhat more neatly dressed than most students, but otherwise typical in appearance. The girl who sat at the table was Chinese. Her command of English was good, but she spoke in such a low hesitating voice that it seemed at first as if she spoke only a little English. The choice of this young woman was fortunate; as the experiment got underway, it became clear that if there were someone at the table willing to discuss the plight of Biafra with passersby, the situation would become too complicated. The observer, a young man, sat at a table piled with books and coats placed some distance from the main table. He appeared to friends who happened by to be using it as a convenient place to study.

Finally, I myself served as interviewer. The problem of bias in recording answers is a serious one and as I interviewed passersby it became clear that the interviewer should not know what answers support the hypothesis. Therefore the attempt to get a random sample of passersby in each condition was abandoned.

Dependent Variable

The observer noted everyone who stopped at the table. He recorded sex and whether they were reading materials, studying the pictures, talking, donating, or buying note cards. Those who had not obviously decided to donate or buy some of the note cards within the observation period but did so after it ended were not recorded as donors or buyers, but simply as readers or talkers. Those who were present before the observation period began were recorded in terms of their activity during the observation period. These somewhat arbitrary rules represent an attempt to reduce observer bias. Some error was introduced this way, particularly in assignment to the control condition of card buyers who probably heard the model but took a long time to decide to buy. Such error, however, is preferable to giving the observer discretion to decide whom to count.

Results

Interviews

As explained above, the attempt to collect interviews in all conditions was abandoned. Those interviews taken indicate that, as in the previous experiment, almost no one disapproved of making donations to Biafran relief. A few people, seemingly echoing the model, said they approved of donating but wondered if it did any good. Some respondents seemed to see the Biafra–Nigeria Committee as a political one in the Questionable Appeal condition, as intended, and would say they did not know enough about it to express an opinion of the Committee. However, they would add that they approved of collecting money for Biafran relief. As the following results also show, the need for Biafran relief was too well known and overshadowed the apparent political concerns of the Biafra–Nigeria Committee.

Donating and Other Activities at the Table

As Table 4 shows, a very large difference in activity was found between experimental and control observation periods. Not only donations, but all forms of activity around the table were increased by both types of model speeches. (The same results are seen if the average number of people present in each type of observation period is calculated.) Furthermore, the positive model action led

TABLE 4A

Proportions of Observation Periods during Which Donations and Other Activities Occurred[a]

Type of activity	Legitimate appeal (%)				Questionable appeal (%)			
	Positive model		Negative model		Positive model		Negative model	
	Experimental	Control	Experimental	Control	Experimental	Control	Experimental	Control
Person(s) stopped to talk or read literature only	28	4	16	4	40	10	15	0
Some charitable activity:								
Card buyers only	0	20	4	8	0	10	0	0
Donation	40	4	36	0	47	0	30	0
No activity	32	72	44	88	15	80	55	100
	100	100	100	100	100	100	100	100

[a]Cell entries are proportion of total number of observation periods in each condition. For the Legitimate Appeal conditions, n = 25. For the Questionable Appeal conditions, n = 20.

TABLE 4B
χ^2 *Analysis of Type of Activity Observed*[a]

	df	χ^2	p
Type of appeal	1	1.22	n.s.
Model *vs.* control	1	43.31	.001
Positive model and control *vs.*			
negative model control	1	8.96	.01
Interactions[b]	4	3.61	n.s.

[a]n.s. = Not significant.

[b]Since there were too many cells with small expected frequencies in the Bought Cards category, it was combined with the Donated category in this analysis. Since more of the interactions approached significance, the combined χ^2 for these terms is reported.

to a significantly greater increase in donating and other activity than did the negative action. The observer also recorded four separate instances of the negative speech turning people away from the table. No such incidents were observed after the positive speech. As before, there is an apparent difference between control periods. This is clearly due to card buyers who were more numerous in the positive model condition and tended to stand at the table for quite some time. Finally, although there is a tendency for the positive model to draw more people to the table in the Questionable Appeal condition than in the Legitimate Appeal condition, this difference is not significant. No other sizable difference between these conditions is apparent.

The large experimental–control difference could be seen from the outset in the observer's recording sheets. The observer was lectured, for a second time, on the problem of experimenter effects, etc., and was himself observed for a time while he worked. Data following this admonition show the same large experimental–control difference as data preceding it. While the matter of observer bias cannot be completely dismissed, it does not seem to offer a full explanation for the large difference seen in the data.

These results, then, replicate those of the first experiment. However, their explanation in terms of perceived legitimacy of the charity has yet to be directly tested. Whatever the explanation, it seems clear that a negative model can have a boomerang effect in some situations.

The interpretation of modeling effects as being due in part to a lowering of restraints against public action also receives support here in the low level of activity in the control conditions and in observations of those involved in the study. It seemed to us as we watched that most people would not stop at the table unless there was already someone there. People seemed to avoid solo action. Perhaps they thought they would be very conspicuous if no one else was at the table, or perhaps they feared having to discuss Biafra with the girl at the table and thus reveal their ignorance, etc.

Furthermore, the model clearly had an impact on those who heard her when she spoke up—whether she had something positive or negative to say. Possibly it was not only what she said, but the fact that she could and would speak up so clearly in public that goaded others into action. We seldom overhear a declaration of intent in a situation like this, even in the politically active Student Union. Whatever the cause of the lack of activity in the control periods, it seemed clear to us that it took a model to "break the ice" — a common phrase that suggests there is both difficulty and the possibility of danger in initiating social action.

REFERENCES

Blake, R.R., Mouton, J.S., & Hain, J.D. Social forces in petition signing. *Southwestern Social Science Quarterly*, 1956, **36**, 385–390,

Blake R.R., Rosenbaum, M., & Duryea, R. Gift-giving as a function of group standards. *Human Relations*, 1955, 8, 61–73.

Bresnahan, J.L., & Shapiro, M.M. A general equation and technique for the exact partitioning of chi-square contingency tables. *Psychological Bulletin*, 1966, **66**, 252–262.

Bryan, J.H., & Test, M.A. Models and helping: Naturalistic studies in aiding behavior. *Journal of Personality and Social Psychology*, 1967, **6**, 400–407.

Freed, A.M., Chandler, P.J., Mouton, J.S., & Blake, R.R. Stimulus and background factors in sign violation. *Journal of Personality*, 1955, **23**, 499.

Helson, H., Mouton, J.S., & Blake, R.R. Petition signing as adjustment to situational and personality factors. *Journal of Social Psychology*, 1958, **48**, 3–10.

Kimbrell, D.L., & Blake, R.R. Motivational factors in the violation of a prohibition. *Journal of Abnormal and Social Psychology*, 1958, **56**, 132–133.

Lefkowitz, M., Blake, R.R., & Mouton, J.S. Status factors in pedestrian violation of traffic signals. *Journal of Abnormal and Social Psychology*, 1955, **51**, 704–705.

Rosenbaum, M. The effect of stimulus and background factors on the volunteering response. *Journal of Abnormal and Social Psychology*, 1956, **53**, 118–121.

Rosenbaum, M., & Blake, R.R. Volunteering as a function of field structure. *Journal of Abnormal and Social Psychology*, 1955, **50**, 193–196.

Schachter, S., & Hall, R. Group-derived restraints and audience persuasion. *Human Relations*, 1952, **5**, 397–406.

Stein, A.H. Imitation of resistance to temptation. *Child Development*, 1967, **38**, 158–169.

CHILDREN'S REACTIONS TO HELPERS:
THEIR MONEY ISN'T WHERE THEIR MOUTHS ARE[1]

James H. Bryan

It seems quite clear that both social institutions and large numbers of individuals are dependent upon, and supportive of, the altruistic behaviors of others (Campbell, 1965). Whether called the norm of social responsibility (Berkowitz & Daniels, 1963) or that of giving (Leeds, 1963), there is widespread expectation that people, virtually of any age and social class, render help to needy others even if such aid is associated with cost. Moreover, it appears that such norms are learned, and apparently accepted, early in the individual's life. That is, most children in middle childhood will verbally, if not behaviorally, support the principle that one should aid the needy. Recently, a series of investigations has suggested the situational determinants and personality correlates affecting the child's willingness to sacrifice a prized object. Aronfreed and Paskal[2], and later Midlarsky and Bryan (1967), have suggested empathy as an important determinant of the development of sharing, while Rosenhan and White (1967) and Hartup and Coates (1967) have demonstrated the role of models in eliciting self-sacrifice.

[1]These investigations were supported by the National Institute of Child Health and Human Development, under Research Grants 1 PO1 HD 1762-01 and 1 RO1 HD 03234-01. Special thanks are due Dr. Wesley Gibbs, and Messrs. Tom Wood, Loy Landers, and Harold Hutchinson, and to the many school teachers serving School Districts 65 and 68 of Skokie and Evanston, Illinois, whose cooperation made these studies possible.

[2]Aronfreed, J., & Paskal V. Altruism, empathy, and the conditioning of positive affect. Unpublished manuscript, University of Pennsylvania, 1965.

Moreover, such personality correlates as need for social approval (Staub & Sherk[3]), age (Handlon & Gross, 1959; Wright, 1942), and the social class status of the recipient (Berkowitz & Friedman, 1967; Berkowitz, 1968) have been shown to be relevant to the aiding reponse.

In spite of the diversity of the determinants and correlates studied, one should note that investigators have focused upon the self-sacrificing act rather than, for example, verbal endorsements concerning the norm of giving. Given the the presumption that such behavior reflects a single underlying process of norm internalization, one would expect that verbal and interpersonal reactions might also be manifest within helping situations. Adoption of standards may be reflected not only in verbal agreements with, and behavioral enactments of, the principle involved, but also in children's responses to others. Thus, if such self-sacrificing acts reflect an adoption of attitudes of social responsibility, then it is also reasonable to assume that children guided by such positions should esteem those who espouse them and reject those who deny them. Reactions to others then becomes a measure which might be assumed to covary with both verbal and behavioral endorsement of the social responsibility norm. The investigations on which this report is based were concerned with these three response classes, sometimes singly and sometimes jointly.

Like responses reflecting norm adoption, the processes by which one might learn, or be reminded of, such norms are multiple (Campbell, 1963). The concerns of the present series of investigations were addressed to the impact of two input processes—that of behavioral example and that of direct tutorials— upon donation behavior and reactions to peers. A series of studies has demonstrated that models can play an important role in affecting the self-sacrificing behaviors of both adults (Bryan & Test, 1967; Test & Bryan, 1969; Wagner & Wheeler, 1969) and children (Rosenhan & White, 1967; Hartup & Coates, 1967). The observation of helping others increases the probability of similar behavior by the observer. Sharing, then, like aggression (Bandura, Ross, & Ross, 1963) and courage (Bandura, Grusec, & Menlove, 1967), can be influenced by the witnessing of such behavior by others. One explanation of such findings is that the model simply reminds the observer of his own social responsibilities and thus increases the probability that the witness will himself commit the act. While work with adults would suggest that the modeling effect contributes more to the behavior than simply that of cognitive cueing (Wagner & Wheeler, 1969), direct evidence of this effect upon the responses of children is not available.

[3]Staub, E., & Sherk, L. Relationships between need approval and children's sharing behavior. Unpublished manuscript, Harvard University, 1968.

If simple reminders of norms were sufficient to provoke charitable responses, then one would expect that direct exhortations of charity or greed would play an important role in affecting such behavior. Interestingly, however, while some attention has been paid to the impact of commands upon altruistic responses—that is, the effects of a powerful other specifying the exact behavior desired of the child (White, 1967)—no attention has been given to the effects of exhortations by either adults or peers upon children's self-sacrificing behavior. Experiments were thus addressed to determining the relative strengths of exhortations and behavioral example upon reactions in helping situations. Moreover, aside from the implications that the study of exhortation may have for the interpretation of the modeling effect, it also seems obvious that many attempts to socialize children are made through reiterations of general moral principles by relatively powerless adults. The present series of investigations thus was addressed to the impact of powerless other's preachings and practices upon both the child's donation behavior and his reactions to the exemplar.

While the degree and locus of effects of preachings and practices are of interest, of no less importance is the relationship between deeds and words. Since Kinsey's, Pomeroy's, and Martin's (1951) survey of sexual practices and LaPiere's (1934) classic study of racial discrimination, it has been realized that people play quite a different game than they preach. It would be surprising indeed if this were not particularly true with regard to socialization agents. Given the generality of the usual preached morality and the considerable complexities governing moral behaviors within specific situations, it would be reasonable to assume that model inconsistency is ubiquitous within the child's world. We have thus been interested in determining the impact, again on both the observer's behavior and his evaluations of the model, of the model's preaching views which he behaviorally contradicts. Indeed, while caveats concerning the detrimental effects of inconsistency and hypocrisy (e.g., preaching charity while practicing greed) flow readily, surprisingly little systematic or experimental work has been completed on this topic.

In summary, then, we have been concerned with the relative influence of two norm-defining techniques and their interactions upon the moral behavior and the interpersonal judgments of the child. In this regard, the present series of investigations follows Campbell's (1963) exhortations for closer study of the relationship between modes of learning and of responding.

Since the details of the experimental procedures have been outlined elsewhere (Bryan, 1968; Bryan & Walbek[4]), only a general overview of them will

----

[4]Both the experiments reported herein are described in further detail in Bryan, J.H., & Walbek, N.H. Preaching and practicing self-sacrifice: Children's actions and reactions. Unpublished mauscript, Northwestern University, 1968.

be given here. The experimental arrangement is such that the child plays a bowling game on two occasions, separated by the introduction of the experimental treatment, and wins a predetermined number of gift certificates. Thus, the experiment is designed to give the child something of value so that he will have something to contribute subsequently. Early in the experiment, the experimenter indicates that the child may desire to donate some of his winnings but stresses that such donations are voluntary. The presumed (and often actual) recipients of such donations have included a variety of unfortunates such as the poor, the crippled, and the orphaned. Initially, the child plays the game for ten trials in the presence of the experimenter. These practice trials allow a measure of the base rate of donations and insure the experimenter that the child understands the rules of the game. Following this practice period, the child is introduced to a model of the same sex who is either approximately the same age as the subject or is an adult. In the entire series of studies, we have used 13 models in all, six children and seven adults. Adult models have been presented "live," while peer models are presented by videotape. Following the instructions to the model, the experimenter leaves the room and the model plays the game. During the game, the model practices either charity or greed. He accomplishes the former by placing one-third of his winnings, on each occasion of winning, into the appropriate cannister. If practicing greed, he simply takes the money with him when he leaves the laboratory (live models) or conspicuously places the money in his pocket (if presented by videotape). In addition to his acts, the model also preaches to the child. The Preaching Charity condition has included such admonitions as: "It is good to give to the poor children (or crippled children)," "One should give to the crippled children," "I am going to give to the poor children." The Preaching Greed condition always employs the same statements as the Preaching Charity condition, except for the insertion of a negative into the appropriate section of the sentence. Finally, as a control condition, the model simply holds a nonexhortative conversation in which he indicates that he is enjoying the game. The preachings and practices are factorially combined so that one-sixth of the children are exposed to our hypocrite (preacher of charity and practitioner of greed) and another one-sixth to what we call our pseudocynic (the preacher of greed who donates). Following the exposure of the child to the model, the child is left alone to again play the game and, if he desires, to contribute to the needy. As far as the child is concerned, the charitable acts are committed in the absence of an audience. In addition, the child is led to believe that neither experimenter nor model will reenter the room and is instructed to return to his class room at the termination of the game.

Finally, a word about the subjects. We have tested approximately 550 children from such geographical locations as Rowland Heights, California; Montgomery, New Jersey; and Skokie and Evanston, Illinois; and have used children from grades one through five. The samples employed, then, have been both large in number and diversified.

Before going into some detail concerning our most recent experiments, I would like to indicate the general nature of our findings. The model effect is often, but not always, found. For example, in the California sample we found that the observation of others, while not increasing the amount donated, did influence the number of children who would contribute (Bryan, 1968). Hence, of the third- to fifth-grade children tested, 26 out of 45 witnessing the adult model contribute, themselves gave gift certificates, while only 14 of the 46 seeing the nondonating model, themselves sacrificed (χ^2 = 6.90 p < .01, two-tailed). That the modeling effect is weak is understandable within the framework of our studies insofar as care is exerted to exclude both the possibility that the model might subtly reinforce the child for imitation or that the child is vicariously reinforced by witnessing the model receive rewards for his donations. While two studies employing adult models have failed to yield the modeling effects, the results have all been in the expected direction. These findings essentially replicate the work of Hartup and Coates (1967), Rosenhan and White (1967), and White (1967). Quite surprising, however, has been the consistent failure to obtain an effect upon acts of donations attributable to the model's exhortations. We have yet to discover those conditions under which hypocrisy or inconsistency uniquely affect donation behavior. Witnessing a preacher of charity and a practitioner of greed produces no unique reactions upon either the children's donation behaviors or their judgment of the model. We have also attempted to assess the relationship between such preachings and practices upon not only self-sacrifice but self-indulgence. Like self-sacrifice, theft rates have not been influenced by exhortations or inconsistency.

The mental gyrations we have used to try to account for the ineffectiveness of exhortations are too numerous and muddleheaded to describe here. We were sufficiently concerned however with the possibility that the marked status discrepancy between the child subject and the adult model attenuated the exhortation effects to pursue it experimentally. We thought that children may feel that what adults say to them and do for themselves are unrelated since each actor adheres to very different standards. Because of this concern, our last two experiments employed peer rather than adult models. With the help of Nancy Walbek and Robert Michaels, 96 boys and 72 girls from the third and fourth grades were exposed to one of six types of models previously described. Some children witnessed a preacher and practitioner of charity, others saw one who preached and practiced greed; some observed a model who did no preaching but acted charitably, or conversely, one who also did no preaching but acted greedily; and finally, some observed one of the two types of inconsistent models. Several innovations were introduced in the procedure. Since we wished to use peers as models, we presented the exemplar by videotape. In addition, we were interested in the child's evaluative responses to the models. Was the hypocrite disliked and the preacher-practitioner of charity particularly esteemed; or, indeed, do statements and deeds conforming to the norms of social responsibility fail to affect evaluation at all? In order to explore such questions, subjects were given a post-experimental questionnaire during which they were asked questions concerning the experimental manipulations and their opinions of the model. Finally, in order to reduce the possibility of the children discovering the purpose of the experiment, four experimenters and four models were employed. Hopefully, the permutations of treatment conditions, models and experimenters would prevent children from deducing that they were participating in the identical experiment. Children of each sex were exposed to one of two models and to one of two experimenters. Each child played the game, was exposed to the model, replayed the game alone, and was given the opportunity to donate to the March of Dimes. The proportion of winnings donated when the child was alone and his judgment of model served as the primary measures.

Because of the marked heterogeneity of variance associated with the amount of money the children contributed, nonparametric analysis of the data was employed. A Mann-Whitney U test indicated that boys exposed to a charitable peer were significantly more generous than those not so exposed ($Z = 2.1$, $p < .03$, two-tailed). Girls were unaffected by the model's practices.

Moreover, and not surprisingly, the number of boy donors varied according to the model practices in the direction expected ($\chi^2 = 7.04$, $p < .01$, two-tailed). However, since 21 of the 96 boys had misperceived the experimental treatments, the data were again analyzed after excluding such subjects. Once again, nonparametric analysis also yielded a significant effect of the model upon amount contributed ($Z = 2.37$, $p < .01$). These findings, then, partially replicate those of

Bryan (1968), Hartup and Coates (1967), and Rosenhan and White (1967) in demonstrating the impact of behavioral example upon altruistic responses. More perplexing is the implied model X sex of subject interaction found in the current study, particularly since similar trends are found in many of our studies. Reports of such interactions do not appear in the literature with the exception of Rosenhan and White's findings that girls were less altruistic than boys after being exposed to a negatively reinforcing model. If such interactions are attributable to other than sampling fluctuations, the explanation for them is elusive.

Neither exhortations nor the variable of inconsistency affected donation or theft behavior. Moreover, exhortations did not combine with behavioral example in any additive fashion to produce greater generosity. However, the fact that exhortations failed to affect children's donations did not indicate that they failed to have any impact whatsoever. The verbalizations of the model were effective in determining the child's subsequent evaluation of him. The main effects of practicing, preaching, and grade on evaluation were all significant (F = 29.19, 85.49, 10.27, respectively, $p < .01$, two-tailed). Models who practiced charity were judged more favorably than those who failed to donate. Similarly, if model preached charity, he was rated more favorably than model who held a neutral conversation. Both of these models were rated more favorably than one who preached greed. Interestingly, those models who held a neutral conversation but failed to donate were not judged any less worthwhile than the model who preached greed but contributed gift certificates. The absence of verbal transgressions against the norms of giving or social responsibility suffices to produce a favorable rating irrespective of the acts accompanying it. That is, the absence of the model's acts to support verbal allegiance to the norm of social responsibility failed to affect the child's judgment of him. Of some interest is the failure of the evaluation of the model to be affected by the discrepancies of words and deeds. That is, if inconsistency is something other than simply the addition of the effects of words and those of deeds, if it is a variable in its own right, then one would expect its impact to be reflected in the interpersonal ratings assigned the model. This was not the case. Indeed, the practitioner of greed and the preacher of charity was rated as favorably as the practitioner of charity and "neutral" preacher.

The results thus suggest that words serve as an important determinant of the attraction of the model, while his acts are the more important determinant of the child's succorant behaviors. Moreover, it would appear that consistency in words and deeds simply fail to affect the child, whether it be in relation to his own self-sacrifice, honesty, or evaluations of the model.

The second experiment was designed to assess not only the impact of practices and exhortations upon donation and evaluative responses, but also to determine their effects upon the child's subsequent cognitions concerning charity. In effect, we were interested in determining the salience of the norm of social responsibility for the participating child, in assessing the determinants of such salience, and finally in assessing the relationship between the child's exhortations and his behavior. The procedures of this particular experiment are similar to those just described. The child is presented a videotaped demonstration of another, slightly older child of the same sex playing the bowling game. The model either practices greed or charity and either exhorts greed or charity, or holds a normatively neutral conversation. One important modification was that of structuring the study as a transmission experiment. After viewing the model, each child was asked to relate his thoughts and feelings about the game, charity, or whatever, by speaking into a microphone. He was told that his message would be relayed, at some future time, to another child. One hundred and thirty-two children were thus tested.

The results of the model's actions were essentially the same as those reported earlier. Since the distribution of donations was highly skewed, nonparametric analysis of the donation behavior was undertaken. Both the number of donors and the amount donated were significantly related to the actions of the model. Twenty-seven of the 66 children exposed to the altruistic model donated, while only 14 of 66 exposed to the nondonating model contributed any of their winnings (χ^2 = 5.98, $p < .02$). Moreover, the modeling effect was primarily due to the influence of the male children. The amount contributed by the children witnessing the generous model was significantly greater by a Mann-Whitney U test than children not so exposed ($Z = 1.94$, $p < .026$, one tailed). Again, the preaching effect was not significant by either χ^2 or Kruskal One-Way Analysis of Variance. Furthermore, attraction ratings, assessed in the manner reported above, showed the same relationship to the variables as in the prior experiment. The main effects of practice and preachings, as well as race of the subjects, were all significant ($F = 11.49, 30.82$, and 12.11, respectively). Preachers of greed were particularly rejected, while practitioners of charity were somewhat esteemed. Again, inconsistency failed to affect evaluation of the model. The model who preached charity but practiced greed was rated no worse than the model who did no preaching but practiced charity.

Of more interest were the preachings of the child. Each child's message was tape-recorded, transcribed, and rated as to the emphasis of the message upon charity or greed by two independent judges. Messages were rated on a scale of 1 to 5 as to their emphasis, with a score of 1 indicating an emphasis upon greed, a score of 3 indicating neutrality, and a score of 5 indicating considerable emphasis upon charity. To assess the impact of the treatment variables upon the subjects' messages, an analysis of variance was completed. The only significant effect was the main effect of the model's preachings ($F = 14.61$). Analysis of the group means showed that the children exposed to either the exhorter of charity or greed were more likely to emphasize charity in their messages than those exposed to the model who failed to verbalize either of these themes. It is interesting to note that the practice of charity by the model did not affect the emphasis of the children's messages nor, presumably, their cognitions concerning their social responsibilities.

To assess the relationship between the preachings of the child and his own behavior, children who had preached greed or failed to mention charity were compared to children who had emphasized charity as to their donation behavior. While the χ^2 value was significant ($\chi^2 = 16.14$), the associated ϕ correlation was a remarkably low .35. It should be noted moreover that this correlation is inflated through the operation of a determinant of giving: exposure to a generous model.

The experiments reported here have been designed to assess the relative strengths of two sources of influence upon two responses which were thought to reflect a single process. It appears increasingly clear that these two response systems are governed by different modes of input and are not highly correlated themselves.

Exhortations designed to make the norms governing the situation salient— norms governing the responsibilities toward the needy — fail to provide enough motivation to affect the child's willingness to sacrifice. Children appear quite indifferent to the norm and fail to respond to general exhortations regarding sacrifice. This does not mean that words do not affect the altruistic act. White (1967) has shown that children exposed to commands to give will be more likely to give when subsequently left alone than children not exposed to such explicit and coercive instructions. The data suggest, however, that exhorters, be they adult or peers, cannot be powerless and still affect responses. Those few studies which have demonstrated the impact of preaching upon self-denial responses (Mischel & Liebert, 1966; Rosenhan, Frederick, & Burrowes, 1968) have employed procedures that have given considerable power to the exhorter. That such power increases the effects of the instructions has been demonstrated by Mischel and Liebert (1967). Whatever the necessary conditions lending power to words, the present studies suggest that simple reminders of the norm of social responsibility are not enough to produce self-sacrificing behavior by children.

What does initiate action on the part of the child are the actions of the model? These findings extend those of previous investigators (Rosenhan & White, 1967; Hartup & Coates, 1967; Bryan, 1968) by demonstrating the impact of a peer model depicted via television upon altruistic responses. The question does remain as to the processes underlying the modeling effect. Special precautions were taken not to directly or vicariously reinforce the subject either materially or socially for imitative acts. Moreover, on the face of it, the imitative act should be aversive to the child. One process underlying the modeling effect may be vicarious fear reduction. While children may hear forms of behavior encouraged by the model, such talk may simply define permissible conversation but not permissible acts. Indeed, given the data concerning the lack of effects attributable to model's inconsistency in words and deeds, it is reasonable to assume that children, by and large, do not employ such verbal material in making predictions concerning the effects of their own behavior. Hence, when a child hears those encouraging words of greed or charity, he may not assume that such words have any implications for the permissibility of specific acts of avarice or succorance. Given the novel context of the laboratory as well as the unusual opportunity to donate, the child may well be inhibited. Recent results reported by Staub and Sherk (1968) indicated that children with high needs for social approval not only donated fewer prized possessions than those with low needs for such approval, but also more frequently failed to claim a legitimate reward. Given the demonstrated importance of vicarious experiences upon children's modeling behavior (Bandura *et al.*, 1967) and the likelihood that children are somewhat inhibited within this novel context, it would not be surprising that the witnessing of unusual behaviors, albeit socially acceptable ones, without reprimand, would subsequently serve a disinhibiting function for the observer. That is, children who are frightened even of doing the right thing may simply become less inhibited upon seeing another peer "get away with it." This suggests that model's practices do not arouse already learned prosocial or anti-social disposition, but rather free the child to act upon those already present.

While exhortations consistently fail to affect donation behavior, it is clear that verbal allegiance to the "norm of giving" (Leeds, 1963) or social responsibility (Berkowitz & Daniels, 1963) plays an important role in the child's evaluation of the model. Moreover, it appears that consistency is not a variable of concern, at least when the words are not backed with power and/or specific instructions. Hypocrisy, in itself, failed to affect either succorant behavior, the evaluative responses of the child, or the child's honesty. Since over 90% of the children in the last experiment agreed during a postexperimental interview that one should give, yet only 31% did so, and since less than 50% of those children who themselves preached charity to others, while having the opportunity to donate actually did so, it is suggested that integration of deeds concerning helping norms is neither a property of nor an expectation held by the young child.

Finally, while Campbell's (1963) thesis that modes of response acquisition combine, perhaps in an additive fashion, in influencing the elicited response may be true generally, these results suggest considerable specificity of modes of learning for modes of response when dealing with self-sacrifice. Neither the intersubstitutability (Campbell, 1963, p. 111) of the expression of such learning nor of the techniques designed to elicit behavior seems great. The intersubstitutability of such learning techniques upon the types of behavior elicited from the child may be considerably less than implied by Campbell (1963). One cannot help but agree, however, with Campbell's assertion that the investigation of the nature of the interactions of various influencing techniques upon behavioral expression represents a most important problem for social, and I might add, developmental psychology.

To conclude and reiterate, children evaluate their peers both on the latter's practices and his preachings concerning aiding, but the effects of each do not interact in influencing the child's behavior. From these and other studies, it is clear that behavior is affected by modeling, but apparently neither boys nor girls are affected in their behavior by the exhortations of the model. Moreover, it is becoming clear that the cognitions of the young child concerning his social responsibilities, as indicated by his preachings and by his reactions to transgressors, bear only slight relationship to his behavior. It does appear, however, to be a just world as one can be assured that children's standards for consistency for others do not exceed those they hold for themselves.

REFERENCES

Aronfreed, J., & Paskal, V. Altruism, empathy, and the conditioning of positive effect. Unpublished manuscript, University of Pennsylvania, 1965.

Bandura, A., Grusec, J.E., & Menlove, F.L. Vicarious extinction of avoidance behavior. *Journal of Personality and Social Psychology,* 1967, **6,** 16–23.

Bandura, A., Ross, D., & Ross, S. Imitation of film-mediated aggressive models. *Journal of Abnormal and Social Psychology,* 1963, **66,** 3–11.

Berkowitz, L. Responsibility, reciprocity and social distance in help-giving: An experimental investigation of English social class differences. *Journal of Experimental Social Psychology,* 1968, **4,** 46–63.

Berkowitz, L., & Daniels, L. Responsibility and dependency. *Journal of Abnormal and Social Psychology,* 1963, **66,** 429–436.

Berkowitz, L., & Friedman, P. Some social class differences in helping behavior. *Journal of Personality and Social Psychology,* 1967, **5,** 217–225.

Bryan, J.H. Actions speak louder than words: Model inconsistency and its effect on self-sacrifice. *Research Bulletin,* **68-16.** Princeton, N.J.: Educational Testing Service, 1968.

Bryan, J.H., & Test, M.A. Models and helping: Naturalistic studies in aiding behavior. *Journal of Personality and Social Psychology,* 1967, **6,** 400–407.

Bryan, J.H., & Walbek, N.H. Preaching and practicing self-sacrifice: Children's actions and reactions. Unpublished manuscript, Northwestern University, 1968.

Campbell, D.T. Ethnocentric and other altruistic motives. In D. Levine (Ed.) *Nebraska symposium on motivation; Lincoln:* University of Nebraska Press, 1965, pp. 283–311.

Campbell, D.T. Social attitudes and other acquired behavioral dispositions. In S. Koch (Ed.), *Psychology: A study of a science.* Vol. 6. New York: McGaw Hill, 1963, pp. 94–172.

Handlon, B.J., & Gross, P. The development of sharing behavior. *Journal of Abnormal and Social Psychology,* 1959, **59,** 425–428.

Hartup, W.W., & Coates, B. Imitation of peers as a function of reinforcement from the peer group and the rewardingness of the model. *Child Development,* 1967, **38,** 1003–1016.

Kinsey, A.C., Pomeroy, W.B., & Martin, C.W. *Sexual behavior in the human male.* Philadelphia: Saunders, 1951.

LaPiere, R.T. Attitudes vs. actions. *Social Forces,* 1934, **14,** 230–237.

Leeds, R. Altruism and the norm of giving. *Merrill-Palmer Quarterly,* 1963, **9,** 229–240.

Midlarsky, E., & Bryan, J.H. Training charity in children. *Journal of Personality and Social Psychology,* 1967, **5,** 408–415.

Mischel, W., & Liebert, R.M. Effects of discrepancies between observed and imposed reward criteria on their acquisition and transmission. *Journal of Personality and Social Psychology,* 1966, **3,** 45–53.

Mischel, W., & Liebert, R.M. The role of power in the adoption of self-reward patterns. *Child Development,* 1967, **38,** 673–683.

Rosenhan, D., Frederick, F., & Burrowes, A. Preaching and practicing: Effects of channel discrepancy on norm internalization. *Child Development,* 1968, **39,** 291–301.

Rosenhan, D., & White, G.M. Observation and rehearsal as determinants of pro-social behavior. *Journal of Personality and Social Psychology,* 1967, **5,** 424–431.

Staub, E., & Sherk, L. Relationship between need approval and children's sharing behavior. Unpublished manuscript, Harvard University, 1968.

Test, M.A., & Bryan, J.H. Dependency, reciprocity and models. *Journal of Social Psychology,* 1969, in press.

Wagner, C., & Wheeler, L. Model, need and cost effects in helping behavior. *Journal of Personality and Social Psychology,* 1969, **12,** 111-116.

White, G.M. The elicitation and durability of altruistic behavior in children. *Research Bulletin,* 67-27. Princeton, N.J.: Educational Testing Service, 1967.

Wright, B.A. Altruism in children and perceived conduct of others. *Journal of Abnormal and Social Psychology,* 1942, **37,** 218-233.

SOCIAL NORMS AND THE SOCIALIZATION
OF ALTRUISM

LEGALITY AND HARMFULNESS OF A BYSTANDER'S FAILURE TO INTERVENE AS DETERMINANTS OF MORAL JUDGMENT

Harry Kaufmann[1]

Recent incidents in a number of metropolitan centers have focused attention on the passivity of witnesses to crimes of various sorts. Not only has this extreme noninvolvement been documented by a number of newspaper articles, but, in a laboratory test of intervention, Kaufmann[2] found that only 19 out of 186 subjects who had been given an accessory task protested when a "teacher" ostensibly gave increasingly severe shocks to a stooge as punishment for learning errors. Of these 19, only ten refused to complete the experiment. Moreover, the willingness to intervene did not appear to be affected by such variables as respective status of the teacher and the subject, the authority for the choice of shock level expectation for future participation, or the moral deservingness of the "learner."

It might be supposed that legal prohibitions would operate as codified "norms" or as influential statements of presumed majority opinion. However, recent studies (Walker & Argyle, 1964; Berkowitz & Walker, 1967) have shown that, in fact, knowledge of "peer" opinion has a greater effect on moral judgment than knowledge of legal prohibition. Psychologically, then, morality and legality are not equivalent. Harmfulness might conceivably be seen as irrelevant to the morality of the bystander's behavior since he was not aware of the

[1]The present study was conducted while the author held a S.P.S.S.I. Grant-in-Aid.

[2]Kaufmann, H. The unconcerned bystander. Unpublished manuscript, Hunter College, 1967.

eventual outcome when he failed to act. However, Piaget (1948) has shown that children under seven judge "naughtiness" only in terms of "damage," while older children are more apt to consider "intentions." On the other hand, common as well as criminal law considers both intention and outcome.

The present study was conducted to assess evaluative attitudes toward non-involvement of a bystander, where such noninvolvement is either legal or illegal, and does or does not result in harm. Intention was not explicitly stated, and might have been assumed to be the same regardless of legality or outcome.

METHOD

Subjects

One hundred and fifty-four male and female students between the ages of 18 and 27 were used as subjects. The students were taking an introductory course in psychology and were given the questionnaire as a group.

Procedure

Subjects were told that the investigator was interested in assessing student attitudes. All students filled out a questionnaire which presented eight situations, In each situation, a potentially harmful event was taking place, and a Mr. X (who was given a different initial for each of the eight situations) failed to attempt to prevent this harm. The situations were ambiguous enough so that failure to intervene could be said to be either legal or illegal. The potential harm either occurred or was prevented by a change in the situation which came about after the bystander had failed to intervene. A sample situations follows.

> A man drowned when he fell through the ice on a frozen lake, 10 feet from shore. Mr. A, who observed the event, did nothing to help. The law does not require a person to render assistance in such a situation. Therefore, Mr. A is not liable to criminal prosecution. (legal-harm condition)

There were four experimental conditions, and each subject was asked to judge two situations for each of these four conditions. The eight situations were arbitrarily divided into four pairs. In each questionnaire, the paired situations were put in the same condition, and an approximately equal number of subjects was given each combination of paired situations and experimental condition. Each pair of situations, therefore, occurred in each of the four conditions an equal number of times. In each questionnaire, the paired situations followed each other, but the order of conditions was varied so that each condition appeared first in an equal number of questionnaires.

After reading about each situation, the subjects answered four questions evaluating either Mr. X or his actions. These four questions and the scales following them are shown in Table 1.

TABLE 1

QUESTIONNAIRE

A. As a question not of law but of morality, is Mr. X's action:

wrong as possible	very wrong	wrong	slightly wrong	not wrong	very right
_____	_____	_____	_____	_____	_____

B. Quite apart from legal aspects, Mr. X:

did not do anything wrong	did slightly wrong	did wrong	did very wrong
_____	_____	_____	_____

C. Leaving legal aspects aside, Mr. X:

should not be censured or punished in any way	should be reprimanded	should be punished slightly	should be punished moderately	should be punished severely	should be punished very severely
_____	_____	_____	_____	_____	_____

D. Although I know very little of Mr. X, my guess is that, as a person, he might be:

very unpleasant	moderately unpleasant	slightly unpleasant	neither pleasant nor unpleasant	slightly pleasant	moderately pleasant	very pleasant
_____	_____	_____	_____	_____	_____	_____

RESULTS

Table 2 shows mean responses for the four questions and the four experimental conditions. Analysis of variance of responses to question A, judging the morality of Mr. X's lack of action, yielded three significant main effects, legality ($p < .001$), harmfulness ($p < .001$), and subjects ($p < .01$), and one significant interaction, legality by subjects ($p < .01$). Regarding the two manipulated variables, illegal failure to intervene was considered significantly less moral than legal failure to intervene, and harmful outcomes rendered these failures significantly less moral than nonharmful outcomes.

TABLE 2

Mean Response to Questionnaire as a
Function of Experimental Condition[a]

	Question	Legally required to intervene		Not legally required to intervene	
		Harm	No Harm	Harm	No Harm
A:	Morality	4.70	4.44	4.46	4.18
B:	Morality	3.12	3.00	2.98	2.74
C:	Deserved punishment	2.82	2.58	2.48	2.14
D:	Pleasantness	5.12	4.79	4.92	4.72

[a]A higher mean indicates a less moral act, an act more deserving of punishment, and a less pleasant Mr. X.

Question B, which raised much the same issue as A, but phrased it differently and provided different responses, yielded the same three main effects ($p < .01$), but no interactions.

For question C, concerning recommended punishment, there were again three significant main effects ($p < .01, < .01, < .05$, respectively), and no significant interactions.

Finally, for question D, concerning the perceived pleasantness of Mr. X, there were three significant main effects, as well as three significant interactions (legality × harmfulness, legality × subjects, harmfulness × subjects). The legality × harmfulness ($p < .05$) interaction reflects the finding that the difference between the judgments in legal and illegal situations was greater when harm was involved than when no harm was involved. The other interactions, both significant at the .01 level, indicate that subjects were differentially affected by the legality or harmfulness variables.

DISCUSSION

In this study, an illegal failure to intervene was seen as more reprehensible (morally wrong and deserving of punishment) than such an act when it is legal. Berkowitz and Walker (1967) suggest that this effect stems from at least two sources: *(1)* the implication of majority opinion, and *(2)* the support of "legitmate authority."

It also appeared in this study that failure to intervene was viewed as more reprehensible when harm occurred, even though the prevention or lack of it could in no way be attributed to the bystander. This result appears to be at variance with Piaget's description of mature moral judgments which take intention into account. However, it should be noted that each case history mentioned both legality and "legal prosecution." Since the law does, in fact, consider outcome as well as intention when determining punishment, the mention of "legal prosecution" may have increased the salience of outcome.

Not surprisingly, subjects differed in the severity of their judgments. However, as was shown by the interaction effects for the "pleasantness" question, they were also differentially susceptible to the experimental manipulations.

Mr. X's personality (his pleasantness) was judged in the context of the situation in which it appeared. He was thought to be most pleasant when involved in a nonharmful and legal nonintervention situation, and least pleasant when involved in a harmful and illegal nonintervention situation. People, it thus appears, are judged by the manner in which their actions and intentions turn out, even if these outcomes are fortuitous.

REFERENCES

Berkowitz, L., & Walker, N. Laws and moral judgments. *Sociometry*, 1967, **30**, 410–422.
Kaufmann, H. The unconcerned bystander. Proceedings of the American Psychological Association, 1968.
Piaget, J. *The moral judgment of the child.* New York: Free Press, 1948.
Walker, N., & Argyle, M. Does the law affect moral judgments? *British Journal of Criminology*, 1964, October, 570–581.

NORMS AND NORMATIVE BEHAVIOR:
FIELD STUDIES OF SOCIAL INTERDEPENDENCE

John M. Darley and Bibb Latané

Altruism presents a problem for psychology. Altruistic behavior may please us as people, but it embarrasses traditional theories of psychology that are founded on the assumption that man is moved only by considerations of reinforcement. The hedonistic tone of traditional reinforcement theory is at variance with the simple observed fact that people do help others in circumstances in which there seem to be no gains and even considerable risk to themselves for doing so.

Reinforcement theory's traditional resolution of this dilemma is to postulate that individuals do, in fact, get rewards for altruistic acts. One line of argument is that the sight of a person in distress arouses sympathetic or empathic feelings in an observer: "Primitive passive sympathy," MacDougall said. The observer, in helping the victim, helps himself. He is motivated not to relieve the victim's suffering but to alleviate his own sympathetic distress. Whether this primitive passive sympathy is instinctive or is the result of complicated classical or instrumental conditioning, its arousal motivates a person to helping action and its termination rewards those actions.

A second resolution that preserves a reinforcement explanation of altruism postulates "norms" which the individual must learn to follow. A basic norm, according to this view, is to help other individuals in distress. If a properly socialized individual within a culture violates the helping norm, he subjects himself to negative consequences which punish him for his failure to help. As with the primitive passive sympathy explanation the onlooker acts altruistically because of the negative consequences of doing otherwise. Unlike the previous explanation, the negative consequences are anticipated in the future rather than in the immediate present, and no empathic distress must be aroused in the observer. Instead, he helps because the specific case he witnesses is covered by the general normative rule.

Several theories suggest various processes by which norms are enforced. For Freudians, rules originally enforced externally, largely by the parents, become internalized in the process of development to form the superego. Norm violation leads to guilt. Other theorists locate these rules, and their enforcing mechanisms, in the other members of the society in which the individual lives. They assert that norms are enforced by the threat of the disapproval of other onlookers and also, perhaps, by more concrete negative consequences that may stem from this disapproval.

It seems to us that many discussions of altruism have confused two basic questions, and that understanding can be more profitably advanced if these questions are separated. The first question asks: "What is the underlying force in mankind toward altruism?" or "What motivates altruistic behavior?" The second question is much more specific: "What determines, in a particular situation, whether or not one person helps another in distress?" The first question is a general one, of enormous social interest and importance, and of a semiphilosophic nature. It probably will never be completely answered by reference to data. The second question is more specific, more mundane, and more amenable to research analysis.

There is no reason to expect that principles used in answering the first question should also be important or even be relevant to answering the second. It is possible, for example, that norms provide a general predisposition to help other people, but that whether or not someone will help in a particular situation is dependent on other factors.

A number of theories do make heavy use of the concept of norms to account for variations in helping from one situation to another, however. Some suggest that different norms are engaged in different situations. The "social responsibility norm" will operate at the sight of a dependent other; the "mind your own business" norm will operate when another is less dependent. The "equal outcomes" norm will operate when there is a disparity in wealth among those present in a given situation; the "do as well for yourself as you can" norm will operate when there is a smaller disparity of wealth. In other situations, other norms, such as "reciprocity," "*noblesse oblige,*" and "to the victor belong the spoils" may be activated. Although, as we shall emphasize below, this diversity of norms seriously weakens their explanatory usefulness, it does allow the "explanation" of almost any kind of behavior.

A second way in which the concept of norms has been used to explain variations in helping from situation to situation is through the notion of norm "salience." A number of experimenters have shown that if one person does something, another person seeing him may be more likely also to do that thing. According to one common explanation for such effects, the model, by his behavior, increases the salience of the relevant norm for the observer, who is consequently more likely to obey this norm.

There may be considerable validity in such norm-centered accounts of behavior. We certainly hope so, since in other contexts we have used normative accounts to explain a variety of data. However, for the sake of argument, and in a mood of sporting perversity, we would like to take a rather radical position here—namely, that norms are, in general, rather unimportant determinants of behavior in specific helping situations, and that they should rarely be invoked unless all other alternative explanations fail. In the remainder of this paper, we will elaborate on some difficulties with the concept of norms, and present some data which illustrate these difficulties.

The main difficulty with norms is that they seem, at least in simple statement, contradictory. In our society, we are told to "do unto others as you would have them do unto you." We usually interpret this to mean that we should help others. Yet we are also taught "don't take candy from a stranger" or, more generally, that it is demeaning to accept help from others. It's good to help others: it's bad to be helped. This normative ambivalence toward helping and being helped is well illustrated by Adam Lindsay Gordon in his forgotten classic, *Ye Wearie Wayfarer.* Gordon exhorts us:

> Question not but live and labour
> Till yon goal be won,
> Helping every feeble neighbor,
> Seeking help from none.
>
> Life is mostly froth and bubble
> Two things stand like stone
> Kindness in another's trouble
> Courage in your own.

Although norms tell us we should not ask for help, we should also be able to look out for ourselves. As Mr. Deeds discovered to his chagrin, the man who attempts to help others at too great expense to himself may be looked on with suspicion and disapproval. As an example of this, a poor man recently found a sack of money that had fallen from a Brink's truck. He returned the money to Brinks (who were much startled, as they had not yet discovered the loss). Although publicized as a hero, he received scores of threatening and vilifying calls and letters castigating him for being a fool and exhorting him to look out for himself in the future.

A final way in which norms of helping conflict with other norms is that we are told to respect the privacy of others. If you intrude into another's distress, even with the best of intentions, you may find yourself resented and reviled. "Mind your own business," you may be told, "don't stick your nose in somebody else's mess." The Bible, as always, has the more elegant way of expressing this point: "He that passeth by, and meddleth with strife belonging not to him, is like one that taketh a dog by the ears (Proverbs, 26:17)."

Norms, then, seem to contradict one another. The injunction to help other people is qualified by strictures not to accept help, to look out for yourself, and not to meddle in other people's business. In any specific situation it is hard to see how norms will provide much guidance to an undecided bystander.

A second problem with norms is that they are usually stated in only the most vague and general way. There are probably good reasons why this is so. To specify norms in sufficient detail to allow them to be useful guides in specific situations would require an elaborately qualified, lengthily stated, integrated set of rules covering a wide variety of situations, many of which will arise only infrequently. It is difficult to imagine an embattled bystander watching an act, wondering what to do, and leafing through his mental rule book to exclaim "Aha! That reminds me! Section 34.62b fits this case!"

A third difficulty with normative accounts of variations in helping in specific situations is that there is little evidence that people actually think about norms when choosing a course of action. In a series of studies in which we have staged realistic emergencies and then observed people's reactions to them (Latané & Darley, this volume), we have found that subjects typically intervene, if they intervene at all, in a matter of seconds. They seem to be guided by their first reactions, and not by a complicated choice among a variety of norms. In postexperimental interviews, we were unable to elicit any indication that subjects made explicit mental reference to norms before they decided whether or not to act. Subjects talked about their interpretations of the facts of the situations, but they did not report that they had thought about norms. This accords with our examination of our own mental processes in the minor emergencies and help-giving situations with which we have been faced. We do not often think about the golden rule when we are confronted by a beggar.

Our final reason for rejecting norm-centered explanations is that they do not seem to fit the facts adequately. For instance, a norm-centered account should argue that the presence of other people would make individuals more likely to behave in a prosocial fashion. Other people should increase the salience of norms and enforce them through the threat of negative sanctions. In our experiments on emergencies, however, the presence of other people consistently dampens altruistic ardor. Individuals seem much more likely to intervene helpfully when they are alone than when they think other people are present.

Norms, then, are contradictory and vague. People do not report thinking about them when deciding what to do. And their behavior does not always correspond to simple predictions derived from normative considerations. Having put forward these arguments, let us now try to shore them up with some data. We would like here to review several studies on helping behavior in nonemergency situations. These studies are modest ones; they were designed to explore rather different issues than the general question of the relevance of norms. It seems clearest and most sporting to present them on their own terms rather than selecting the data that best fit the point that we are trying to make. What follows, then, is rather a smorgasbord of studies in which, occasionally, immediate relevance to the central question of this paper may be sacrificed for clarity of presentation.

PARAMETRIC STUDIES OF COMPLIANCE WITH A SIMPLE REQUEST

A major difficulty with laboratory studies of helping is that they are hard to relate to real life situations. On the one hand, subjects are under unusual pressures in the laboratory—they have been pulled out of their daily routine and are shorn of many of their usual defenses. They cannot easily leave the situation, and they may find it hard simply to ignore a request. They are known by name to the experimenter and sometimes to other subjects, and they may be anxious to gain favorable evaluations from them. These lowered defenses and heightened pressures may make the laboratory subject much more vulnerable to a request for help than the man on the street.

A second dissimilarity between laboratory helping situations and life is that in order to make a request for help believable in its laboratory context, and in order to increase the measurement utility of the response, subjects may be faced with rather unusual demands. "How many hours are you willing to spend in sensory deprivation?" "Will you help stack these papers?" "How shall we allocate these points?" Although laboratory experiments constitute an invaluable technique for testing theoretical derivations, they may not tell us much about the determinants of helping in everyday situations.

Over the past 3 years, 93 students in introductory social psychology courses at Columbia University have gone out on the streets of New York and made a variety of simple requests of some 4400 passers-by. They asked for different kinds of help, and they asked for it in different ways. The varying responses to their requests provide some information about the prevalence of altruistic compliance and the parameters influencing it.

Subjects

Students, for the most part relatively cleancut, well-dressed male (76%) undergraduates, descended on Manhattan Island in the springs of 1966–1968. Students avoided the Columbia area, but spread out over the East and West sides and the Village. Sixty-one percent of the people they asked were male, 47% were alone, 70% were moving at the time of request. Thirty percent of the requests were made in indoor locations such as subway stations and railway terminals, and 70% were made outdoors. Sixty percent of the requests were made in fairly crowded surroundings, with five or more other people within about 30 feet.

Students participated in the study as part of a class assignment. For the most part, they seemed interested in the study and found the task rather easy. The few who felt too embarrassed to "beg on the streets" were allowed to take other projects. A number of checks supported the accuracy and veracity of the students' reports of their results; the number of fabricated cases was almost certainly less than 5% of the total. Students were asked to be as unselective as possible in choosing whom to "hit"; several devices were used to prevent systematic sampling of subjects and to assign subjects randomly to experimental conditions. Although there probably was still a tendency to avoid the most seedy or most threatening prospective donees, the sample is probably not too unrepresentative of New Yorkers who show themselves in public places.

Type of Request

As Table 1 shows, the type of request made a major difference in the likelihood of receiving help. Students were very successful in getting the time, directions, or change for a quarter. They were considerably less successful in getting a dime or the name of the passerby. Less than 40% of those asked for it

TABLE 1

Frequency of Response to Different Requests

"Excuse me, I wonder if you could . . .	Number asked	Percentage helping[a]
a. tell me what time it is?"	92	85_a
b. tell me how to get to Times Square?"	90	84_a
c. give me change of a quarter?"	90	73_a
d. tell me what your name is?"	277	39_b
e. give me a dime?"	284	34_b

[a]Conditions which do not share the same subscript are significantly different by χ^2 ($p < .05$).

gave their names, and then usually only their first names. Subjects usually seemed surprised when asked for their names, and the students reported that those who gave them often seemed to do it out of sheer reflex.

Manner of Request

A bold request for a dime worked in about one-third of the cases; requests including more information were markedly more successful, as Table 2 shows. If the subject gave his name before asking for a dime, he had about a 50–50 chance of getting help, and if he claimed that he needed to make a telephone call or had lost his wallet, he was helped two-thirds of the time.

Information preceding the request had as striking an effect when students asked for names. Students who asked simply, "Could you tell me what your name is?" were answered 30% of the time. When they said, "Excuse me, my name is ____. Could you tell me what your name is?" 59% of the 64 asked gave their names ($p < .01$ by χ^2).

Sex of Subject and of Requester

Sex had no effect on giving minor assistance. Sex affected the request for a dime: female requesters were helped by 58% of the subjects; males were helped by only 46% ($p < .02$). Sex of the subject had no effect on the request for a

TABLE 2

Frequency of Response as a Function of Manner of Request

Manner of request	Number asked	Percentage helping[a]
a. "Excuse me, I wonder if you could give me a dime?"	284	34$_a$
b. "Excuse me, I wonder if you could give me a dime? I've spent all my money."	108	38$_{ab}$
c. "Excuse me, I wonder if you could tell me what time it is?" . . ."and could you give me a dime?"	146	43$_{ab}$
d. "Excuse me, my name is _____ . I wonder if you could give me a dime?"	150	49$_b$
e. "Excuse me, I wonder if you could give me a dime? I need to make a telephone call."	111	64$_c$
f. "Excuse me, I wonder if you could give me a dime? My wallet has been stolen."	108	72$_c$

[a]Conditions which do not share the same subscript are significantly different by χ^2 ($p < .05$).

dime. Sex also had a large effect on the request for a name, but a different pattern of results emerged. Females were more likely to receive an answer, but only if the subject was male. Sixty-eight percent of male subjects gave their name to a female; other sex pairings achieved response rates of 37–39% ($p < .01$).

Number of Requesters

If a person, for the same cost, can help two people rather than just one, will he be more likely to help? To answer this question, male and female students asked 1440 passers-by for 20 cents for the subway. They asked either alone or in pairs. The pairs were composed either of one male and one female, or of two males or two females. The form of request was standard in all cases: "Excuse me, could you help me (us)? I (we) have to get downtown and need 20 cents for the subway?" Table 3 presents the results.

TABLE 3

*Frequency of Helping as a Function of Sex and
Number of Requesters for a Dime*

Sex of requester	Alone		Same sex pair		Mixed sex pair	
	Number asked	Percentage helping[a]	Number asked	Percentage helping[a]	Number asked	Percentage helping[a]
Female	319	57$_b$	240	72$_a$	323	53$_b$
Male	442	30$_c$	360	25$_c$	317	50$_b$

[a]Conditions which do not share the same subscript are significantly different by χ^2 ($p < .05$).

The results were straightforward. Females were almost twice as likely to receive help as males when alone and three times as likely when in same sex pairs. The presence of a second female increased the response to a female ($p < .01$); the presence of another male slightly decreased the response to a male (n.s.). These results seem to suggest that subjects responded mainly to the person making the request, and that the presence of another person had little influence upon helping. Results from the mixed-sex pairs, however, change this picture. A female accompanied by a male was slightly less successful than a single female (n.s.), but a male accompanied by a female was much more successful than a single male ($p < .01$). It appears as if subjects do respond to the second member of a pair. They do not respond to the sum of the needs of the two persons. If there are two people asking, the response seems to be averaged.

Discussion

These results can easily be explained in terms of norms. People gave the correct time, change of a quarter, or directions because there is a norm to "help thy neighbor." They were less likely to give money because there is a norm to "look out for yourself." They often did not give their names because there is a norm against invading privacy. If the requester gave his name before asking for a name or a dime, he was more successful because there is a norm of reciprocity. Females were more successful than males in getting money because there is a norm to help the weak. Males were more likely to give their names to females because there is a norm to be gallant. Couples were . . . but stop. We are citing one new norm to explain each successive comparison. To continue in this fashion would be nothing more than giving *ad hoc* explanations for results that we could not have predicted in advance. Further, the explanations are not really very clear. We are not convinced that normative explanations really help our understanding of the results.

THE EFFECT OF SOCIAL CLASS AND FAMILIARITY OF
ENVIRONMENT ON HELPING

An individual was identified sitting far enough removed from other people to be functionally isolated from them. A young man approached him on crutches, with his left knee bent and heavily taped. Suddenly the young man fell to the ground, clutching his knee in great pain. A rater stationed some distance away unobtrusively observed the incident and noted the reactions of the bystander to it.

Sixty such incidents were staged in each of two public locations, an underground subway station and La Guardia Airport. The results were startlingly different. In the subway, 83% of the people helped; in the airport, only 41% did ($p < .01$). This result obviously can be explained by socioeconomic differences. Middle and upper class citizens, who are much more likely to be present at airports, may be less inclined to help others. They may put a higher value on the privacy of others and thus be less likely to intrude even when the others are in distress. Lower classes, who are more frequently found in subways, have no such inhibitions. Differences in norms between social classes can obviously account for this difference in helping—or can they?

Roger Granet, who ran the studies as a class project at New York University, had a rather different hypothesis in mind. His expectation was that familiarity with the environment was the determining factor. Persons who were familiar with the physical location in which the emergency took place would be more likely to help the victim. The major reason for greater helpfulness in subways is that subway users grow familiar with the subway setting in a way that few people ever do with airports. To determine if familiarity influenced functioning in emergency situations, after each bystander had responded to the staged incident and the rater had judged the adequacy of his response, another experimenter appeared to interview the bystander about his familiarity with subways or airports. Subjects were asked about how often they used the facility and their knowledge of its entrances, exits, telephone booths, etc. The questionnaire was short, and the person administering it, though goodnatured, was large. There were only two refusals to answer. One other variable was also coded: the socio-economic class of the bystander as judged on a five point scale from the external cues of dress and bearing. Various correlations between the class and familiarity scales gave us some confidence that they were valid. As we would expect, the socioeconomic class of bystanders in the airport was higher than that of by-standers in the subway. People were, on the average, considerably less familiar with the airport environments. More subtle results also conform to our general expectations: the higher the socioeconomic class of the respondent, the more likely he was to be familiar with the airport and the less likely he was to be famil-iar with the subway station.

The results on helping are quite clear. In both the airport and the subway, there was a significant correlation ($r = .29, p < .05; r = .31, p < .05$, respectively) between familiarity and responding to the emergency. In neither case was there a significant correlation between social class and helping behavior. As one would expect from this pattern of results, the relationship between familiarity and emergency functioning was not much affected by partialling out the effect of socioeconomic class. The overall pattern of the results is clear: increased famil-iarity with a setting is associated with an increase in the helping behavior. Socio-economic class is not.

Granet's interpretations of these results seem to us to be the appropriate ones: a person who is more familiar with the environment is more aware of the way in which the environment works. He is not overloaded with stimuli, and his fears of embarrassment or, in the subway, actual physical harm, have moderated. He may have a greater stake in keeping that environment safe. Thus he is more likely to help. But the norms supporting helping behavior are equally relevant, regardless of environmental familiarity. Again norms do not account for the be-havior of the subjects.

DOWN IN THE SUBWAY

The next study took place in the subways of New York City, and was done by Harvey Allen as a Ph.D. dissertation at New York University. A subject was riding in a subway, and a second person stood or sat near him. A bewildered looking individual approached and asked whether the subway is going uptown or downtown. The other bystander gave the wrong answer—if the subway was going uptown, he replied "downtown," and vice versa. The dilemma for the subject was clear; should he give the right information, correcting the other bystander, or not?

The situation was, of course, prearranged. Both the question asker and the misinformer were experimenters. The dependent measure of the study was whether the bystander corrected the misinformer. In the first study, Allen varied the direction in which the original request for information was aimed. In the first condition, the request was aimed at the subject; in a second condition, the question was aimed at both bystanders; and in the third condition, the misinformer-to-be was directly addressed. These variations had major effects. When the misinformer cut in to answer the question asked of the naive subject, subjects almost always corrected him and did so immediately, impatiently, and indignantly. When the original question was addressed generally toward the two-person group, subjects corrected considerably less frequently. Finally, when the question was directed at the misinformer, subjects corrected least frequently of all. Even though norms governing response should be fairly constant, situational variables can have a strong effect on the frequency of help (Table 4).

Allen's second study demonstrates that people behave in accordance with their estimates of the cost to themselves for doing so. Again, someone asked for directions and was misinformed, putting pressure on the naive subject to correct him. (In this experiment, the question was always aimed at both the confederate and the naive bystander since that gave nearest to a 50–50 split of responding in the previous study.) Unlike the previous study, the misinformer-to-be created a character for himself before the question asking incident occurred. He sat with his legs stretched in front of him in the subway car. Another individual (yet another confederate) walked past him and stumbled over his feet. The misinformer-to-be responded in one of three ways: by doing nothing, by looking up from his magazine on muscle-building and shouting threats of physical harm at the helpless stumbler, or by making embarrassing comments about him. Thus, in the last

TABLE 4

Direction of the Asker's Question and
Number of Corrections Made [a]

Direction of question	Number asked	Percentage helping
Misinformer	30	27
Group	30	47
Bystander	30	93

[a]$\chi^2 = 31.44$, $p < .01$.

two conditions the misinformer-to-be established that he was quickly ready to resort to physical violence or noisy vituperation when crossed. When he subsequently misinformed the direction seeker, he presented an acute dilemma for the real subject. For him to offer the correct information required contradicting the misinformer, who might react badly to this correction.

In the third condition the misinformer-to-be made no response to the tripping incident, thus not establishing himself as belligerent. In a fourth condition, in which Allen wished to make it clear to the subject that there was a very low probability of confrontation with the misinformer, the misinformer gave a tentative answer to the request for directions (e.g., "Uptown, but I'm not sure"), making it apparent that he was not confident about his answer.

The effects of variations in potential nastiness of the misinformer are quite clear, and much as you would expect them to be. The subject was most reluctant to correct the physically threatening person and least reluctant to correct the tentatively answering person. The other two conditions fell in between in the expected positions. Clearly, subjects calculated the cost of help and modified their behavior accordingly (Table 5).

One further result is of note: if the subject had not corrected the misinformer after 30 seconds, the misinformer walked away out of ear shot, thus eliminating, for the subject, the problem of correcting the misinformer in order to help the question asker. Among subjects who had failed to correct by the time the misinformer had left, correction was still less likely among those subjects for whom the misinformer had established a threatening or an embarrassing character for himself.

TABLE 5

Degree of Threat and Number of Corrections [a]

Degree of threat	Number asked	Percentage helping
Physical threat	50	16
Embarrassment	50	28
Control	50	52
Reduced embarrassment	50	82

[a] $\chi^2 = 51.56$, $p < .001$.

In both these studies, differences between conditions showed up even though norms for helping should have been equally strong. Allen's third study tried to vary norms directly by varying the character of the direction asker, who was later to be misinformed. In one condition he was dressed as an obvious tourist, carrying a travel bag with stickers from the Midwest, and dressed in a semi-western hat. This should arouse norms about helping strangers to the situation. In a second condition, the future direction asker established himself as a helping person. A female confederate (by this time you must have the feeling that roughly half of the population of New York served as confederates—Allen had the same feeling when he paid them), heavily laden with packages, spectacularly dropped them. The future direction asker helped her to pick them up, hopefully engaging norms of reciprocity as well as modelling a help-giving act. The third condition was a control condition; no particular character was established for the direction asker.

Although the effects were in the direction one might anticipate, no significant differences were found. In a situation in which it seems plausible to assume that norms of helping strangers and norms connected with reciprocity of helping actions were aroused, no significant differences were produced in helping behavior (Table 6).

TABLE 6

Character of Question Asker and
Number of Corrections

Character of question asker	Number asking	Percentage helping
Tourist	50	62
Helpful	50	68
Control	50	48

$^a\chi^2 = 4.38$, n.s.

FRISBEE STUDY

We are all familiar with the frisbee, or pluto platter, that appears on college campuses in the spring. It is a circular, almost pie plate-shaped disk which, when propelled by an expert, can be made to fly or float through the air in complex and graceful arcs. The amount of time college students take off from more scholarly activities to devote to the study of frisbees suggests that the activity is pleasurable and even fascinating. In a study conducted in a senior social psychology seminar at New York University, Sheri Turtletaub and Harriet Ortman cleverly capitalized on this fascination to study the promotion of inter-action among groups of strangers. They were concerned with factors promoting interaction among previously nonorganized groups in public places. Most specific-ally, their task was to turn the Grand Central Station waiting room into a frenzy of flying frisbees.

A girl sat on a bench in the waiting room at Grand Central. Soon another girl sat on a bench facing her. They recognized each other and began a conversa-tion. One girl had been shopping, and announced that she had just bought a fris-bee. The other girl asked to see it, and the first girl threw it to her. They then be-gan to toss it back and forth. Apparently by accident, the frisbee was thrown to a third person and the reaction of this third person (an experimental confeder-ate), was the independent variable of the study. That person either enthusiastic-ally joined in throwing the frisbee or accused the two girls of being childish and dangerous, and kicked the frisbee back across the gap.

Whichever of these two variations occurred, the two girls continued throw-ing the frisbee back and forth and soon sent it to one of the 3–10 bystanders seated on the benches. They continued this until all the bystanders on the two facing benches had been probed. A bystander was counted as participating in the activity if he returned the frisbee at least twice. The percentage of bystanders present who joined in the frisbee fest was the dependent measure of the study. In all, 170 people took part in the study.

When the experimental confederate joined in the play, the other spectators were extremely likely to do so also. Over four cases, 86% of the 34 available people responded, often coming from other areas of the waiting room to partici-pate. Indeed, in this condition the problem was not to start interaction but to terminate it so that the experimenters could leave for the next waiting room and run further incidents.

On the other hand, if the confederate refused to play, and instead negative-ly sanctioned the girls' activity, in four cases no other bystander of the 24 ever joined in the action. Instead, people sitting nearby would frequently get up and move to other seats to avoid being thrown a frisbee, muttering their disapproval while doing so.

The finding seems to require a normative analysis. When certain norms are made salient, they inhibit action. It also seems to fit a modelling explanation. If the third confederate participates, others do also; if she does not participate, others do not. However, the girls went on to run another condition that seemed to eliminate a simple modelling explanation. In this control condition, the confederate did not join in the action but allowed the frisbee to bounce off her accidentally and be retrieved by one of the two original girls. In this condition, a high percentage of bystander participation was observed: of 25 subjects, 74% in four cases, not significantly different from the positive participation condition. A person who was a model for nonaction failed to inhibit participation by the bystanders.

At this point we concluded that what the confederate did was less important than what the confederate said. The one treatment that significantly inhibited interaction was the one in which the confederate loudly denounced the frisbee throwers. This seemed to require a norm-centered interpretation of the results since it was to various norms that the confederate appealed. The experimenters carefully ran other conditions to tease apart exactly what norms were operative in the situation. In these further conditions, the confederate carefully confined her negative comments to an appeal to one norm. In one situation, she cited the danger to others that was caused by throwing the frisbee, in another she accused the participants of indulging in childish behavior.

These two kinds of sanctions were not significantly different from one another in the amount of action they inhibited. The overall percentage of action was about 27% of 79 subjects in 16 cases. At this point, one would be prone to conclude that both of these norms are about equally effective in inhibiting interactions since making either of them salient inhibits participation roughly equally.

However, the girls did one more manipulation, the results of which call a norm-centered account into question. The manipulation crosscut the negative sanction manipulation and consisted simply of whether or not the sanctioning person stayed to watch the frisbee players after she gave the sanctions or immediately left the waiting room. When the sanctioning individual stayed, the usual result occurred—play was greatly inhibited (11% in 33 subjects in eight cases, as reported above). But when the sanctioning person left, the percentage of participation of bystanders rose to near its original rate (60% of 46 subjects in eight cases, not significantly different from the 80% average of the other positive conditions). It was not simply the sanctioning speech given by the confederate that inhibited play, but the sanctioning speech plus her continued presence.

It might be argued that the continued presence of the sanctioning individual made the norm that she had evoked more "salient" and thus more inhibitory. This, we think, stretches the meaning of the word "salience." Even when the denouncer left, she had previously shrieked out a denunciation of the frisbee throwers. Clearly, the norms she cited were salient to bystanders in that they were forcefully reminded of the existence of these norms. However, they still participated. One explanation of the result is that the bystander simply considered the costs of participating. When the spoilsport confederate stayed around, it was clearly possible that she might yell at other bystanders who participated, call the police, or otherwise punish or embarrass the participants. We see no necessity to talk about norms to account for these data.

Discussion

These four studies, as designed, obviously have little in common with each other. They do, however, illustrate the points we feel are important about the relationship of norms to behavior. The data on responses to simple requests indicate that any serious attempt to deal with the variations in response rates in normative terms must involve the postulation of a proliferation of norms—about as many norms as Dr. MacDougall had instincts. In cases where the norms governing help can be assumed to be constant, such as the collapse of a man on crutches, environmental variables cause strong changes in the rates of helping. Finally, in the last two studies where normative and cost explanations are roughly pitted against each other, cost explanations prevail. All in all, norm-centered explanations of helping seem difficult to apply.

We have argued that a person's helping behavior is too complexly determined by situational factors to be accounted for by norms. Yet one question remains: why do some people explain their own helping behavior in normative terms? Surely this argues for the necessity for, and validity of, norm-centered accounts of helping behavior.

But perhaps not. We are familiar with other cases in which a person explains his behavior in ways that have little to do with the causes of it. The obsessive has a perfectly good account of his reasons for washing his hands—they are dirty. Or the awakened subject complies with the posthypnotic suggestion of the hypnotist and begins dancing at the sound of music, but has an explanation for why he did so if he is pressed for one. "Just practicing for a dance I'm going to," he reports.

Even when we do not infer unconscious motives from the discrepancy, we are familiar with cases in which a person's actions are not really accounted for by his explanations of them. The college student who wants permission to turn in a late paper is aware of a socially acceptable set of excuses which he is likely to offer instead of the real reasons for his tardiness. Or, nearer home, the deductive, logically sequenced steps of the normal journal article, if our cocktail confessions are correct, may grossly misrepresent the intuitive, post hoc way a good deal of research gets done in psychology.

Looking at helping actions from this perspective, it is possible to see how a good deal of childhood training involves teaching children to give normative explanations of behaviors that are, in fact, somewhat more complexly determined. The child sees the parent giving money to a Salvation Army Santa Claus and asks why. "We should share our nice things with less fortunate others," the father tells him. Thus, the child learns two things: the specific norm, and that it is appropriate to give a "should," or norm-centered account for helping behavior. Later, when the child gives away some valued family possession to an artful beggar, the parents' anguished explanation of why they took it back teaches the child that although norms "are very thoughtful of you, dear," their relation to behavior should not be too close.

These considerations seem to lead to a picture of norms as explanatory fictions used to explain actions after the fact, but having no behavior-guiding force of their own. But, although this is a possible conclusion to our argument, it is not a necessary one.

Some events occur and are responded to without a great deal of rational thought. This is true of emergencies; it is probably also true of the Milgram (1965) and Brock and Buss (1962) experiments, in which subjects found themselves administering electric shocks to people. It is also true in real life situations, such as confronting a beggar, in which we have our refusal speech begun before he is half through his appeal. Only later, thinking back over the incident, does it come clear to us that ethical norms are relevant to our actions and that, under pressure of time and circumstance, we behaved in a fashion not entirely in keeping with these norms. Then we may cope with this realization in ways that have implications for our future behavior. As the research of Berscheid and Walster (1967) shows, if an opportunity to compensate the victim appropriately appears, we may take it. On the other hand, as Lerner's studies demonstrate, we may also justify our behavior toward the victim by derogating him or otherwise convincing ourselves that "he deserved what he got."

In this fashion, although normative considerations may not be important in predicting responses to sudden appeals for help, after his response the person may reflect on the discrepancies between norms and his behavior. This reflection may cause him to desire to compensate or make restitution, either toward the specific previous victim of his failure to act or to all people in distress. A person in this frame of mind might actually seek out opportunities to help and even be a wandering "good Samaritan." Less happily, the tensions between actions and norms may lead a person to rationalize the rightness of his actions by arguing that a person who needs help always deserves the difficulties in which he finds himself, which will make him even less likely to help people in distress in the future.

REFERENCES

Berscheid, E., & Walster, E. When does a harm-doer compensate a victim? *Journal of Personality and Social Psychology*, 1966, 6, 435–441.
Brock, T. C., & Becker, L. A. "Debriefing" and susceptibility to subsequent experimental manipulations. *Journal of Experimental Social Psychology, 1966*, 2, 314–323.
Brock, T.C., & Buss, A.H. Dissonance, aggression, and evaluation of pain. *Journal of Abnormal & Social Psychology*, 1962, 65, 197-202.
Milgrim, S. Some conditions of obedience and disobedience to authority, *Human Relations*, 1965, 18, 57-75

THE SOCIALIZATION OF ALTRUISTIC AND SYMPATHETIC BEHAVIOR: SOME THEORETICAL AND EXPERIMENTAL ANALYSES

Justin Aronfreed[1]

The focus of this volume is on certain forms of human social behavior which are widely interpreted as the expression of altruistic and sympathetic dispositions. I am going to confine my own contribution primarily to some theoretical and experimental analyses of the origins of these dispositions—more particularly, to an analysis of the affective and cognitive mechanisms through which they are originally acquired. The purpose of the analysis is to show that an adequate psychological conception of altruism and sympathy cannot be mounted without a broader developmental perspective into the process of socialization. I would like to begin the analysis by calling to your attention some of the problems which are associated with any attempt to specify the criteria for the identification of altruistic and sympathetic actions. Then I would like to make a few general observations, of a developmental and even comparative nature, which follow from these problems of criteria. Finally, I want to use the naturalistic socialization of children as a context in which to place two different types of experimental inquiries into children's acquisition of their dispositions toward altruism and sympathy.

[1]Vivian Paskal was a warm and intelligent collaborator in the experiments which are outlined in the latter part of this paper. Her untimely death in January of 1969 has only temporarily delayed the plans for co-authored reports of the full empirical details of the experiments.

Perhaps the most significant way of characterizing the consequences of socialization is to say that children become capable of their own internalized control over their behavior. Their acquired patterns of social behavior begin to show, quite early in the course of development, many signs of persistence even in the absence of explicit rewards or punishments. The fact that children do come to maintain certain forms of conduct, under conditions which would not support their expectation of direct external reinforcement, and sometimes even without the presence of agents of socialization, is a phenomenon of major importance for an understanding of altruism and sympathy. It indicates that children are able to monitor their behavior in the absence of control by actual or anticipated external outcomes which have immediate consequences for themselves. If we assume that the child's choices among behavioral options must have some consequences which are reinforcing, in order to account for any stability in the maintenance of the choices, it then follows that the child's direct experience of rewards and punishments is at least partially dispensable as the medium of reinforcement.

I have suggested elsewhere, in more detailed analyses of the phenomena of internalization (Aronfreed, 1968a,b), that internalized control of the child's behavior rests on the coupling of potentially reinforcing changes of affectivity to internal monitors. These internal monitors are sometimes directly inherent in the feedback from the behavior itself. But they take their move powerful form in cognitive representations which are highly mobile with respect to both the child's behavior and its immediate external environment. Because the child's capacity for cognitive representation becomes relatively independent of any direct correlation to overt action, or to the observable consequences of action, it assumes anticipatory as well as reactive functions in the control of the child's behavior. For the purposes of this volume, I want only to point out that a broad conception of the mechanisms of internalization is required for an understanding of the specific character of altruistic and sympathetic actions. I am also going to argue that the inference of empathic or vicarious mediation of affectivity is the central criterion for the identification of altruism and sympathy.

Altruism and sympathy cannot be identified as distinct forms of behavior. They may be more accurately identified as dispositional components of actions. Moreover, their identification requires close attention to the conditions under which an act occurs, rather than merely a knowledge of the consequences of the act. In the case of altruism, for example, the altruistic act sometimes has been analyzed as though its critical feature were the absence of reinforcing (or valued) consequences for the actor (Durkheim, 1951, pp. 217-240). However, the fact that an act has no directly rewarding external consequences for the actor does not imply that the act functions entirely without reinforcing consequences. From the point of view of the requirements for a more general conception of internalized control of behavior, we would do better to assume that altruistic acts are indeed governed by the affective value of their anticipated outcomes, and that they often do have reinforcing consequences for the person who carries them out. Even when an altruistic act may have a directly experienced aversive outcome for the actor, the value of its total set of outcomes can nevertheless be preferred to the value of the outcomes of another less altruistic alternative.

The assumption that altruistic behavior does have reinforcing consequences is not to be taken as equivalent to an assertion which can be found in a number of recent analyses of altruism—the assertion that altruistic action can be treated as a form of social exchange (Gouldner, 1960; Homans, 1961; Thibaut & Kelly, 1959). The concept of altruism can more usefully be restricted to the choice of an act which is at least partly determined by the actor's expectation of consequences which will benefit another person without benefit to himself. But the expected consequences for the other person are not necessarily without affective (and reinforcement) value for the actor, even though directly beneficial outcomes for the actor are not specified by the altruistic component of the act.

When the consequences of an act for another person are concrete and visible, their affective value for the actor may be mediated by his capacity for empathic or vicarious response to social cues which immediately transmit the other person's experience (for example, to expressive cues which may convey the affective state of the other person). Alternatively, the actor may experience the empathically or vicariously reinforcing affective consequences of altruistic behavior through his capacity to give a cognitive representation to the effects of the behavior on another person. The affective support for the altruistic act therefore does not require that the effects of the act be directly observable. Of course, the affective value that is attached to such cognitive representations will sometimes be filtered through the normative self-evaluative systems which people may apply to their actions. But changes of self-esteem or other consequences of self-evaluation cannot have a criterial status in the specification of the affective or cognitive mechanisms of altruistic behavior. A concept of altruism must focus on a component of behavioral control that is directed to effects which will be produced in the experience of another person. Regardless of whether such effects are directly observable or are given a cognitive representation by the actor, the altruistic component of their affective value must be transmitted by the actor's empathic or vicarious experience. Empathic or vicarious control is the criterion of the truly altruistic act.

Although empathic or vicarious experience is also a prerequisite of sympathetic behavior, a concept of sympathy must be distinguished from a concept of altruism in certain other respects. The concept of sympathy often has been used to refer to a complex of affective and cognitive dispositions toward empathic or vicarious experience (Allport, 1954; Asch, 1952, pp. 171–172; Heider, 1958, pp. 277–282; McDougall, 1908, pp. 150–179). But its more behaviorally immediate usage is in reference to a disposition to relieve the distress of others—a disposition which appears to influence the behavior of all of the primate species (DeVore, 1965) as well as the behavior of many other species, and which is most prevalent in the behavior of mothers toward their offspring. To state the criterion for the presence of this disposition in human social behavior, we may say that an act is sympathetic to the extent that it is elicited through the actor's empathic or vicarious affective response to the actual or anticipated distress of another person. An act cannot be identified as sympathetic, of course, merely because it has the effect of relieving another person's distress. It might have been motivated, for example, by the actor's simultaneous experience of the same distressful events, or even by the actor's anticipation of aversive consequences which he will directly experience as a result of his failure to come to the aid of another.

The requirement of empathic or vicarious distress specifies that sympathetic behavior is under aversive affective control. A sympathetic component of an act, therefore, has a narrower potential affective base than does an altruistic component, since altruism may be under either positive or aversive affective control. However, the contingencies of reinforcement for sympathetic behavior are less restrictive than are the contingencies for altruistic behavior. A sympathetic act may be altruistic to the extent that it is controlled by the anticipated consequence of the reduction of empathic or vicarious distress which the actor will experience when another person's distress is relieved. Altruistic components may be present, for example, in some recent demonstrations of the conditions under which both children and college students will display sympathetic actions (Buss, 1966; Lenrow, 1965; Rosenhan & White, 1967; Schopler & Bateson, 1965). But sympathetic actions also are very often under the control of the anticipation of direct social rewards, or of subsequent reciprocity from another person, even though the disposition toward sympathy itself requires a capacity for empathic or vicarious experience of distress. Observations in naturalistic settings have shown that the sympathetic behavior of children frequently is predicated on their expectation of social approval or of mutual benefits in a shared difficulty (Isaacs, 1933; Murphy, 1937). The sympathetic act can be dependent, then, on external outcomes which are to be directly experienced by the actor. In contrast, independence of such outcomes is a criterion for the altruistic component of an act.

Since empathic or vicarious experience is taken to be a prerequisite of both altruism and sympathy, I would like to summarize here, in an abbreviated form, a more extended analysis of the essential properties of this experience (Aronfreed, 1968a). There is actually an interesting distinction which can be made between the concepts of empathic and vicarious. Empathy might be used for a person's affective response to the expressive behavioral cues of another person's affective experience, whereas vicarious experience might be a more appropriate term when a person's affect is elicited by information about the external events which have an impact on another person. The distinction may be very useful in the observation and experimental analysis of social behavior. But it can be overlooked in a rough outline of the larger problems which are posed in an account of altruistic and sympathetic dispositions. Accordingly, I will use the single term *empathy* here to denote an individual's affective experience when it is elicited by social cues which transmit information about the corresponding affective experience of another person—either by expressive cues which are direct indices of another person's affective state, or by other kinds of cues which convey the affective impact of external events upon another person.

It should be noted that the concept of empathy is tied to observations which allow the inference that a person's affectivity is elicited by the observation (or cognitive representation) of social cues which transmit another person's *experience*. The requirements of this inference would not be met merely by a demonstration that one person's behavior had been influenced by observation of the rewarding or punitive outcomes of another person's behavior. A great many such demonstrations have been conducted with both children and adults as subjects (Bandura, 1965; Bandura, Grusec, & Menlove, 1967; Bruning, 1965; Craig, 1967; Ditrichs, Simon, & Greene, 1967; Kanfer & Marston, 1963; Lewis & Duncan, 1958; Marston, 1966; Rosekrans, 1967; Rosekrans & Hartup, 1967; Walters, Parke, & Cane, 1965; Wheeler & Smith, 1967). In none of these demonstrations is it possible to distinguish between the observer's affective response to the perception of another person's experience and the observer's more direct response to the information that is carried in the observed reward or punishment itself. The same difficulty of interpretation is present in the findings of experiments which have been addressed to the question of whether mere observation of another person's aggression will strengthen or reduce an observer's subsequent disposition toward aggression (Bandura, Ross, & Ross, 1963; Berkowitz & Geen, 1966; Feshbach, 1961; Rosenbaum & deCharms, 1960; Wheeler & Caggiula, 1966).

More persuasive demonstrations of empathic experience can be found in the results of experiments which have used peripheral autonomic indices of an observer's anxiety or distress in response to either expressive or objective cues of another person's pain or distress (Bandura & Rosenthal, 1966; Berger, 1962; Haner & Whitney, 1960; Lazarus, Speisman, Mordkoff, & Davidson, 1962; Miller, Caul, & Mirsky, 1967). However, these latter experiments have not been designed to demonstrate how empathic experience functions in the control of overt social behavior. Empathic affective control of choices of action can perhaps be examined most convincingly when the social cues which are used to elicit empathic control are made the contingent outcomes of the observer's own overt performance of an act. It would then be possible to assess the value of these outcomes for control of the observer's behavior, even though they have no directly rewarding or punitive consequences for the observer.

Since the specific qualitative properties of a change of affective state are determined by its cognitive housing, empathic reactions will require some common elements between the cognition of the observer and the cognition of the person whose experience is being observed. For this reason, it is usually quite difficult to identify truly empathic control of an observer's behavior. For example, a child's reactions to another person's expressive affective cues, or to the impact of external events upon that person, often may be partially attributable to its experience of the observed social stimuli as impinging directly upon itself— perhaps because of some generalization of affectivity from the child's direct experience of the stimuli in the past, or because the child perceives the stimuli as signals which portend correlated events of corresponding affective value that it will experience directly. But the concept of empathy is used too broadly to have any utility unless it is restricted to that component of an observer's affectivity which is elicited by the perception of another person's experience, and which is independent of the perception of social stimuli as having an impact on one's self. The application of such a criterion clearly must rest on experimental operations or conditions of observation which permit certain kinds of inferences to be made about the observer's cognition of concrete social cues. It is interesting to note that the criterion is not met, for example, by experiments which have demonstrated response indices of an observing animal's aversion to the distress cues of another animal (Church, 1959; Miller, 1961; Miller *et al.*, 1967). These demonstrations have been conducted under conditions in which the distress cues might have retained their original conditioned value as signals of directly aversive experience for the observer.

Bearing in mind these suggested criteria of empathic experience, we can now turn our attention more closely to the problem of the identification of altruistic and sympathetic acts. Comparative psychologists sometimes have suggested that the higher species of animals may have innate dispositions toward altruism and sympathy—particularly in their reactions to the distress of others (Hebb & Thompson, 1954; McBride & Hebb, 1948). More recently, a number of ethologists have argued that evolutionary selection in animals will favor a certain amount of behavior that is altruistic in the sense that it benefits others, even at some cost in survival to the altruistic individuals—for example, alarm calls at the approach of predators (Hamilton, 1964; Maynard Smith, 1965; Wynne-Edwards, 1962). Campbell (1965) has proposed that humans also may have unlearned altruistic dispositions which are selected for their adaptive value in meeting environmental stress. While some of the kinds of behavior in question might well be classified as sympathetic—for example, reactions to the distress of the young—it is very doubtful that a concept of altruism gains anything when it is applied indiscriminately to any behavior that may benefit another member of the same species. It is reasonable to suppose that grooming, retrieval, and some other behavior patterns of the higher animals might be forerunners of human altruistic behavior. But the distinctive utility of a concept of altruism would be much diluted if we were to treat these types of animal behavior as equivalent to the more highly internalized altruistic acts of which human beings are capable. For example, the extensive grooming behavior of many primates (DeVore, 1965) is not properly described as altruistic, because it is usually reciprocal and is sometimes a source of edible insects for the groomer. Correspondingly, cleaning, retrieval, and other components of nurturance of the young may have directly experienced pleasurable or distress-reducing consequences for the female adults of many species.

Altruism is a more useful concept when it is limited to contingencies from which it can be inferred that the behavior of one individual is controlled by the anticipation of its consequences for another individual. The problem of the identification of altruism in the behavior of animals also hints at the need for caution in the application of concepts of both altruism and sympathy to observations of human social behavior. The act of helping another person to attain desirable ends, for example, or the act of relieving another person's distress, may be controlled by the expectation of social approval or of subsequent reciprocal assistance, or by the sense of contract or equity which is acquired from previous experience as the recipient of help. Likewise, the conditions under which people are likely to respond with aid to the circumstances of others who are ill or in danger may often be influenced primarily by their anticipation of potential external social reactions to their initiative, their effectiveness, or their good judgment. The fact that help or aid has been extended to another person obviously does not, therefore, require us to assume that the observed behavior is controlled by altruistic or sympathetic dispositions. A very considerable part of the problem of interpretation here clearly arises out of our inability to classify the relevant behavior on the criteria of either its form or its consequences. Classification must rest on inferences about the affective and cognitive determinants of the behavior.

The magnitude of the problem of the identification of altruistic and sympathetic components in social behavior is indicated by the ambiguity of numerous experimental observations of the dispositions of children to share possessions with or extend aid to their peers (Doland & Adelberg, 1967; Fischer, 1963; Hartshorne, May, & Maller, 1929; Hartup & Coates, 1967; Lenrow, 1965; Murphy, 1937; Rosenhan & White, 1967; Ugurel-Semin, 1952; Wright, 1942). The same ambiguity is apparent in demonstrations of the behavior with which adults produce beneficial consequences for others (Berkowitz & Daniels, 1964; Berkowitz & Friedman, 1967; Darlington & Macker, 1966; Goranson & Berkowitz, 1966; Schopler & Matthews, 1965). Similar demonstrations have been carried out with other primates (Crawford, 1941; Mason, 1959; Mason & Hollis, 1962; Nissen & Crawford, 1936). And some investigators have attempted to show that there are analogous dispositions in rats (Holder, 1958; Ulrich, 1967). With the exception of the studies which are reported by Lenrow (1965) and by Rosenhan and White (1967), it is very difficult to determine whether an altruistic status should be assigned to the behavior that has been observed in these demonstrations. In a number of instances, the behavior is reinforced by direct and explicit rewards. In other cases, the behavior appears as part of a cooperative effort to produce beneficial outcomes for both self and other. And virtually all of the remaining demonstrations with human subjects are conducted under conditions which cannot be used to separate the altruistic component of the observed behavior from strong implicit incentives for the expectation of social approval.

Some experiments with both humans and other primates are particularly effective illustrations of the difficulty of establishing the presence of an altruistic component in cooperative behavior or sharing (Boren, 1966; Daniels, 1967; Horel, Treichler, & Meyer, 1963). These experiments uniformly show that cooperative behavior breaks down when it no longer has direct and fairly immediate reciprocal reinforcing consequences for one of the partners. Experiments which have been designed to demonstrate the aversive reactions of monkeys to the distress of their peers also are difficult to interpret as evidence of either altruistic or sympathetic dispositions (Masserman, Wechkin, & Terris, 1964; Miller, Banks, & Ogawa, 1963; Miller et al., 1967). It cannot be determined that the behavior with which the monkeys reduce or prevent the distress of a peer actually has an altruistic or sympathetic character, because there is little evidence to support the inference that the behavior is empathically controlled by its consequences for the peer. The design of the experiments makes it equally plausible that the subjects are acting to avoid stimulation (either electric shock or distress cues) which they experience as directly aversive to themselves. The results of other experiments with rats (Lavery & Foley, 1963; Rice & Gainer, 1962), in which the subjects were given opportunities to terminate either white noise or the distress squeals of a peer, also tend to confirm the suspicion that acts which reduce the distress of another are not necessarily empathically motivated, but may be controlled instead by the directly aversive experience of distress cues by the actor–observer.

From the point of view of the developmental psychology of socialization, the ingredients of altruistic and sympathetic behavior can be divided into two basic classes of phenomena. The first class establishes the child's capacity for empathic experience. It consists of the coupling of changes in the child's affectivity to social cues which transmit information about the experience of others. Some of these social cues can then serve as motivational elicitors of the child's altruistic and sympathetic dispositions. Other kinds of social cues can begin to function as empathically reinforcing outcomes of the child's overt acts. The origin of the child's empathic reactions can be found in contingencies of socialization which have certain essential properties of a paradigm for the conditioning of changes of affective state. The prerequisite contingencies for this conditioning process may take a number of different forms (Aronfreed, 1968a). But their common and crucial feature—a feature that is indigenous to the child's earliest social experience—is an initial temporal association between cues which transmit the affective experience of others and closely related events whose affective value is directly experienced by the child. As a result of this temporal contiguity, the cues which transmit the experience of others will acquire their own independent value for the elicitation of changes in the child's affectivity, under conditions where they are no longer perceived by the child as signals of other events which it will experience directly. These social cues must be concretely observable in order to function in the earliest period of socialization. But they can gradually be given a cognitive representation that also exercises affective control over the child's behavior.

The second basic class of phenomena in the socialization of altruistic and sympathetic behavior lies within the establishment of the instrumental value of overt acts. The child often finds the outcome value of overt acts of altruism or sympathy in its empathic experience of the effects of the acts upon others. The empathically reinforcing effects of an altruistic or sympathetic act may take the form of social cues which are directly observable contingent outcomes of the act. Or the effects may have their value transmitted, even when they are not observable, through their cognitive representation by the child. Of course, as was noted earlier, an act may have a sympathetic component even when its reinforcing consequences are directly experienced rather than empathically mediated—that is, the sympathetic component of an act does not confer upon it an altruistic status.

The act may be motivated in part by the expectation of direct rewards or mutual benefits.

Behavior-contingent learning is one path for the establishment of the instrumental value of a child's altruistic and sympathetic actions. In the behavior-contingent paradigm of learning (Aronfreed, 1968a), the child would find that its overt performance of certain actions could produce either pleasurable or distress-reducing outcomes in the experience of others. These outcomes in turn would elicit the child's own empathically reinforcing changes of affective state. Opportunities for the child's behavior to be brought under the control of such outcomes pervade the socialization process. In the socialization of sympathetic behavior, for example, dispositions which the child already has begun to acquire—such as giving, sharing, or the expression of affection—may be more selectively channeled into sympathetic action when the child finds that they can be instrumental to the reduction of another person's distress. The reinforcing reduction of empathic distress that the child experiences, when it observes social cues which indicate relief of another person's distress, will also attach some potentially reinforcing change of affectivity to the intrinsic correlates of the actions with which it has reduced the other person's distress. And as the child's cognitive capacities expand, the intrinsic affective value of sympathetic acts may come to be carried in the child's cognitive representation of their consequences for others. The maintenance of the child's sympathetic behavior will then have acquired some independence both of its directly experienced consequences for the child and its directly observable consequences for others.

The speed and accuracy with which altruistic and sympathetic dispositions often appear in the behavior of the young child, together with the rapid spread of these dispositions toward a variety of real and surrogate social objects, indicates that behavior-contingent learning will provide only a very partial account of their origins. Imitative modeling and other forms of observational learning may make an even more important contribution to the emergence of the child's altruistic and sympathetic behavior (Aronfreed, 1969). The opportunity for observational learning of the form and value of sympathetic behavior, for example, would occur whenever the child observed another person's sympathetic actions in conjunction with its own direct or empathic experience of relief of distress. It might be expected that the most frequent and potent foundation of this learning in the child's social experience would be the many occasions on which the child is the recipient of actions that others direct to the relief of its own distress. The result of such experience would be an attachment of intrinsic affective value, corresponding to relief of distress, at first to the child's cognitive representation of the sympathetic actions of others, and then to the representational correlates of its own potential repertoire of sympathetic behavior. The child could then reduce its empathic distress, in response to the perceived or anticipated distress of another, by reproducing the sympathetic actions which it had learned by observation. And since the child's representation of a sympathetic act, and of its consequences, would already have acquired some internalized distress-reducing value on the basis of past observational learning, its overt performance of the act could have reinforcing consequences which were to some degree independent of directly observable effects on others.

The learning of altruistic behavior can be demonstrated in the findings of an experiment which was conducted by the author and Vivian Paskal (Aronfreed & Paskal, 1965). Six- to eight-year-old girls were used as subjects, and an adult female acted as the agent of socialization. The experimental paradigms of socialization consisted of two immediately successive phases, which were respectively designed to control the following processes: first, the attachment of a child's empathic positive affectivity to the expressive cues of a corresponding affective state of the adult agent; second, the establishment of the altruistic value of an overt act that the child could use instrumentally to produce the agent's expressive cues. During the initial phase of socialization, the agent sat close enough to the child to allow body contact. She demonstrated the operation of a choice box which automatically dispensed a small candy as the outcome of the movement of one lever and a 3-second red light as the outcome of the movement of another lever. Each outcome was programmed so that it would occur unpredictably, however, on only 60% of the occasions on which the appropriate lever was moved. The child merely watched while the agent varied her choices equally between the two levers over the course of 20 trials. The agent displayed no reaction when her choices did not produce explicit outcomes. Nor did she show any reaction when her choices produced candy. But when one of her choices activated the red light, she displayed one of three patterns of behavior which represented variations in the contingencies between her expressive cues and her behavior toward the child. These variations were constructed to support the inference that the reinforcement value of the agent's expressive cues, when they were later used as outcomes of the child's own choices among alternative acts, during the second phase of socialization, could be attributed to their conditioned elicitation of the child's empathic positive affective experience.

In the basic experimental paradigm, the children were repeatedly exposed to a very close relationship in time between the agent's expressive cues of pleasure and their own direct experience of the agent's affection. Whenever the agent's choice of a lever activated the red light, she stared at the light and smiled. Simultaneously, the agent gave one of four exclamations in a pleased and excited tone of voice. All of these exclamations were roughly equivalent to: *"There's the light!"* The agent's exclamation terminated her expressive cues. It was followed immediately by a firm hug of the child, for which the agent used one arm. At the same time, she inclined her head toward the child and displayed a very broad direct smile. The physical affection and social warmth were emitted as though they were the spontaneous overflow of the agent's pleasurable reaction to the light. Two control paradigms were used to eliminate different segments of the contingencies which occurred in this experimental paradigm. In one of the control paradigms, children were exposed only to the agent's expressive affective cues (and were given no experience of affection from the agent); whereas in the second control paradigm, the children experienced only the agent's affection (and were not given the opportunity to observe the agent's preliminary expressive cues).

The second phase of socialization consisted of a performance task which was designed as a common test of the effects of the three paradigms of the first phase. During the second phase, the child herself operated the choice box over a great many trials. The agent used a pretext to deactivate the red light on the face of the box, the illumination of which had sometimes been the outcome of her choices during the first phase. The agent now sat directly across from the child, facing the rear of the box. Her gaze was fixed on another red light that was visible only to her. The child was told of the presence of this auxiliary light, and also was told that it could be illuminated by her choice of the light-producing lever. The child was further informed that she could keep all candies which came out of the box (but that she could not eat them until completion of the task). While the child was engaged in the performance of the task, the agent remained impassive when the child's choice of a lever produced no explicit outcome. The agent was likewise unreactive when the child's choice produced candy for herself. But whenever the red light was illuminated by the child's choice of the appropriate lever, the agent would smile while staring at the light, and would at the same time exclaim: *"There's the light!"* Thus, the agent emitted the same cues which she had used to express her pleasure during two of the three paradigms of the initial phase. The child therefore found herself in a position where she had to choose repeatedly between an act that could produce candy for herself and an act that could produce only observably pleasurable consequences for another person. The situation therefore simultaneously tested both the child's altruistic disposition and her empathic responsiveness.

Variations in the contingencies of experience during the first phase of the paradigms had a strong effect on the children's choices during the test for altruism. It will be recalled that the basic experimental paradigm initially placed the agent's expressive affective cues in very close conjunction with the child's direct experience of affection. The children who had been exposed to this contingency were significantly more willing to surrender opportunities to obtain candy, during the test for altruism, than were the children whose earlier experience had included only an association between the red light and the agent's expressive cues of positive affect (without physical affection). They also showed significantly more altruism than did the children who had been exposed previously only to physical affection in association with the red light (without the expressive cues which the agent then used during the test task). The majority of the children who had been in the basic social conditioning paradigm in fact produced the light for the agent more frequently than they produced candy for themselves. In the case of each of the control paradigms, however, the children typically chose the candy-producing lever more frequently.

For the children in the basic experimental paradigm, the establishment and demonstration of the value of the agent's expressive affective cues was a variant of a more general procedure that is commonly used to establish and test the acquired positive reinforcement value of a "neutral" stimulus. However, the expressive cues and the child's direct experience of affection were paired under contingencies which were analogous to those of a Pavlovian conditioning paradigm. Since the child was only an observer during these contingencies, the pairing was not contingent on its overt performance of the critical act. There are some experiments with animals which also appear to demonstrate that the positive secondary reinforcement value of a stimulus can be acquired under Pavlovian contingencies—that is, where the pairing with the unconditioned stimulus is not produced by the subject's overt behavior (Ferster & Skinner, 1957; Kelleher & Gollub, 1962; Knott & Clayton, 1966; Stein, 1958). The performance test for altruism was an index of the potential reinforcement value that had been acquired by the agent's expressive cues. It was apparent that these cues had acquired some empathic affective value for the children who initially had been exposed to the basic conditioning paradigm.

The relationships among the different contingencies of the three initial paradigms, and their relationship in turn to the contingencies of the subsequent performance paradigm, were devised with the aim of assuring that differences among the groups in their altruistic test behavior could not easily be attributed merely to differences in the children's perception of approval when the agent reacted to their choices with expressive cues of pleasure. Since the agent's expressive cues were unrelated to the children's overt behavior during the initial paradigms, but were made contingent on the overt choices of all of the children during the test, it seems clear that the experimental effect could not have been the result of the already established value of the cues as evidence of direct social approval. It is also of some interest to note that the agent's cues of pleasurable affect appeared to have a highly durable value for the reinforcement of the altruistic choices of children in the experimental group. These children made essentially as many altruistic choices during the second half of the test trials as they did during the first half. The inconsistent scheduling of both the expressive cues and the agent's affection, with respect to the agent's choices during the initial phase and the child's choices during the test, possibly may account for the fact that the value of the cues showed such strong resistance to extinction. The findings of other experiments with children also have suggested that the acquired positive secondary reinforcement value of a stimulus event can be maintained independently for longer periods of time when the event is scheduled inconsistently during extinction, and when the event originally was associated with a more "primary" event that was used as an inconsistent outcome of behavior (Myers & Myers, 1963; Myers, 1960; Myers & Myers, 1966).

The author and Vivian Paskal also have used experimental paradigms of socialization in a more detailed examination of the mechanisms for children's learning of sympathetic behavior (Aronfreed & Paskal, 1966). This experiment was conducted with seven- and eight-year-old girls as subjects. And an adult female was again the agent of socialization. The experimental paradigms were constructed around three distinct but immediately successive phases of socialization. The first phase was designed to condition a child's distress to the observed distress cues of another person. The second phase gave the child the opportunity to observe the sympathetic actions with which the agent relieved the child's own distress. The last phase placed the child in a situation where it could respond sympathetically to the distress of another child. Five separate sequences or experimental groups were used to vary the contingencies of socialization within one phase at a time. During each phase of any of the sequences, the child classified a number of small toys which were replicas of real objects. She was assigned the task of classifying each toy in accordance with whether she thought it most appropriate for a house, a dog, or a school. Twelve discrete toys were classified in each of the three phases. And the set of toys was changed for each new phase. The child showed her classification of each toy by pushing down one of three levers on a choice box. The word which labeled the category appeared on a panel above each lever. The middle lever was used for the dog category, and the toys were selected to make its use inappropriate, so that it would ordinarily be chosen very infrequently or not at all. Since choices of the middle lever were not instrumental to the task of classification, it became possible to use them as an index of sympathetic behavior during the third or test phase of all of the experimental sequences.

The first of the five experimental sequences was designed as the prototype of the contribution of both empathy and observational learning to children's acquisition of sympathetic behavior. A summary of its three phases can be used to describe the essential ingredients of the same phases within any of the sequences. The first phase was devised to be a paradigm of the original acquisition process for the establishment of a child's empathic affective response to the expressive cues which indicate another person's distressful experience. The crucial contingencies for conditioning of the child's empathic experience were introduced in a temporal contiguity between the agent's observable distress cues and the child's own direct experience of aversive stimulation. Both the child and the agent wore earphones, on the pretext of having to monitor periodic noise from within the choice box. The child was told that the noise in the agent's earphones would be even louder than the noise in her own earphones. Following six of the child's 12 classifications of toys, she heard through her earphones a highly aversive loud noise which had a duration of 7 seconds. The occurrence of the noise was unpredictable across trials, and was not determined by the child's choice. The noise began at a point well into the intertrial interval that followed the classification of a toy. The agent began to show cues of distress (apparently because of the noise in her own earphones) by placing her head in her hands 3 seconds before the onset of the noise. Her distress cues continued throughout the duration of the noise.

The second phase was designed to give the child the opportunity to form a cognitive representation of an act–outcome contingency that was observable in the agent's sympathetic actions toward the child. The agent now wore no earphones and therefore showed no evidence of distress. As soon as the child had classified each toy, the agent operated another choice box to show how she would classify the same toy. She had told the child beforehand that she might be able, while she was using her own choice box, to turn off the noise that the child would still sometimes hear through her earphones. When the child had finished her classification of each toy, the agent would begin her classification by poising her finger above one of the two outer levers in the array of three on her choice box. The outer levers represented house and school, and were clearly the only correct choices for almost all of the toys. After 2 or 3 seconds of apparent thought, the agent did actually choose one of the two outer levers on six of the 12 trials. On the remaining six trials, however, the child at this point began to hear the noise through her earphones. The noise remained at the same highly aversive intensity as had been used during the first phase, in order to maximize the distress-reducing value of the agent's sympathetic actions toward the child. As had been true earlier, the noise was unpredictable across trials and unrelated to the child's choice. It lasted only for 3 seconds, at which point the agent pushed the middle lever on her choice box, and at the same time said that she was choosing the middle lever in order to turn off the noise. Her action in fact did terminate the noise. It was clear that she had reduced the child's distress by temporarily giving up the task of making a correct classification.

The third phase of the first sequence was constructed as a test of whether the subject had acquired a disposition to reproduce the previously observed sympathetic actions of the agent. The subject was given a number of opportunities to reduce her empathic experience of distress, in response to the distress cues of another child, by making the same choice (of the middle lever) as the agent had made earlier in order to reduce the subject's own direct exposure to the noise. The contingencies of this phase also were arranged so that elimination of the other child's distress cues would be a potentially reinforcing outcome of the subject's choices. The subject's sympathetic dispositions thus could be brought under the control of external events which provided both the empathic motivation and the empathic reinforcement for her behavior.

Another girl was introduced as a new subject for the third phase. The new girl actually had been a subject earlier, and then had been trained to the role of a more or less innocent dummy. She was now to emit distress cues at critical junctures in the test of the primary subject's sympathetic dispositions. The primary subject was given the task of classifying each toy, following its classification by the dummy, by using the levers on the second choice box—the same role that the adult agent had performed during the preceding phase. Only the dummy now wore the earphones, so that the subject was no longer vulnerable to the direct experience of aversive stimulation. The agent sat behind the subject as an observer. Dummy and subject made their successive choices without incident in the classification of six of the 12 toys. But on the remaining six trials, the dummy placed her head in her hands, in response to a low signal from her earphones, just when the subject was about to make her own choice. The dummy's distress cue was the same, of course, as the one that the agent had emitted originally during the first phase of the socialization sequence. If the subject now chose the middle lever—the same sympathetic choice which the agent had made to reduce the subject's own distress during the second phase—the dummy would immediately terminate her distress cue by raising her head in response to the termination of the low signal in her earphones. But if the subject made a task-oriented, non-sympathetic choice of one of the two outer levers, the dummy would maintain her distress cue for a duration of 5 seconds after the subject had made her choice (such a choice would therefore be deprived of empathically mediated reinforcement).

The four remaining experimental sequences were designed primarily as a series of controls on the basic contingencies which had been used in the three phases of the first sequence. But they were also structured to support certain key inferences concerning the affective and cognitive mechanisms in the acquisition of sympathetic behavior. The second sequence was identical to the first, with the exception that the agent's distress cues were not paired with the aversive noise that the child heard during the first phase. Although the noise occurred at the same six intertrial intervals at which it had occurred for the first sequence, the agent's distress cues were emitted only during the noiseless intervals which followed the remaining six trials. This sequence exposed the children, of course, to the same frequencies of occurrence of noise and distress cues as had been used in the first sequence. But the children were not exposed to the temporal contiguity which was required for the conditioning of empathic distress.

The third experimental sequence differed from the first only in one feature of the second phase, where the noise that the child occasionally heard was sharply reduced to a very mild intensity (in contrast to the first sequence, in which the noise continued to be highly aversive). It was expected that the third sequence would be relatively ineffective in establishing the child's disposition to reproduce the agent's sympathetic actions, since it minimized the potential distress-reducing value of the actions for the child. The fourth and fifth experimental sequences introduced two levels of reduction of the social cues which were used, during the third phase of the first sequence, to elicit and reinforce the children's sympathetic choices. During the third phase of the fourth sequence, the dummy wore earphones but emitted no distress cues. In the third phase of the fifth sequence, the dummy did not even wear the earphones.

Differences among the effects of the five sequential paradigms strongly confirmed the contribution of the mechanisms of both empathic conditioning and observational learning to the acquisition of sympathetic behavior. In all of the sequences, the children were highly task oriented in their classification of the toys across the twelve trials of each of the first two phases. They would choose the task-inappropriate middle lever (classification in the dog category) only once or twice. But during the third phase, the children from the basic first sequence moved to a marked preference for the middle lever. Half of them chose the middle lever on six or more trials—that is, at least on all of the occasions on which the dummy emitted distress cues. With few exceptions, the remainder of the children from the first sequence showed a sharp increase in the frequency of their choice of the middle lever. They typically now made a sympathetic choice four or five times (among the six trials on which the dummy showed distress cues), and each time forfeited the opportunity to make a correct classification.

The children from all of the other four sequences continued to show a strong task orientation during the test for sympathetic behavior. Although some of the children made small increases in the frequency of their choice of the middle lever (particularly those from the fourth sequence), the frequency distribu- tions of their choices during the third phase were generally quite similar to the corresponding distributions for the first two phases. There was a powerful and highly reliable difference between the effect of the first sequence and the effect of each of the other sequences, when all sequences were compared with respect to the shifts, between the first two phases and the test phase, in the frequencies of the children's choices of the middle lever. The distributions of frequency shifts in choices of the middle lever were very similar among the groups of children from the second through the fifth sequences—although the children from the fourth sequence departed somewhat from this pattern in a rather interesting way.

The difference between the effects of the first and second sequences shows that the empathic experience of distress is a prerequisite for the establishment of sympathetic behavior. During the first phase of the second sequence, the agent's distress cues and the children's direct experience of aversive stimulation were not placed under contingencies which would condition the children's distress to observation of the cues alone. These children showed little sympathetic behavior during the test phase. Even though they previously had many opportunities to observe the sympathetic action which the agent had directed toward them, and even though the same action was easily available for their choice, they seldom chose to use it to relieve another child's observable distress. Clearly, reproduction of the agent's sympathetic actions was not elicited merely by the knowledge that another child was now experiencing distress. The children's behavioral expres- sions of sympathy appeared to require some empathic reinstatement of the con- ditions of affective experience under which the agent's actions originally had acquired value for them.

The absence of sympathetic behavior among children from the third se- quence indicates that the sympathetic actions of children from the first sequence were not simply attributable to a generalized disposition to be influenced by observation of the previous choices of an adult. Such a generalized disposition would not account for the difference between the two groups even if we were to assume that its behavioral expression was narrowed, under the conditions of the test situation, by the further requirement that the subject experience em- pathic distress in response to the cues from the dummy. This requirement would not have been realized for children from the second sequence, who were not exposed to the contingencies for conditioning of empathic distress during the first phase of the experiment. But children from both the first and third sequences did experience the contingencies which were designed to attach their empathic responsiveness to the distress cues of the agent, and which would also have made them responsive to the distress cues of the dummy. Certainly both of these groups had equal access to the sheer informational value of the observation of which actions the agent could most effectively direct to their own welfare during the second phase of the experiment. Both groups were therefore in an equal position to know that reproducing the agent's actions would reduce the dummy's distress during the test. The single difference between the experiences of the two groups occurred in the intensity of the aversive stimulation to which they were exposed during the second phase. The agent's sympathetic actions terminated a highly aversive noise for children in the first sequence, but only a mild noise for children in the third sequence. It therefore seems necessary to conclude that the effect of this difference was to give different amounts of acquired value to a sympathetic act which the children could potentially reproduce in their own behavior, during the test situation, in order to reduce their empathic reaction to the dummy's distress. Although both groups had the same opportunity for observational learning of sympathetic act–outcome contingencies, their behavioral reproduction of the observed sympathetic actions seemed to be determined by the magnitude of the change of affectivity which they originally had experienced when the actions had been directed toward themselves.

The relatively unsympathetic behavior of the children from the fourth and fifth sequences, during the test phase, confirms the obvious functional value of the dummy's distress cues as elicitors of the children's sympathetic dispositions. Unlike the children from the first sequence, the children from the last two sequences did not show sharp increases in the frequency of their choice of the action with which the agent previously had reduced their own distress, even though their exposure to the contingencies for empathic conditioning and the opportunity for observational learning had been identical during the first two phases. Of course, the importance of external distress cues in the affective control of the children's sympathetic behavior was also apparent in the fact that the children from the first sequence generally confined their choice of the middle lever to the six trials on which the dummy emitted distress cues. These findings make it clear once again that the second phase of the experiment provided only the basis for observational learning of the actions and consequences which could be produced by a sympathetic agent. The children's own dispositions to reproduce these actions required the affective control of their empathic experience of distress.

There are some other aspects of the experimental findings which reveal that onset and termination of the dummy's distress cues, while crucial to the choices of children from the first sequence during the test, were not the only determinants of their sympathetic behavior. As was pointed out earlier, the experience of children from the third sequence would have given them the empathic motivation to terminate another child's distress cues, and also the necessary information about the distress-reducing consequences of a choice of the middle lever. Yet when they were given the opportunity to use their potentially sympathetic resources, they did not show a significant increment in their frequency of choice of the middle lever. Their failure to do so suggests the inference that the same act had acquired some additional intrinsic value for children from the first sequence, who earlier had experienced the relief of their own relatively intense (rather than mild) distress in direct conjunction with the observation of the agent's sympathetic actions. Because the difference between the effects of the two sequences cannot be attributed to the children's control of external outcomes in the dummy's distress cues, it seems plausible to conclude that the children's potentially sympathetic actions differed in the amount of inherent value that the actions had acquired as representations of an earlier external sample of behavior.

There was another indication of representational control over the value of sympathetic behavior in the behavior of children from the fourth sequence. Despite their maintenance of a fairly strong task orientation during the test for sympathetic behavior, these children showed discernible increments in the frequency of their choice of the middle lever. Their behavior was in fact closer to that of children from the first sequence than was the behavior of the children from any of the other control sequences. It was especially interesting to note that they chose the middle lever, during the test situation, reliably more often than did the children from the fifth sequence, whose dummies wore no earphones as well as emitted no distress cues. Of course, since the dummy did not emit distress cues for the children in the fourth sequence, the children distributed their choices of the middle lever more or less unpredictably among the 12 test trials. It seems likely that their choices were under the control of their cognitive representations of the distress-reducing (or distress-avoiding) consequences of their actions for another child who was wearing the earphones. Their behavior suggested that the internalized affective value of a sympathetic act also can be mediated in part by the cognitive representation of outcomes of the act.

During a verbal inquiry that followed most of the experimental sessions, the children gave introspective reports which provided some additional evidence of the role of cognitive representation. Among the children in the three groups which received distress cues from the dummy, almost all perceived the cues as indicators of loud noise in the dummy's earphones. However, many of these children seemed unable or unwilling to report a clear recognition that their choices of the middle lever would have relieved the dummy's distress. Among the children in the first sequence, reported awareness of this contingency was a highly reliable predictor of maximal sympathetic behavior. Among the children in the second and third sequences, reported awareness of the contingency was unrelated to their behavior.

REFERENCES

Allport, G. W. The historical background of modern social psychology. In G. Lindzey (Ed.), *Handbook of social psychology*. Vol. 1. *Theory and method*. Cambridge, Mass.: Addison-Wesley, 1954, Pp. 3–56.

Aronfreed, J. *Conduct and conscience: The socialization of internalized control over behavior*. New York: Academic Press, 1968. (a)

Aronfreed, J. The concept of internalization. In D. A. Goslin (Ed.), *Handbook of socialization theory and research*. Chicago: Rand-McNally, 1969. (b)

Aronfreed, J. The problem of imitation. In L. P. Lipsitt & H. W. Reese (Eds.), *Advances in child development and behavior*. Vol. 4. New York: Academic Press, 1969.

Aronfreed, J., & Paskal, V. Altruism, empathy, and the conditioning of positive affect. Unpublished manuscript, University of Pennsylvania, 1965.

Aronfreed, J., & Paskal, V. The development of sympathetic behavior in children: An experimental test of a two-phase hypothesis. Unpublished manuscript, University of Pennsylvania, 1966.

Asch, S. E. *Social psychology*. Englewood Cliffs, New Jersey: Prentice-Hall, 1952.

Bandura, A. Influence of models' reinforcement contingencies on the acquisition of imitative responses. *Journal of Personality and Social Psychology*, 1965, **1**, 589–595.

Bandura, A., Grusec, J. E., & Menlove, F. L. Some social determinants of self-monitoring reinforcement systems. *Journal of Personality and Social Psychology*, 1967, **5**, 449–455.

Bandura, A., & Rosenthal, T. L. Vicarious classical conditioning as a function of arousal level. *Journal of Personality and Social Psychology*, 1966, **3**, 54–62.

Bandura, A., Ross, D., & Ross, S.A. Imitation of film-mediated aggressive models. *Journal of Abnormal and Social Psychology*, 1963, **66**, 3–11.

Berger, S. M. Conditioning through vicarious instigation. *Psychological Review*, 1962, **69**, 450–466.

Berkowitz, L., & Daniels, L. R. Affecting the salience of the social responsibility norm: Effects of past help on the response to dependency relationships. *Journal of Abnormal and Social Psychology*, 1964, **68**, 275–281.

Berkowitz, L., & Friedman, P. Some social class differences in helping behavior. *Journal of Personality and Social Psychology*, 1967, **5**, 217–225.

Berkowitz, L., & Geen, R. G. Film violence and the cue properties of available targets. *Journal of Personality and Social Psychology*, 1966, **3**, 525–530.

Boren, J. J. An experimental social relation between two monkeys. *Journal of the Experimental Analysis of Behavior*, 1966, **9**, 691–700.

Bruning, J. L. Direct and vicarious effects of a shift in magnitude of reward on performance. *Journal of Personality and Social Psychology*, 1965, **2**, 278–282.

Buss, A. H. Instrumentality of aggression, feedback, and frustration as determinants of physical aggression. *Journal of Personality and Social Psychology*, 1966, **3**, 153–162.

Campbell, D. T. Ethnocentric and other altruistic motives. In D. Levine (Ed.), *Nebraska symposium on motivation.* Vol. XIII. Lincoln, Neb.: University of Nebraska Press, 1965.

Church, R. M. Emotional reactions of rats to the pain of others. *Journal of Comparative and Physiological Psychology,* 1959, 52, 132–134.

Craig, K. D. Vicarious reinforcement and noninstrumental punishment in observational learning. *Journal of Personality and Social Psychology,* 1967, 7, 172–176.

Crawford, M. P. The cooperative solving by chimpanzees of problems requiring serial responses to color cues. *Journal of Social Psychology,* 1941, 13, 259–280.

Daniels, V. Communication, incentive, and structural variables in interpersonal exchange and negotiation. *Journal of Experimental Social Psychology,* 1967, 3, 47–74.

Darlington, R. B., & Macker, C. E. Displacement of guilt-produced altruistic behavior. *Journal of Personality and Social Psychology,* 1966, 4, 442–443.

DeVore, I. (Ed.) *Primate behavior: Field studies of monkeys and apes.* New York: Holt, Rinehart & Winston, 1965.

Ditrichs, R., Simon, S., & Greene, B. Effect of vicarious scheduling on the verbal conditioning of hostility in children. *Journal of Personality and Social Psychology,* 1967, 6, 71–78.

Doland, D. J., & Adelberg, K. The learning of sharing behavior. *Child Development,* 1967, 38, 695–700.

Durkheim, E. *Suicide.* Glencoe, Ill.: Free Press, 1951.

Ferster, C. B., & Skinner, B. F. *Schedules of reinforcement.* New York: Appleton-Century-Crofts, 1957.

Feshbach, S. The stimulating versus cathartic effects of a vicarious aggressive activity. *Journal of Abnormal and Social Psychology,* 1961, 63, 381–385.

Fischer, W. F. Sharing in preschool children as a function of amount and type of reinforcement. *Genetic Psychology Monographs,* 1963, 68, 215–245.

Goranson, R. E., & Berkowitz, L. Reciprocity and responsibility reactions to prior help. *Journal of Personality and Social Psychology,* 1966, 3, 227–232.

Gouldner, A. W. The norm of reciprocity: A preliminary statement. *American Sociological Review,* 1960, 25, 161–178.

Hamilton, W. D. The genetical evolution of social behavior. I and II. *Journal of Theoretical Biology,* 1964, 7, 1–16, 17–52.

Haner, C. F., & Whitney, E. R. Empathic conditioning and its relation to anxiety level. *American Psychologist,* 1960, 15, 493. (Abstract)

Hartshorne, H., May, M. A., & Maller, J. B. *Studies in the nature of character.* Vol. 2. *Studies in service and self-control.* New York: Macmillan, 1929.

Hartup, W. W., & Coates, B. Imitation of peers as a function of reinforcement from the peer group and rewardingness of the model. *Child Development,* 1967, 38, 1003–1016.

Hebb, D. O., & Thompson, W. R. The social significance of animal studies. In G. Lindzey (Ed.), *Handbook of social psychology.* Vol. 1. *Theory and method.* Cambridge, Mass.: Addison-Wesley, 1954. Pp. 532–561.

Heider, F. *The psychology of interpersonal relations.* New York: Wiley, 1958.

Holder, E. E. Learning factors in social facilitation and social inhibition in rats. *Journal of Personality and Social Psychology,* 1958, 51, 60–64.

Homans, G. C. *Social behavior: Its elementary forms.* New York: Harcourt, Brace & World, 1961.

Horel, J. A., Treichler, F. R., & Meyer, D. R. Coercive behavior in the rhesus monkey. *Journal of Comparative and Physiological Psychology,* 1963, 56, 208–210.

Isaacs, S. *Social development in young children.* London: Routledge & Kegan Paul, 1933.

Kanfer, F. H., & Marston, A. R. Human reinforcement: Vicarious and direct. *Journal of Experimental Psychology,* 1963, **65**, 292–296.

Kelleher, R. T., & Gollub, L. R. A review of positive conditioned reinforcement. *Journal of the Experimental Analysis of Behavior,* 1962, **5**, 543–597.

Knott, P. D., & Clayton, K. N. Durable secondary reinforcement using brain stimulation as the primary reinforcer. *Journal of Comparative and Physiological Psychology,* 1966, **61**, 151–153.

Lavery, J. J., & Foley, P. J. Altruism or arousal in the rat? *Science,* 1963, **140**, 172–173.

Lazarus, R. S., Speisman, J. C., Mordkoff, A. M., & Davison, L. A. A laboratory study of psychological stress produced by a motion picture film. *Psychological Monographs,* 1962, 76(34, Whole No. 553).

Lenrow, P. B. Studies of sympathy. In S. S. Tomkins & C. E. Izard (Eds.), *Affect, cognition, and personality: Empirical studies.* New York: Springer, 1965. Pp. 264–294.

Lewis, D. J., & Duncan, C. P. Vicarious experience and partial reinforcement. *Journal of Abnormal and Social Psychology,* 1958, **57**, 321–326.

McBride, A. F., & Hebb, D. O. Behavior of the captive bottle-nose dolphin, *Tursiops truncatus. Journal of Comparative and Physiological Psychology,* 1948, **41**, 111–123.

McDougall, W. *An introduction to social psychology,* London: Methuen, 1908.

Marston, A. R. Determinants of the effects of vicarious reinforcement. *Journal of Experimental Psychology,* 1966, **71**, 550–558.

Mason, W. A. Development of communication between young rhesus monkeys. *Science,* 1959, **130**, 712–713.

Mason, W. A., & Hollis, J. H. Communication between young rhesus monkeys. *Animal Behaviour,* 1962, **10**, 211–221.

Masserman, J. H., Wechkin, S., & Terris, W. "Altruistic" behavior in rhesus monkeys. *American Journal of Psychiatry,* 1964, **21**, 584–585.

Maynard Smith, J. The evolution of alarm calls. *American Naturalist,* 1965, **99**, 59–63.

Miller, N. Acquisition of avoidance dispositions by social learning. *Journal of Abnormal and Social Psychology,* 1961, **63**, 12–19.

Miller, R. E., Banks, J. H., & Ogawa, N. Role of facial expression in "cooperative-avoidance conditioning" in monkeys. *Journal of Abnormal and Social Psychology,* 1963, **67**, 24–30.

Miller, R. E., Caul, W. F., & Mirsky, I. F. Communication of affects between feral and socially isolated monkeys. *Journal of Personality and Social Psychology,* 1967, **7**, 231–239.

Murphy, L. B. *Social behavior and child personality: An exploratory study of some roots of sympathy,* New York: Columbia University Press, 1937.

Myers, J. L., & Myers, N. A. Effects of schedules of primary and secondary reinforcement on extinction behavior. *Child Development,* 1963, **34**, 1057–1063.

Myers, N. A. Extinction following partial and continuous primary and secondary reinforcement. *Journal of Experimental Psychology,* 1960, **60**, 172–179.

Myers, N. A., & Myers, J. L. Secondary reinforcement as a function of training and testing schedules. *Child Development,* 1966, **37**, 645–652.

Nissen, H. W., & Crawford, M. P. A preliminary study of food-sharing behavior in young chimpanzees. *Journal of Comparative Psychology,* 1936, **22**, 383–419.

Rice, G. E., Jr., & Gainer, P. "Altruism" in the albino rat. *Journal of Comparative and Physiological Psychology,* 1962, 55, 123–125.

Rosekrans, M. A. Imitation in children as a function of perceived similarity to a social model and vicarious reinforcement. *Journal of Personality and Social Psychology,* 1967, 7, 307–315.

Rosekrans, M. A., & Hartup, W. W. Imitative influence of consistent and inconsistent response consequences to a model on aggressive behavior in children, *Journal of Personality and Social Psychology,* 1967, 7, 429–434.

Rosenbaum, M. E., & deCharms, R. Direct and vicarious reduction of hostility. *Journal of Abnormal and Social Psychology,* 1960, 60, 105–111.

Rosenhan, D., & White, G. M. Observation and rehearsal as determinants of pro-social behavior. *Journal of Personality and Social Psychology,* 1967, 5, 424–431.

Schopler, J., & Bateson, N. The power of dependence. *Journal of Personality and Social Psychology,* 1965, 2, 247–254.

Schopler, J., & Matthews, M. W. The influence of the perceived causal locus of partner's dependence on the use of interpersonal power. *Journal of Personality and Social Psychology,* 1965, 2, 609–612.

Stein, L. Secondary reinforcement established with subcortical stimulation. *Science,* 1958, 127, 466–467.

Thibaut, J. W., & Kelley, H. H. *The social psychology of groups.* New York: Wiley, 1959.

Ugurel-Semin, R. Moral behavior and moral judgment of children. *Journal of Abnormal and Social Psychology,* 1952, 47, 463–474.

Ulrich, R. Interaction between reflexive fighting and cooperative escape. *Journal of the Experimental Analysis of Behavior,* 1967, 10, 311–317.

Walters, R. H., Parke, R. D., & Cane, V. Timing of punishment and the observation of consequences to others as determinants of response inhibition. *Journal of Experimental Child Psychology,* 1965, 2, 10–30.

Wheeler, L., & Caggiula, A. R. The contagion of aggression. *Journal of Experimental Social Psychology,* 1966, 2, 1–10.

Wheeler, L., & Smith, S. Censure of the model in the contagion of aggression. *Journal of Personality and Social Psychology,* 1967, 6, 93–98.

Wright, B. A. Altruism in children and the perceived conduct of others. *Journal of Abnormal and Social Psychology,* 1942, 37, 218–233.

Wynne-Edwards, V. C. *Animal dispersion in relation to social behavior.* New York: Hafner, 1962.

MORAL DECISION MAKING AND BEHAVIOR

Shalom H. Schwartz[1]

In the recent proliferation of research on the antecedents of prosocial and antisocial behavior, attributes of the actor and of the interaction setting have been emphasized. With few exceptions (e.g., Schopler & Thompson, 1968), investigators have not examined closely the perceptual and cognitive processes underlying decisions that lead to action. This paper outlines an approach to understanding moral behavior through analysis of the process of moral decision making. By studying how people perceive and define their situation when they face moral decisions, I hope to identify a limited number of dimensions in the decision-making process through which situational and personality variables exercise their impact on behavior.

A glance at the diversity of the situational and personality correlates of morally relevant behavior that have been studied shows the desirability of organizing these variables more parsimoniously. It has been demonstrated that such prosocial actions as giving help, charity, and comfort, for example, are related to the behavior of models (Bryan & Test, 1967; Rosenhan & White, 1967; Hornstein. Fisch, & Holmes, 1968), the attractiveness of the other (Davis & Jones, 1960; Lerner & Matthews, 1967), the dependence of the other on the self (Berkowitz & Daniels, 1964), previous favors received (Schopler & Thompson, 1968), guilt arousal (Darlington & Macker, 1966; Freedman, Wallington, & Bless, 1967), and

[1]The research reported in this paper was supported in part by Grant No. GS2048 from the National Science Foundation.

127

Internal-External Control (Gore & Rotter, 1963; Strickland, 1965). Such anti-social behavior as aggression, cheating, and exploitation have been shown to be influenced by the behavior of models (Berkowitz & Rawlings, 1963; Walters, Llewellyn, & Acker, 1962), proximity of the victim and of authority (Milgram, 1965), delay of gratification (Mischel & Gilligan, 1964), judgment of ethical risk (Rettig & Pasamanick, 1964), and Level of Moral Thought (Schwartz, Feldman, Brown, & Heingarter, 1969).

Literature concerned with defining the domain of morality (Baier, 1958; Kohlberg, 1964; Lee, 1931; Miller & Swanson, 1960) suggest three distinctive attributes of moral decisions. First, moral decisions necessarily lead to interpersonal actions having consequences for the welfare of others. Second, decisions are classified as moral only when the decision maker is considered a responsible agent—a person who has chosen an action knowingly and willingly when he could have done otherwise. Finally, the actions resulting from moral decisions and the agent held responsible for them are evaluated as good or bad according to the consequences the actions have for others' welfare. Cultural specifications of what constitutes good and bad interpersonal behavior, i.e., moral norms, are the reference points for these evaluarions.

These three attributes of moral decisions are observed in the conception of morality tacitly employed in everyday social interaction (cf. Schmitt, 1964). Each attribute provides one dimension along which the perception and definition of the decision-making situation may vary. In elaborating on these dimensions I will illustrate how variations on them may cut across and tie together findings in some of the studies referred to above.

DYNAMICS OF MORAL DECISIONS AND BEHAVIOR

Awareness of Consequences

Whenever the welfare of one person potentially depends upon the actions of another, the latter may face a moral decision. It is only with awareness of this dependence that the process of moral decision making can commence. The first step is to become aware that particular actions have consequences for the welfare—physical or psychological—of the other person. Those actions and consequences to which attention is directed determine which personal standards and group norms are seen as pertinent to the action decision. Without recognition of real or imagined consequences for another, one would not perceive himself to be faced with a moral choice at all.

The probability that a person will become aware of particular consequences for others of his potential actions depends on situational and individual factors such as those cited above. The behavior or models, for example, may draw attention to certain lines of actions and sets of consequences rather than to others, thereby increasing the likelihood of prosocial (e.g., helping, Bryan & Test, 1967) or antisocial (e.g., aggressive, Berkowitz & Rawlings, 1963) behavior. Individual differences in the tendency to delay gratification may partly determine whether attention is focused on short-range or long-range consequences of potential action, thereby influencing whether people resist or yield to temptation (Mischel & Gilligan, 1964).

Ascription of Responsibility

Having recognized that a moral decision may be in order by becoming aware of potential consequences for others of certain actions, a person must next decide if he himself is responsible for these actions and their consequences. He may ascribe responsibility to himself in greater or lesser degree, or he may ascribe responsibility away from the self to other potential actors, to chance, to role demands, to provoking circumstances, etc. Whether or not one does accept some personal responsibility is a function both of the structure of the situation and of his own individual tendencies. For situations in which moral norms are widely and unequivocally accepted, I hypothesize that conditions which increase the probability of ascribing responsibility to the self foster socially desirable behavior; conditions promoting ascription of responsibility away from the self reduce the likelihood of socially desirable behavior. Several of the studies of prosocial and antisocial behavior can be reinterpreted and unified in light of this hypothesis. A number of examples will indicate the thrust of this approach.

Milgram (1965) observed that the closer the experimenter was to the subject and the more prestigious the research organization supposedly sponsoring his research, the greater the proportion of subjects who inflicted serious pain upon a supposed victim. Self-reports by the subjects indicate that under these conditions they tended to ascribe responsibility for their actions away from themselves and to the experimenter. Schopler and Matthews (1965) found that powerful subjects were less helpful to dependent partners when they believed the latter had volunteered to be dependent than when they believed the dependency had been imposed upon them. It was probably easier to ascribe responsibility for acting away from the self when the other could be defined as responsible for his own predicament.

Subjects in an experiment by Lerner and Matthews (1967), who perceived themselves to be responsible for their partner's assignment to an anxiety-provoking task, tended to find this partner less attractive than those in a condition where the partner was seen as responsible for choosing his own fate. Despite the lesser attractiveness of partners in the former condition, more subjects offered to comfort them in this condition. Thus comfort was offered more readily when ascription of responsibility away from the self was more difficult.

Hornstein *et al.* (1968) report that subjects returned a lost wallet significantly more frequently when given a model who was characterized as similar rather than dissimilar to themselves. Similarity can be viewed as determining whether the model's acceptance of personal responsibility to help is seen by the observer as calling for similar ascription of responsibility to himself.

Darley and Latané (1968) interpreted the negative relationship they observed between the number of bystanders and the likelihood of help being offered to a seizure victim as evidence for diffusion of responsibility among the bystanders. In the terminology of this chapter, the presence of others provided the individual with alternatives to the self to who to ascribe responsibility.

Horowitz (1968) found that subjects who were free to help or not to help a dependent other gave more help than subjects who were compelled by the experimenter to help. The amount of help may be viewed as a function of the extent to which subjects perceived themselves, rather than the experimenter, as responsible for their decision to help.

These translations of situational variables into variations in ascription of responsibility are speculative; no doubt other determinants of decisions were also at work. The examples should suffice to illustrate, however, that focusing on this one dimension of perception and definition in the decision-making situation may permit a more parsimonious understanding of the process of moral choice and behavior.

Moral Norms

Social specifications of desirable behavior in particular situations provide the actor with potential directions for his action to take. These moral norms may be internalized wholly or partially, or they may be perceived as expectations held by significant others. As noted above, in order for a given moral norm to be activated, the actor must become aware of interpersonal consequences of actions governed by that norm. Whether the activated norm will then influence behavior depends on whether or not the actor ascribes some personal responsibility to himself for the actions and consequences to which the norm refers.

According to this analysis, awareness of consequences and ascription of responsibility to the self are conducive to behavior congruent with the norms the actor defines as pertinent in a choice situation, but they are not necessarily conducive to prosocial behavior. Most experimental research on antecedents of prosocial and antisocial behavior has ignored differences between individuals in the norms they accept and in the intensity with which they endorse particular norms. The research has usually assumed generalized agreement regarding prescriptions to give help and proscriptions against inflicting harm. The main source of moral conflict for subjects has been taken to be the self-sacrifice required to comply with norms. Analyzing moral decision making in terms of the activation of norms permits consideration of normative differences among individuals and of the possibility that conflicting norms may be activated simultaneously in one person.

Defensive Redefinition of the Situation

It is evident even to the most casual observer of human behavior that awareness or endorsement of moral norms is no guarantee of conforming behavior. The major barriers to acting in conformity with pertinent moral norms are the absence of the resources and opportunities needed to conform (e.g., interpersonal skills and spatial proximity) and various countervailing motives (e.g., selfish interests). The presence of countervailing motives renders the process of moral decision making more complex.

If a person plans to act in conformity with moral norms, he is likely to feel anticipatory virtue, pride or security—emotions which enhance the likelihood of behaving as planned. But if, due to countervailing motives, he plans to violate pertinent moral norms, he is likely to feel guilt, shame or fear (cf. Aronfreed, 1968). Such emotions may inhibit behavior or they may motivate a redefinition of the choice situation that would permit performing the behavior without experiencing the disturbing emotions. Redefinition can occur by defensive changes on one or more of the three key dimensions of moral decisions:

1. Denial of consequences: Having once recognized potential consequences, the person may subsequently deny to himself that his acts will have these anticipated consequences and attend to other consequences or to none at all.

2. Denial of responsibility: Initially having seen himself as a responsible agent, he may now deny his responsibility by changing his perception of how free or capable he is to control what may happen to others.

3. Transformation of norms: In conjunction with the denial of consequences and responsibility, a person may change his view of which moral norms legitimately apply to him in the situation. Any modification in the consequences perceived or in the ascription of responsibility may increase the salience of some norms while decreasing that of others.

Any one of these defensive redefinitions may suffice to deactivate a moral norm that has aroused inhibiting emotions, although combinations of defenses may be required. It should be emphasized that these defensive redefinitions occur prior to or during the decision-making process, permitting actions to be taken that might otherwise have been inhibited (cf. Sykes & Matza, 1957).

In summary, a three-step decision process has been outlined leading to behavior congruent with moral norms. The person must first recognize the dependence of another on him by becoming aware that a potential action has consequences for the other. He must then have knowledge of moral norms pertinent to this action and its consequences. Finally, he must ascribe some responsibility to himself for the action. At each of these steps moral norms may be prevented from influencing his behavior. This may occur spontaneously—he may not take note of consequences, have knowledge of relevant moral norms, or see himself as a free, responsible agent—or it may be due to a defensive redefinition of the situation once disturbing anticipatory emotions have been aroused. A similar set of steps has been proposed by Latané and Darley (1968) to describe the process of deciding to intervene in an emergency—a special case of moral decision making.

A Note on Self-Conscious Cognition

While I hypothesize that the process described above occurs in moral decision making, I am not asserting that people are always aware of thinking about consequences, norms, and responsibility. The whole process may be painfully self-conscious—as when a team of doctors decides which patient is to receive a heart transplant, or it may be without conscious thought and telescoped in time—as when an adult pulls a child from the path of an onrushing vehicle. As part of a current study, I am exploring factors that influence the degree of self-consciousness in moral decision making. Some factors to be considered are the speed and certainty with which consequences of action may materialize, the seriousness of consequences in terms of immediate suffering and/or permanent damage to the dependent other, the clarity and singularity of relevant moral norms, and whether the proximate cause of dependence is social or impersonal. It should also be recognized that behavior judged by observers as morally desirable may represent overlearned responses and involve no decision making at all.

EMPIRICAL FINDINGS

Research designed to examine some aspects of the above theoretical scheme has been reported elsewhere (Schwartz, 1968a, b). The following summary of empirical findings points to major conclusions, unexamined questions, and new issues raised in this research. The general proposition tested was that awareness that one's potential acts have consequences for the welfare of others and ascription of responsibility for these acts and their consequences to the self are necessary conditions for the activation of moral norms. This proposition implies that there is a significant positive association between the moral norms endorsed by individuals and their actual interpersonal behavior only when people perceive relevant consequences and accept responsibility for them in the decision situation. In the absence of awareness of consequences or ascription of responsibility to the self, no such association is expected.

One hundred and eighteen male undergraduates (the membership of nine self-contained residential units) who had lived together for at least four months served as subjects. During these three sessions held in the house of each group, I measured each individual's personal norms and obtained peer ratings of his behavior in a variety of everyday situations involving considerateness, reliability, and helpfulness toward peers. Summary indexes of norms and behavior will be referred to in this report. While the probabilities of perceiving interpersonal consequences and accepting responsibility can be affected both by individual tendencies and by situational cues, only individual tendencies were measured in this research.

Awareness of consequences (AC) was tapped by a projective test in which subjects described the thoughts and feelings that might run through the minds of protagonists in stories who faced decisions having interpersonal consequences. Responses were scored blindly by two coders who attained 93% agreement within one point on a five-point scale measuring "the extent to which the actor is aware of the potential consequences of his behavior for the welfare of others as part of his decision-making process." AC scores were related neither to endorsement of prosocial norms nor to Social Desirability scores (Crowne & Marlowe, 1964). Scores were based on thoughts and feeling prior to reaching a decision to act; hence they probably indexed primarily initial tendencies to perceive decision situations in terms of consequences for others. The impact of redefinition of the situation through defensive denial of consequences is therefore yet to be studied.

The following story exemplifies the items in the AC instrument:

> When the alarm rang at 7:30 on Saturday morning, Bob rolled over and shut it off with a groan. He had been up very late and had no desire to climb out of bed into the cold air now. Then he remembered that his friends were schedduled to pick him up at 8:00 A.M. They were planning to spend the day skiing, and had agreed to leave early to beat the traffic and the crowds. Bob had looked forward to the day. He knew that if he didn't get going immediately, he would keep everyone waiting. Lying in bed, Bob struggled to get up. *Question:* What thoughts and feelings might be going through Bob's mind as he debates with himself about what to do now?

Ascription of responsibility to the self (AR) was measured by agreement with 24 opinions and self-descriptive items. Each item referred to actions with interpersonal consequences and provided a rationale for ascribing responsibility for these actions away from the actor. Acceptance or rejection of the rationales was interpreted as a sign of a tendency to ascribe responsibility away from or to the self, respectively. The major rationales built into the scale which also emerged in factor analyses of later forms are: extreme provocation, role requirements, conformity, lack of intentionality, just deserts for victim and prior harm by others. Internal reliability correlations for several samples have ranged between .67 and .78, and a test–retest reliability of .63 has been obtained. AR scores were not related to the norms endorsed by subjects nor to their Social Desirability scores.

In addition to evidence for validity reported in Schwartz (1968a), AR scores have been found to predict participation in voluntary social service activities among samples of male and female undergraduates, and to have a low positive correlation with verbal intelligence. AR scores probably reflect tendencies for defensive denial of responsibility, since in over two thirds of the scale items responsibility is assigned for acts already completed. The influence on moral decisions and behavior of differences in the initial perception of responsibility thus remains unexamined. The following illustrative items are marked to indicate the response receiving a point for ascription of responsibility to the self:

Disagree   You can't blame basically good people who are forced by their environment to be inconsiderate of others.

Agree   Being very upset or preoccupied does not excuse a person for doing anything he would ordinarily avoid.

Disagree   If a person is nasty to me, I feel very little responsibility to treat him well.

Assuming that AC and AR scores index the probability that people will define decision situations in terms of consequences for others and of personal responsibility, the proposition that these are necessary conditions for the activation of moral norms and their influence on behavior was tested. The total sample was divided into subsamples differentiated by level of AC. I then examined the correlations between personal norms and peer ratings of behavior within each subsample. A similar division of the sample was carried out for AR scores. I predicted that the correlations would be near zero within the subsamples scoring lowest on the personal tendencies and increasingly positive within subsamples scoring higher. Analysis of the data confirmed the prediction both for AC and AR separately (first two rows of Table 1). Further analysis demonstrated that the systematic increases in correlations were not attributable to differences in the variances of either norms or behavior across the subsamples nor to possible biases introduced by combining behavior ratings of subjects from different peer groups.

TABLE 1

Correlations between Summary Indexes of Personal Norms
and Peer Ratings of Behavior for Subsamples Split
on Awareness of Consequences and Ascription
of Responsibility

Measure	Level[a]			
	I (Low)	II	III	IV (High)
Awareness of consequences (AC)	−.02 (27)	.08 (28)	.21 (40)	.39[b] (23)
Ascription of responsibility (AR)	.02 (27)	.15 (30)	.20 (33)	.37[b] (28)

Measure	Level[a]		
	Low	Mixed	High
AC and AR split at median	.01 (29)	.17 (54)	.47[c] (35)

[a]Number of subjects on whom correlation is based is shown in parentheses.

[b] $p < .05$ (one-tailed).

[c] $p < .01$ (one-tailed).

I proposed above that the activation of moral norms requires both awareness of consequences and ascription of responsibility to the self; the absence of
either—initally or through defensive denial—would prevent moral norms from
influencing behavior. I therefore predicted an interaction between AC and AR
in their effects on the congruence of norms and behavior. This prediction was
tested by splitting the sample at the median on each tendency and forming subsamples, Low on both, High on both, and Mixed. The correlations in the last
row of Table 1 are consistent with this prediction. Among those most likely both
to perceive consequences and to accept responsibility (High), there is a substantial correlation between norms and behavior. The correlations in the Mixed and
Low subsamples are not significantly greater than zero.

For a more refined test of the predicted interaction, correlations were
calculated within four levels of each tendency, within subsamples divided at the
median on the other tendency. Despite the resulting small samples, the findings
clearly support an interaction interpretation (Table 2). Among those below the
median on each tendency, the impact of increases in the other tendency on the
correspondence between norms and behavior was small; among those above the
median, the impact was quite strong. Thus, only with the probable presence of
either awareness of consequences or ascription of responsibility to the self (as indicated by scores above the median for AC or AR) did the presence of the other
condition for activating moral norms have a substantial impact.

TABLE 2

*Correlations between Summary Indexes of Personal Norms and Peer Ratings of Behavior
for Subsamples on Each Personal Tendency across Levels on the Other*

Measure	Level[a]			
	I (Low)	II	III	IV (High)
	Awareness of consequences			
Ascription of responsibility (AR)				
Low	−.02 (14)	.03 (15)	.10 (19)	.22 (9)
High	.03 (13)	.10 (13)	.32 (21)	.58 (14)
	Ascription of responsibility			
Awareness of consequences (AC)				
Low	−.03 (14)	.05 (15)	.09 (14)	.14 (12)
High	.11 (11)	.20 (15)	.37 (19)	.54 (16)

[a]Number of subjects on whom correlation is based is shown in parentheses.

Because these findings are based on aggregate rather than individual data, the evidence for an interaction as against an additive effect of AC and AR is only suggestive. Future research can test the interaction hypothesis directly by deriving a score for each individual measuring the congruence between his norms and behavior, and by examining whether or not there is a significant interaction term for AC $\times$ AR in the regression equation predicting congruence scores. The importance of studying both the separate effects of AC and AR and their interaction is reinforced by noting that these two tendencies are uncorrelated ($r =$ $-.07$, with no curvilinearity). This is contrary to my anticipations based on assumptions about the kinds of socialization experiences likely to promote the development of both tendencies (cf. Piaget, 1932; Kohlberg, 1963; Hoffman, 1968). Further exploration of the relationships between AC and AR and of their antecedents is thus called for.

Variation in the strength and direction of personal norms endorsed by subjects was great enough to permit analysis of the congruence between norms and behavior in the research. Nonetheless, the preponderance of the norms they endorsed favored some degree of action promoting the welfare of others. Viewing AC and AR scores as indexes of the probability that these available norms would be activated, and hence influence behavior, I predicted that AC and AR scores would be positively associated with peer ratings of prosocial behavior for the whole sample. The following correlations, all significant beyond the .01 level of confidence, confirmed this prediction: AC $\times$ behavior, $r = .27$; AR $\times$ behavior, $r = .22$; AC and AR $\times$ behavior, multiple $r = .36$.

In my discussion of the dynamics of moral decision making, I suggested that awareness of interpersonal consequences and acceptance of responsibility increase pressure to behave in accordance with those moral norms that the individual endorses. If a person feels that behavior conventionally considered antisocial or amoral is appropriate, does this mean he is more likely to behave "antisocially" when his norms are activated? Or does attention to consequences for others and to personal responsibility lead to changes in the content of the decision-maker's viewpoint or promote the salience of only prosocial norms? Because such a small proportion of the norms expressed by subjects in the research oppose peer welfare, this question could not be answered. Answering the question requires research on interpersonal behavior toward which a broad range of normative stances may be adopted.

PROBLEMS FOR THE FUTURE

In this section, I will point to aspects of the theoretical scheme of moral decision making yet to be examined empirically, and consider the limits of the conclusions drawn thus far. The relationship of moral decisions to behavior outlined above was intended as a general description of moral decision making. The empirical research, however, was necessarily confined to a narrow range of conditions. The behavior studied occurred in everyday contacts among peers, required little self-sacrifice or special effort, and probably was not seen by the actors as having long range significance for their own welfare. It is therefore necessary to investigate whether the theoretical scheme also applies more generally—for example, to decisions in emergencies, among strangers, when the consequences of action have serious immediate or career implications for the actor, or when the people involved have differential statuses or power.

Behavior in the research reported was directed toward and observed by others in a key membership group who were likely to respond with sanctions supporting prosocial behavior. Would the dynamics of moral decision making be similar in the absence of significant others, with no threat of sanctions, or when the norms held by the potential actor contradicted norms he attributed to others? Perhaps the tendency to ascribe responsibility to the self fosters rejection of others' contradictory expectations in favor of one's own.

In the brief review of research on antecedents of prosocial and antisocial behavior above, I suggested that the observed effects of situational variations were partly, perhaps largely, traceable to their impact on the person's perceptions of consequences and of responsibility as he weighs his decision. No direct test of this aspect of the theoretical scheme has been completed thus far. A study is planned in which the content of appeals for blood donation will be varied to manipulate the salience of consequences of action for others and the salience of personal responsibility. Measurements of norms held by the subjects relevant to donating blood and their scores on AC and AR will be obtained under independent auspices. Some of the questions pertinent to the theory that these data will open to examination are: How do variations in situational cues about consequences and responsibility affect prosocial behavior? How do they influence the congruence between norms and behavior? Do they interact with personal tendencies (AC and AR) to affect behavior and to affect the congruence of norms and behavior? What is the relative importance of situational cues versus personal tendencies in decision making?

Analysis of the impact on behavior of joint variation in the situational cues for consequences and responsibility and the personal tendencies indexed by AC and AR scores may help to reveal whether the personality instruments tap primarily (*a*) spontaneous tendencies to perceive consequences and responsibility or (*b*) defensive tendencies to redefine consequences and responsibility in the decision setting. I hypothesize that situational pressures interact differently with spontaneous and defensive tendencies. If perception of consequence or of responsibility tapped by the personality instruments are matters of spontaneous response, strong situational pressures to take note of consequences or to accept responsibility should virtually eliminate differences due to these individual tendencies: people should accept the definition of the situation presented to them. Situational pressures may have little impact, however, if AC or AR scores reflect defensive tendencies.

In the study reported here, it was not possible to question subjects about how they reached the decisions for which indexes of their behavior were obtained. Inquiry shortly after a decision is made into how people defined their choice situation—the elements perceived, ignored, distorted, and defended against—would provide information on the validity of the personality instruments, on the success of situational manipulations, and on the accuracy of the view of moral decision making I have propounded. Since people often do not weigh decisions self-consciously, it will be necessary to gather such information in research that maximizes the probability of self-conciousness. Attention to the phenomenology of decision making in studies of prosocial behavior may clarify to what degree the three dimensions and their relationships proposed here can help unify our understanding of the effects of numerous situational and individual variables.

REFERENCES

Aronfreed, J. *Conduct and conscience: The socialization of internalized control over behavior.* New York: Academic Press, 1968.

Baier, K. *The moral point of view.* Ithaca, N.Y.: Cornell University Press, 1958.

Berkowitz, L., & Daniels, L.R. Affecting the salience of the social responsibility norm: effects of past help on the response to dependency relationships. *Journal of Abnormal and Social Psychology,* 1964, **68,** 275–281.

Berkowitz, L., & Rawlings, E. Effects of film violence on inhibitions against subsequent aggression. *Journal of Abnormal and Social Psychology,* 1963, **66,** 405–412.

Bryan, J.H., & Test, M.A. Models and helping: naturalistic studies in aiding behavior. *Journal of Personality and Social Psychology,* 1967, **6,** 400–407.

Crowne, D.P., & Marlowe, D. *The approval motive: Studies in evaluative dependence.* New York: Wiley, 1964.

Darley, J.M., & Latané, B. Bystander intervention in emergencies: Diffusion of responsibility. *Journal of Personality and Social Psychology*, 1968, 8, 377-383.

Darlington, R.B., & Macker, C.E. Displacement of guilt-produced altruistic behavior. *Journal of Personality and Social Psychology*, 1966, 4, 442-443.

Davis, K.E., & Jones, E.E. Changes in interpersonal perception as a means of reducing cognitive dissonance, *Journal of Abnormal and Social Psychology*, 1960, 61, 402-410.

Freedman, J.L., Wallington, S.A., & Bless, E. Compliance without pressure: The effect of guilt. *Journal of Personality and Social Psychology*, 1967, 7, 117-124.

Gore, P.M., & Rotter, J.B. A personality correlate of social action. *Journal of Personality*, 1963, 31, 58-64.

Hoffman, M. Childrearing antecedents of moral internalization. In M. Hoffman (Ed.), *Moral character and moral processes: A symposium*. Chicago: Aldine, 1968.

Hornstein, H.A., Fisch, E., & Holmes, M. Influence of a model's feeling about his behavior and his relevance as a comparison other on observers' helping behavior. *Journal of Personality and Social Psychology*, 1968, 10, 222-226.

Horowitz, I.A. Effect of choice and locus of dependence on helping behavior. *Journal of Personality and Social Psychology*, 1968, 8, 373-376.

Kohlberg, L. Moral development and identification. In H. Stevenson (Ed.), *Child psychology: The sixty-second yearbook of the national society for the study of education*. Part I. Chicago: University of Chicago Press, 1963.

Kohlberg, L. Development of moral character and ideology. In H. Hoffman (Ed.), *Review of child psychology*. New York: Russell Sage Foundation, 1964.

Latané, B., & Darley, J.M.,Group inhibition of bystander intervention in emergencies. *Journal of Personality and Social Psychology*, 1968, 10, 215-221.

Lee, H.N. The differentia of moral value. *International Journal of Ethics*, 1931, 41, 222-229.

Lerner, M.J., & Matthews, G. Reactions to suffering of others under conditions of indirect responsibility. *Journal of Personality and Social Psychology*, 1967, 5, 319-325.

Milgram, S. Some conditions of obedience and disobedience to authority. *Human Relations*, 1965, 18, 57-75.

Miller, D.R., & Swanson, G.E. *Inner conflict and defense*. New York: Holt, Rinehart & Winston, 1960.

Mischel, E., & Gilligan, C. Delay of gratification, motivation for prohibited gratification, and responses to temptation. *Journal of Abnormal and Social Psychology*, 1964, 69, 411-417.

Piaget, J. *The moral judgment of the child*. New York: Harcourt, Brace & World, 1932.

Rettig, S., & Pasamanick, B. Differential judgment of ethical risk by cheaters and non-cheaters. *Journal of Abnormal and Social Psychology*, 1964, 69, 109-113.

Rosenhan, D., & White,G.M. Observation and rehearsal as determinants of prosocial behavior. *Journal of Personality and Social Psychology*, 1967, 5, 424-431.

Schmitt, D.R. The invocation of moral obligation. *Sociometry*, 1964, 27, 299-310.

Schopler, J., & Matthews, M.W. The influence of the perceived casual locus of partner's dependence on the use of interpersonal power. *Journal of Personality and Social Psychology*, 1965, 2, 609-612.

Schopler, J., & Thompson, V.D. Roles of attribution processes in mediating amount of reciprocity for a favor. *Journal of Personality and Social Psychology*, 1968, 10, 243-250.

Schwartz, S.H. Words, deeds, and the perception of consequences and responsibility in action situations. *Journal of Personality and Social Psychology,* 1968, **10**, 232–242. (a)

Schwartz, S.H. Awareness of consequences and the influence of moral norms on interpersonal behavior. *Sociometry,* 1968, **31**, 355–369 (b)

Schwartz, S.H., Feldman, K., Brown, M., & Heingartner, A. Some personality correlates of conduct in two situations of moral conflict. *Journal of Personality,* 1969, 37, 41-57.

Strickland, B.R. The prediction of social action from a dimension of internal-external control. *Journal of Social Psychology,* 1965, **66**, 405–412.

Sykes, G.M., & Matza, D. Techniques of neutralization: A theory of delinquency. *American Sociological Review,* 1957, **22**, 664–670.

Walters, R.H., Llewellyn, T.E., & Acker, C.W. Enhancement of punitive behavior by audiovisual displays. *Science,* 1962, **136**, 872–873.

THE SELF, SELFISHNESS, AND ALTRUISM[1]

Leonard Berkowitz

Discussions of altruism frequently contrast this form of behavior with egoism (Durkheim, 1951; Friedrichs, 1960; Sorokin, 1954). Egoism involves a high level of self-concern which presumably lessens the individual's inclination to help others unless he anticipates some benefits for his effort. Proceeding on this kind of assumption, the Society of Brothers in Paraguay, for example, trains its members to behave altruistically toward all others and to regard themselves as responsible for the others in their group. But more than this, they are also taught not to want to enhance their self-value relative to other people.. The men in this order believe that pride and the will to push oneself forward makes the individual less disposed to help others in need (Sorokin, 1954).

There are a number of different factors in heightened self-concern which, it seems to me, can lower the likelihood of altruistic acts. For one thing, self-preoccupation might keep the person from being immediately aware of social ideals calling for helpful behavior in certain situations. Daniels and I (Berkowitz & Daniels, 1963, 1964) have suggested that people in our society often help those who are dependent upon them because such behavior is prescribed by a social norm. Social standards are not always salient, however, even in the minds of persons who ordinarily adhere to these rules. Worry about one's self, thoughts and misgivings about one's self-worth, dreams of success or fear of failure in im-

[1]The author's research reported in this paper was sponsored by grant GS-1890X from the National Science Foundation.

portant activities, all may distract the person so that (momentarily, at least) he does not think of the helping ideal.

Self-concern might also interfere with empathy. Aronfreed (1966) maintains that altruism is generally motivated by empathy, and few would dispute this contention. Somewhat more problematic is the source of this empathic reaction. Aronfreed views the empathy as the helper's anticipatory experience of the pleasure the help recipient would feel at having his wants satisfied, but it probably is unwise to define empathy this narrowly. Other kinds of empathic reactions may also heighten motivation to help people in need, as Stotland (1969) has noted. Hornstein's paper in this volume suggests one important addition to the Aronfreed conception. Upon learning that someone else has been helpful, the observer's own inclination to give assistance is apparently influenced by his perception of whether or not the first helper had enjoyed rendering aid. The information about the helping model's feelings—especially when this person was relatively similar to the observer—presumably caused the observer to think he would feel the same way should he also give assistance. The observer, we might say, had empathized with the similar model and had been influenced by the resulting feelings, even when the model may not have been thinking of the help-recipient's pleasure at being aided.

A recently completed experiment by David Aderman and myself also demonstrates that the altruism-heightening empathy need not be solely with the help recipient. The male undergraduates in this experiment listened to a brief tape-recorded discussion between two students, in which one of the men said that he had a good deal of library work to do. In one version of the tape, the second student did not volunteer to help the man in need; however, he did offer to help in a second version, and in a third tape, he offered to help and then was thanked. Within each of these three conditions, each subject was asked to pay close attention either to the student in need or to the potential helper. At the conclusion of the tape recording, the experimenter said that the second part of the study would soon begin, and then asked the subject to help him, if he so desired, by scoring a big batch of data sheets from "another study," until the next phase could begin. The number of pages scored by each subject in the 10 minute waiting period is taken as an index of his resulting motivation to aid the experimenter.

Two conditions yielded the greatest help giving: (a) attending to the person in need who was not helped, and (b) attending to the potential helper who volunteered to help and then was thanked. In the first of these groups, according to the subject's reports of their mood, the subjects generally emphasized with the dependent-but-not-helped individual in the tape recording and came to feel relatively sad and resentful. This experience apparently made them think other people requiring assistance would also be unhappy, and induced them to help the experimenter. In contrast, the subjects in the second group—who had attended to the thanked helper—generally were least unhappy and had the strongest feelings of pleasantness of all the conditions. This felt pleasure arising from empathy with the rewarded helping model seems to have also led to a comparatively great willingness to aid the dependent experimenter.

The empathic reactions motivating altruism can be either pleasant or unpleasant, and can arise from thinking of either the person requiring help or the rewarded helper. But whatever the exact source of the empathy, a person who is preoccupied with himself might not readily "take the role" of either the dependent other or the observed helper so that he does not experience the help-stimulating feelings.

Further, self-concern, or at least uncertainty about self-worth, might lead to derogation of those in need of help. Lerner and Simmons (1966), and Lerner in this volume, have proposed that there is a widespread tendency to assume that a person deserves his fate. The hapless victim of circumstances beyond his control is presumably downgraded because of this "need to believe in a just world," while a lucky winner of some prize supposedly becomes a much more attractive individual. Instead of being helped, therefore, the unfortunate victim is neglected, if not shunned. Findings obtained by Patrick Johnson and myself are relevant here. They indicate that the men (but not the women) who were made to fail on an assigned activity and then were led to be uncertain whether this failure was their own or their partner's fault, were particularly likely to employ this type of "deserved fate" assumption in thinking about someone else. Thus, men (at least) who are doubtful about their own merits might refuse to aid people who have been victimized by fate, perceiving these unfortunates as deserving of their misfortune.

I suspect that self-concern is also responsible for some of the phenomena highlighted by social exchange or equity analyses of social interaction (Adams, 1963; Blau, 1964; Homans, 1961). Implicit in these analyses is the notion that the individual often compares his rewards, costs, and investments with those of other people. This comparison between self and others may be most likely to arise when the individual is uncertain of his own worth or is otherwise greatly self-concerned. Schopler (1967) has suggested that men are less apt to help a dependent peer than are women because men are more disposed to compare their own outcomes with the benefits the dependent person stands to gain. If their help will cause the other to get more from the situation than they themselves can get, men theoretically will resent this anticipated difference in outcomes and they then will become less willing to assist him. My own research demonstrates, nevertheless, that men do not always exhibit this type of reaction. It may arise primarily when self-concern is high.

Finally, and certainly not least, self-concern probably increases the resentment produced by the threat of a reduction in behavioral freedom. Whatever other costs may arise from aiding a person in need—muscular effort, the risk of bodily harm, an unwanted expenditure of money, or the inability to pursue other more enjoyable activities—we may also refrain from helping someone because we dislike the possibility that this person will control or restrict our actions. Whether we are confronted by an explicit call for help or only a felt obligation to aid someone, we are faced with a bothersome loss of our freedom. Brehm (1966) has advanced a somewhat similar notion. He contends that "psychological reactance" arises when the individual faces a possible restriction of his behavioral freedom. The results, Brehm says, is hostility as well as an increased desire to do whatever it is the individual believes he may not be able to do. I will describe several research findings, some obtained by Brehm and some by my co-workers and myself at Wisconsin, which suggest that people become less willing to help someone else when they are concerned about their self-worth, presumably because the self-preoccupation makes them less able to tolerate restrictions on their behavioral freedom.

In an experiment by Brehm and Cole (1966) male undergraduates were given either an innocuous introduction to the study that played down its importance or were told that their chances of being a success in life would soon be assessed. This latter statement presumably increased the men's self-concern. Then, supposedly before the experiment proper got underway, another person (the experimenter's confederate) did the subject a favor: he gave the subject a soft drink. No such favor was given to the other half of the subjects. When the experiment ostensibly began, the confederate was assigned a dull and arduous task. The subject could help him if he desired. The investigators found that when self-concern was not aroused, 93% of the men reciprocated the favor done them by the confederate and aided that person. However, when the subjects' chances of success in life were to be measured later so that they presumably were self-preoccupied, only about 13% of the men helped the person who had done them the favor earlier. This level of help giving was even lower than that displayed by the subjects who had not received an earlier favor. All in all, the men who were induced to be self-concerned evidently resented the pressure they felt to return the confederate's favor. As a consequence, they became even more incline to resist the implied demand, and thus were least likely to help the confederate.

Another experiment, this one carried out at Wisconsin, also points to the help-dampening effects of self-concern in men. The subjects in this study first participated in a personality assessment of a same-sex peer. This consisted of listening to one person read an autobiographical statement and then hearing another individual "evaluate" the first speaker. (The evaluation was favorable in half of the cases and unfavorable in the other instances, but this variation did not affect the subjects' subsequent help giving.) Then, in the second phase of the experiment, supposedly as part of an entirely unrelated study, each subject was assigned the role of a Worker operating under the guidance of a Supervisor. The supervisor, who was said to be the person who had been evaluated in the first phase, was eligible for a $5 prize, but there was no prize for them. Half of the subjects were informed that 80% of the supervisor's grade would be based on their productivity (creating High Dependency), while the remaining subjects were told only 10% of the supervisor's grade would be based on their work (Low Dependency). In all cases, the experimenter and the subject were of the same sex. The major dependent variable here is the number of cardboard boxes assembled in a 10-minute work period minus twice the number of boxes made during an earlier, 5-minute practice period; the practice was given before any of the experimental manipulations and before the preliminary "evaluation."

The findings with the help-giving measure represent a fairly major departure from previous results contained in the writer's program, and are consistent with Schopler's notion regarding sex differences. For the first time in our Wisconsin studies there was a significant Sex X Dependency interaction: The women generally exhibited a reliably greater increase in productivity in behalf of their supervisor than did the men, with significantly greater effort under High than under Low Dependency, as is usually found. However, the men showed relatively low effort and were comparatively unaffected by their peer's degree of dependency on them. The men in the study, unlike men in other Wisconsin studies, were less responsive than women to someone else's need after they had participated in the evaluation of a peer, presumably because this evaluation made them more preoccupied with their own self-worth than the men in the previous studies.

A recent investigation by Aderman, Johnson, and myself provides additional evidence. Each subject was first asked to make judgments of photographs taken from the University yearbook. Self-concern was presumably aroused in half of the cases by telling the subject that these judgments would serve as a reliable indicator of his "social intelligence." In the remaining cases, intended to be low in self-concern, the experimenter was ostensibly only interested in student preferences in facial appearances. When the task was completed, the experimenter said they could not proceed with the main part of the study since the person designated to be the subject's partner had failed to show up. The subject would get credit for participating in the study, the experimenter went on, but since he had the time, the experimenter would like the subject to help him by scoring data from another study. As they walked to the location where this would be done, the experimenter introduced the second variation by saying that he was either an undergraduate like the subject (Low Status help recipient) or a graduate student about to receive his Ph. D. (High Status help recipient). (In order to keep the perceived importance of the task constant, all subjects were told their work would ultimately benefit a graduate student). The helping index here was the number of pages scored by the subject, supposedly for the experimenter, in the 15-minute work period. As in all our research, the experimenter and subjects were of the same sex.

The experimental treatments did not significantly affect the women's behavior. For the men, however, there was a significant main effect for the experimenter's status; the higher his status, the greater was the help he was given. This is in accord with exchange theorizing, but more interestingly, self-concern evidently lowered the subjects' motivation to assist the high-status individual. The men induced to think about their self-worth exerted about the same low level of effort while working for the High-Status person as did the subjects working for the Low-Status undergraduate, and they did reliably less work for the High-Status person than the other subjects in the High-Status group who were not self-preoccupied. The least effort was exerted by the self-concerned men working for the Low-Status experimenter, as we would expect, but this was not significantly different from the work performance in the other Low-Status group.

Yet another experiment, by Patrick Johnson, Bonnie Hildebrand, and myself, inquired further into the effects of self-concern and sex differences. We wondered if the women in the previous studies might not have been insufficiently self-preoccupied, and if a more sensitive performance measure might not have yielded significant results for the female subjects. In order to improve the performance (helping) measure, a baseline work rate was first determined for each subject. This was done by telling him (or her) that his partner had not yet arrived and asking him to help the experimenter by scoring data for a few minutes until the other person came. The experimenter then stopped the subject after 5 minutes, saying that he supposed the other subject was not going to arrive but that they would proceed with part of the experiment, nevertheless. The subject was shown a set of ten pictures, each portraying a group. In two conditions, he was asked to identify the group leader and the group attitude toward this person. One of the two conditions was informed that these pictures comprised a test of "social sensitivity," while the other condition was told that the picture test was a measure of the individual's "supervisory ability." Finally, in a third, control condition, the subjects were only to indicate their liking for the pictures. Our expectation here was that the female subjects would become more self-preoccupied if they thought the test was a measure of "social sensitivity" rather than "supervisory ability," while the opposite would be true for the men. (Further information provided to the subject was designed to heighten the importance of the "supervisory ability" test to the men.) Then, to make the subjects still more self-concerned, they were told that the experimenter would go off to score the test results and that they would learn their results in a few minutes. Before departing, however, the experimenter again asked the subjects to help him by scoring the other data he had collected. The influence of the presumed self-concern is assessed in terms of the difference in work rate between the first, baseline period and this later, 10-minute, posttest period.

Analysis of these changes-in-work-rate scores yielded a significant Sex by Experimental Treatment interaction, with the conditions differing as we had expected. The men increased their work rate after taking either the "social sensitivity" or "preference" tests, but their rate of work actually slowed down to a degree reliably different from the other groups when they thought the test had measured their "supervisory ability." In the case of the women, on the other hand, as we had predicted, the lowest increase in work arose after the women though they had taken a test of their "social sensitivity." All in all, the men and women seemed to have different concerns, but whatever made them self-preoccupied, the arousal of self-concern evidently lowered their willingness to help the experimenter.

If these results should prove to be as general as the findings I have cited indicate, they have an obvious implication for several contemporary approaches to education and psychotherapy. A number of educators and philosophers dating back as far as Rousseau and the French *philosophes,* to say nothing of Carl Rogers and Abraham Maslow, have advocated what I believe is a doctrine of self-preoccupation. They urge the individual to search for self-actualization, i.e., to pursue his self interests with little regard for the wishes and opinions of other persons. This romantic conception, it seems to me, is all too likely to breed the sort of self-concern which will dampen altruism. Indeed, writers such as Ayn Rand have recognized this quite explicitly. Miss Rand believes that altruism is one of the major sins of our age, and calls on people to be concerned, deliberately, with their own goals and feelings in an effort to maximize their self-worth.

Finally, let me bring up two more points relevant to the present discussion. Self concern may lead to greater amounts of helping in at least two ways. People may well assist those in need when they think this action will bring approval and enhance their value in the eyes of other persons. A recent experiment by Vanneman, Peterson and myself demonstrated that the arousal of high "evaluation apprehension" will lead to strong effort in behalf of a peer when the individual believes this work is probably instrumental to obtaining a favorable evaluation. This result was obtained, furthermore, for both men and women. Second, even in the absence of external sources of approval, the individual may want to be consistent with his image of himself. If he thinks of himself as a helpful person, he might act in a helpful manner in order to conform to his ideals and his self-conception. Nevertheless, this type of self picture will not always be salient, even in people who usually regard themselves as very helpful. On some occasions they may be thinking about themselves in more negative ways and might even be preoccupied with the question of how good they are. Brooding about themselves in this way, they may well be inclined to be less altruistic than when they have confidence in their own self-worth.

REFERENCES

Adams, J.S. Towards an understanding of inequity. *Journal of Abnormal and Social Psychology,* 1963, 67, 422–436.
Aronfreed, J. The origins of altruistic and sympathetic behavior. In Altruism Symposium presented at the American Psychological Association, 1966.
Berkowitz, L., & Daniels, L.R. Responsibility and dependency. *Journal of Abnormal and Social Psychology,* 1963, 66, 429–436.
Berkowitz, L., & Daniels, L.R. Affecting the salience of the social responsibility norm: Effects of past help on the response to dependency relationships. *Journal of Abnormal and Social Psychology,* 1964, 68, 275–281.
Blau, P.M. Exchange in power in social life. New York: Wiley, 1964.
Brehm, J.W. *A theory of psychological reactance.* New York: Academic Press, 1966.
Brehm, J.W., & Cole, A.H. Effect of a favor which reduces freedom. *Journal of Personality and Social Psychology,* 1966, 3, 420–426.
Durkheim, E. *Suicide,* Glencoe, Ill.: Free Press, 1951.
Friedrichs, R.W. Alter vs. ego: An exploratory assessment of altruism. *American Sociological Review,* 1960, 25, 496–508.
Homans, G.C. *Social behavior: Its elementary forms.* New York: Harcourt, Brace, 1961.
Lerner, M.J., & Simmons, C.H. Observer's reaction to the "innocent victim": Compassion or rejection? *Journal of Personality and Social Psychology,* 1966, 4, 203–210.
Schopler, J. An investigation of sex differences on the influence of dependence. *Sociometry,* 1967, 30, 50–63.

Sorokin, P.A. *Forms and techniques of altruistic and spiritual growth.* Boston: Beacon Press, 1954.
Stotland, E. Exploratory studies of empathy. In L. Berkowitz (Ed.), *Advances in experimental social psychology,* Vol. 4. New York: Academic Press, 1969.

GUILT, EQUITY, JUSTICE, AND RECIPROCATION

TRANSGRESSION, COMPLIANCE, AND GUILT

Jonathan L. Freedman

In the past few years, there has been a considerable amount of work on the effect of transgression on subsequent compliance. I will review this work briefly, describe some as yet unpublished studies on the same topic, and then explain why I think the effects can be explained, at least in part, in terms of guilt. I shall also describe the manipulations that have been used and the effects they have produced.

In one study (Carlsmith & Gross, 1969), subjects delivered either electric shocks or only loud buzzes to a confederate who was posing as another subject. The situation was the familiar learner–teacher setup with the real subject serving as the teacher and punishing the confederate whenever he made an error. After the "learning" part of the study was over, the subject and the confederate were asked to fill out a brief questionnaire. It is very important to note that the confederate did not know whether the subject thought he was delivering shocks or just buzzes. (Since the amount of compliance that was elicited was probably extremely dependent on how the request by the confederate was made, I believe it was essential for the person making the request to be blind as to what condition the subject was in.) While they were filling out these questionnaires, the confederate at one point turned to the subject and said something like, "Hey, I wonder if you could do me a favor. I'm working on a committee which is trying to enlist support to save the Redwoods in California. I am supposed to call a lot of people and I wonder if you could do some of the calling for me?" The subject

155

said either yes or no, and if he said yes, the confederate said, "How many names would you be willing to take? I would really appreciate it if you could take as many as 50." The subject then indicated how many he would be willing to take and that terminated the experimental part of the study.

The results were very impressive. Whereas only one-quarter of the subjects who had delivered buzzes agreed to take any names, three-quarters of those who delivered shocks were willing to help. In other words, getting one person to deliver shock to another produces three times as much compliance to the other's request for help as getting him to deliver buzzes. Any time we in social psychology find a manipulation which triples some behavior, I, at least, am very impressed.

In another phase of the same study, a third confederate, also posing as a subject, watched the subject deliver the shock. When he subsequently made a request of the subject, there was even more compliance than when the actual recipient of the shock made the request. Exactly why this occurred is not clear, but for the present, the important fact is that delivering shock to person A greatly increased compliance to a request from person B even when the request in no way involved person A, and even though in this situation there was no clear restitution to the victim.

A second study (Freedman, Wallington, & Bless, 1967) induced a subject to tell a lie to the experimenter. While waiting to take part in the experiment, some subjects were told something about the test they were going to take while other subjects were not told anything. A confederate posing as a real subject delivered this information. When the actual experiment began, the experimenter told the subject that it was absolutely essential that he knew nothing about the test he was going to take, and was asked whether he had heard anything about it. Virtually all subjects said they had not heard anything. Thus, some subjects (those who actually had heard something) told a lie, while others did not. After taking an innocuous test, they were thanked for taking part in the study and were paid. At this point the experimenter said that she had been asked to inquire whether any of the subjects would be willing to take part in another study for which, unfortunately, they could not be paid. Our measure is simply whether or not they agreed. Those who had told a lie complied twice as often as those who had not told a lie.

In two other studies by the same authors, subjects were induced to knock over a table containing some index cards which were supposedly being used by a graduate student writing a thesis. It was made clear that the index cards were originally in careful order and that in the upsetting, this order was lost. After doing this, subjects took part in an innocuous study and were then asked whether or not they would be willing to participate in a further experiment for which they could not be paid. The other experiment was, in one case, supposedly being run by the graduate student whose cards had been knocked over, and in another case, by some entirely unrelated graduate student. I have simplified the design here somewhat because for our present purposes the important finding was that students who had knocked over cards complied much more than did students who had not knocked over cards. Again we see that the manipulation produced a large increase in compliance.

A number of studies have involved what we can call machine breaking. In one (Wallace & Sadalla, 1966) the machine smoked slightly and the experimenter reported that it had been broken. In others (Brock & Becker, 1966) machines exploded in a marvelous display of fireworks or simply broke more quietly. The data from these studies are somewhat more mixed than those from the studies cited above, and the research is weakened by the fact that in no case was the experimenter blind as to what condition the subject was in. Nevertheless, there was a general tendency for subjects who believed they had broken the machine to comply more than those who had either not broken the machine or who had done less serious or dramatic damage.

In a study by Berscheid and Walster (1967), female subjects were led to harm another woman during the course of a game by depriving her of trading stamp books. In a second game they had a chance to compensate the deprived woman. The proportion of women who elected to compensate her ranged from 42 to 73% depending on conditions. When there had been no previous harm, the proportion of subjects conferring a benefit on the other ranged from 2 to 26%. Although inadequacy or excessiveness of the available compensation significantly lowered the proportion of compensators, the difference between harm doers and the other subjects remains impressively large. This is not compliance in the same sense as in the other studies, because the victim did not ask the subject to do anything for her. But it is clear that the subject was trying to make up for what she did and this produced more than three times as much benefit to the other person as when no harm had been done.

Finally, a study has recently been completed at Stanford by Carlsmith, Ellsworth, & Whiteside in which subjects were induced to cheat on a test. Before taking the test, they were given some information by a confederate posing as a subject. This information made it easier to do well on the test and was, in a sense, an entirely unfair clue. Other subjects were not given the information. After tak-

[1]Carlsmith, J.M., Ellsworth, P.G., & Whiteside, J., Guilt, confession and compliance. Unpublished manuscript. Stanford University, 1968.

ing the test, those who cheated were told they had done extremely well and that, in fact, their scores were so high that the experiment was virtually ruined for the person doing it. The experimenter acted upset and generally gave the impression that the whole experiment had been a disaster. Later the subjects were paid by the secretary for taking part in the study and were asked to sign a receipt. At this point, the secretary simply handed them a sheet on which they were asked to volunteer for a number of future experiments being conducted in the psychology department. Once again, those who had cheated complied much more than those who had not cheated. An additional condition in this study we might call confession: Some of the subjects who cheated were given the opportunity to confess that they knew something about the test ahead of time. Subjects in this confession condition did not comply more than those who had not cheated in the first place. This effect has recently been replicated by Regan[2] under more controlled conditions.

This is not an exhaustive list of research on this problem. I have tried to give some notion of the range of manipulations which have resulted in increased compliance. I know of only one study on this problem that did not demonstrate an increase in compliance — one by Silverman (1967). However, it is flawed by self-selection of subjects, too high a compliance rate in the control groups, and a number of other problems which make the data uninterpretable. Except in the results of that one study, the effects of wrong doing on compliance have been remarkably consistent and powerful.

How can these data be summarized and explained? The simplest way of characterizing the manipulations used in this research is to say that causing someone to transgress against a moral or social code or to harm someone results in an increase in subsequent compliance. This increase in compliance apparently extends to behavior not involving the actual victim of the transgression. Even someone quite unaffected by the act of transgression and entirely unrelated to the victim elicits more compliance to his requests than he would if there had been no transgression in the first place. Delivering a shock, telling a lie, upsetting some cards, breaking a machine, taking money from someone, cheating on an exam are all quite different behaviors. The only common thread running through them is that they all involve some sort of transgression. Transgression, then, leads to greater compliance. Why?

I have made the assumption that the effect is produced by some internal feeling common to any situation in which there has been transgression. The problem now is to specify the characteristics of this internal feeling. Although I do not know in detail what its characteristics are, I do know that it produces an increase

---

[2]Regan, J. W., Unpublished doctoral dissertation, Stanford University, 1968.

in compliance. I also know from other work that it causes subjects to tend to minimize their wrongdoing or to deny that they did anything wrong. In addition, when they know that they can be hurt in return, they show less tendency to compensate the victim. What shall we call an internal state that has all of these properties?

One possibility is to make up a name and call it, let us say, "tulig." People who transgress a moral value feel tulig. This seems to me to have an appropriate unpleasant, rather biting sound to it. It happens, however, that there is already a word in English and in psychology which many people have traditionally applied to the kind of internal state which we are talking about. This word is "guilt." Since the word already exists in the language, it seems fairly reasonable for us to use it, even though, as I said, we could use another word if for some reason we dislike this one.

However, there is one problem with using the word guilt, and that is that it refers to a very rich, somewhat vague concept about which people have not always agreed. It is not a perfect concept for our purposes because we do not know enough about it and because so many people have said so many different things about it that it is hard to keep clearly in mind what it is. Nevertheless, many of the people who have said things about it have probably said very wise things. The word is in common usage and we all have at least vague notions what we are talking about when we use it, and most formulations of guilt do fit the data very nicely. Therefore, despite the minor difficulties that are introduced whenever you use an emotionally laden word such as guilt, I think it is the only sensible course to pursue.

Now let us see what we can say about guilt in this context. A large number of ideas about guilt have been promulgated in the literature. Guilt leads to expiation; it leads to self-punishment; it leads to confession; it causes people to want to reduce guilt in any way they can, to deny their guilt, to minimize it, and so on. These are all possible consequences of arousing guilt and on an a priori basis there is no reason to give more credence to one than to another. I have a tendency to accept them all. I think the least likely is the notion of self-punishment because, except in extreme circumstances, people just do not like to suffer if they can possibly avoid it. I think the most likely effects of guilt are compensation, expiation, and the various kinds of denials of responsibility.

If we now turn again to the findings, we see that causing someone to transgress makes him more compliant, increases his tendency to compensate his victim, and also makes him deny his responsibility. All of these findings fit in very nicely with traditional conceptions of guilt. There is, at the moment, no evidence that people seek self-punishment, but this has not really been very well tested yet. In any case, the failure to find support for one of the many notions about guilt surely in no way detracts from an explanation in terms of guilt. Rather what it does is to tell us more about guilt. In other words, what I am saying is that we now have a fairly potent way of studying this intervening variable which has been called guilt. We have a way of studying how people react when they have transgressed a moral code, how their internal state will affect their behavior. If someone objects to using the word guilt for this internal state, another word can be substituted, but it seems to me that the traditional notion of guilt is probably not far from the truth.

I might note that unfortunately it is difficult to measure guilt directly. Various attempts to construct paper and pencil or interview measures of guilt have been notoriously unsuccessful and therefore we have never tried to collect them in our work. Although it would be preferable to have a direct measure, it is certainly not a fatal flaw since many other concepts (e.g., dissonance) are used without our having any direct measure of them. The important thing is that guilt, as an intervening variable, ties together a large number of experimental findings. One of the reasons I find the explanation in terms of guilt so attractive is that it is very difficult to construct a plausible alternative explanation which can tie together all of this work.

Walster (in this volume) tends to explain her results primarily in terms of equity. When you have hurt someone, you want to compensate him. There is not really any controversy between this view and the idea of guilt. Surely compensation is one aspect of guilt. The weakness of the equity notion is that it should not apply to nonvictims. If it is expanded to some sort of "world equity," it begins to sound very much like a concept of guilt.

I would like to conclude by saying that calling this response guilt in no way ends the discussion. Even if we agree that the important point is one's feeling of responsibility and regret at what he has done (which we might call guilt), we are still left with the long and difficult task of specifying the details of this feeling and its implications for behavior. In a sense, all we have done is to say that the critical factor is the subject's feeling that he should not have done what he did (which is another way of saying that he believes he has transgressed the moral code), that this feeling is unpleasant, and that he will do whatever he can to remove it. He has several ways of removing it and, as usual, we know relatively little about what determines which way he chooses. At the moment, we do know that one very strong tendency is to expiate his feeling by doing something good in return, by compensating his victim, or by agreeing to help someone else. We also know that there is a tendency to deny responsibility and, therefore, the feeling. What else is important, where confession fits in, if at all, whether or not self-punishment will occur are all questions which remain to be answered. Hopefully, further research will tell us more about both compliance and guilt.

REFERENCES

Bercheid, E., & Walster, E. When does a harm-doer compensate a victim? *Journal of Personality and Social Psychology,* 1967, **6,** 435–441.

Brock, T.C., & Becker, L.A. "Debriefing" and susceptibility to subsequent experimental manipulations. *Journal of Experimental and Social Psychology,* 1966, **2,** 314–323.

Carlsmith, J.M., Ellsworth, P.C., & Whiteside, J. Guilt, confession and compliance. Unpublished manuscript, Stanford University, 1968.

Carlsmith, J.M., & Gross, A.E. Some effects of guilt on compliance. *Journal of Personality and Social Psychology,* 1969, **11,** 232–239.

Freedman, J.L., Wallington, S., & Bless, E. Compliance without pressure: The effect of guilt *Journal of Personality and Social Psychology,* 1967, **7,** 117–124.

Regan, J.W. Guilt, confession and compensation. Unpublished doctoral dissertations, Stanford University, 1968.

Silverman, I.W. Incidence of guilt reactions in children. *Journal of Personality and Social Psychology,* 1967, **3,** 338–340.

Wallace, J., & Sadalla, E. Behavior consequences of transgression: I. The effects of social recognition. *Journal of Experimental Research Personality,* 1966, **1,** 187–194.

REACTIVE GUILT AND ANTICIPATORY GUILT IN ALTRUISTIC BEHAVIOR[1]

Edna I. Rawlings

The cry of distress is the summons to relief
Judge Benjamin Cardozo

According to Webster's Third Edition, altruism is an "uncalculated consideration of, regard for, or devotion to others' interests sometimes in accordance with an ethical principle." We can assume that altruism is a moral value within American society, perhaps an aspect of a more general social responsibility norm. According to Berkowitz and Daniel's formulation, the social responsibility norm prescribes that people should help those who are dependent upon them (Berkowitz & Daniels, 1963). In general, people will conform to the social responsibility norm to the extent that they are aware of this ideal at the appropriate time and are motivated to adhere to it (Daniels & Berkowitz, 1963; Goranson & Berkowitz, 1966; Schopler & Bateson, 1965; Schopler & Matthews, 1965).

[1]This experiment was supported in part by Grant 1-F1-MH-22, 048-01 from the National Institute of Mental Health to the author and in part by a project sponsored by Grant GS-345 from the National Science Foundation to Leonard Berkowitz. Parts of the report were included in the author's Doctoral dissertation, partially fulfilling the requirements for the Ph. D. degree at the University of Wisconsin. The author gratefully acknowledges the assistance of Dr. Berkowitz in all phases of the study.

The above studies represent a sociological approach to moral behavior in that the moral behavior, help giving, is considered to be a special case of conformity to norms. Another major theoretical approach to moral behavior has its origins in psychoanalytic theory. According to this view, such behavior is often a reaction to guilt or anxiety (cf. Miller & Swanson, 1960). Guilty persons may expiate their guilt by punishing themselves or doing something good (Walster *et al.,* this volume; Freedman, this volume). Thus, Darlington & Macker (1966) showed that individuals who believed they had harmed another were more apt to agree to donate blood to a local hospital. The results of Freedman, Wallington, and Bless (1967) indicate that the motive for attempting compensation of harm done to another person is often expiation of guilt.

The sociological and psychoanalytic approaches are supplementary rather than being in opposition. Both views propose that behavior is often influenced by immediately preceding conditions, and both postulate at least some common intervening mechanisms. But where the sociological approach typically places greater emphasis on factors governing motivation to adhere to social norms (e.g., reminding a person of the social ideals), the psychoanalytic approach generally makes greater use of the assumption that heightened guilt or anxiety produces moral behavior in an attempt to lessen the aversive internal state. These approaches can readily be integrated.

Guilt means different things to different theorists. I will define it here as a particular type of discomfort either (*a*) aroused by the anticipation of violating an internal standard of "right" or "wrong" conduct or (*b*) following an actual transgression (Mussen, Conger, & Kagan, 1963). I will refer to the first as Anticipatory Guilt and the second as Reactive Guilt. Whatever the precipitating situation, whether a temptation or a transgression, guilt may not arise unless there is an awareness of a sizable discrepancy between the behavior—anticipated or performed—and the individual's internalized values. These values, it is suggested, serve as standards for evaluating the "goodness" or "badness" of the actions the individual might perform or has carried out. Thus, if someone feels guilty after violating a moral norm, it is because he presumably is aware of the discrepancy between his action and this norm. Similarly, Anticipatory Guilt is not produced unless the person is aware that the behavior he is tempted to perform violates his moral standards. Perhaps because of this Anticipatory Guilt, reminding the individual of the ideals or norms of his group often results in an increased adherence to these values (Charter & Newcomb, 1958). The norm reminder heightens the person's awareness that a transgression is a serious departure from his moral standards (assuming he has internalized the group norms), causing even the thought of a possible transgression to lead to an Anticipatory Guilt reaction. Increasing the salience of moral norms can therefore have much the same effect in producing conformity to social ideals as actual moral transgressions as long as the individual has adopted the group norms as his own values; in both cases the resulting behavior is an attempt to lessen or avoid guilt.

Investigators who focus on guilt-induced altruism (e.g., Darlington & Macker, 1966) have assumed that the altruism they observed was a function of Reactive Guilt, i.e., such behavior was an attempt to expiate guilt aroused by having harmed another individual. It is possible, however, that the awareness of harm done to the victim may heighten the salience of the social responsibility norm and make the person more willing to aid others. If the latter explanation is plausible, then the guilt which produced the altruistic response would be considered Anticipatory Guilt. Thus, studies of reactive guilt should include an additional comparison group that witnesses the harm to a victim but is not personally responsible for this harm.

Guilt may be further differentiated into external and internal guilt (Aronfreed, 1963). External guilt promotes conformity to norms or resistance to temptation through shame or anxiety, insofar as the individual fears being caught and punished or ridiculed; he will avoid violating social norms. Internal guilt, produced by strong internal standards, promotes moral behavior without the prod of immediate social pressures. Variations in internalization of these moral standards are presumed to be a function of antecedent social learning conditions. According to Aronfreed (and somewhat similarly, Bronfenbrenner, 1961; Sears, Maccoby, & Levin, 1957), induction discipline techniques (such as reasoning) are especially effective in fostering the development of internalized moral standards. In contrast, sensitization techniques such as withdrawal of love, verbal criticism, and physical punishment focus on the painful consequences of the behavior and encourage inhibition of the act only in order to avoid punishment. In the study described below, all subjects were given a parental discipline scale to assess the relationship of various types of parental discipline to the subjects' behavior. On theoretical grounds, we expected that those persons who received frequent inductive punishment would have more internalized controls and, when guilt was aroused, would be more inclined to behave in a socially acceptable manner than those whose parents used sensitization techniques.

In the present experiment reactive guilt was manipulated by shocking S's partner (P_1) whenever S made an error. This experience would presumably make Ss remorseful for the harmful consequences of their actions to P_1 and motivated them to compensate for this harm. However, S was given no opportunity to compensate for the harm to the original partner (P_1). In a second part of the study, S was given an opportunity to partially alleviate the distress of a new partner (P_2) by sharing the punishment. The reactive guilt hypothesis predicts that Ss will behave altruistically, presumably in order to lessen their guilt feelings. As noted above, the treatment designed to arouse reactive guilt feelings might have also increased the saliency of the altruism ideal. To assess the effects of heightened norm salience, a group was included which observed a victim receiving punishment, but the Ss in this group were not personally responsible for the harm to the victim. If this group also showed heightened altruism one could attribute their behavior to anticipatory guilt rather than reactive guilt. Additional control groups involved were one in which neither S nor P_1 received shock and one in which both S and P_1 were shocked.

METHOD[2]

Pretest Sessions

All Ss who participated in the study had been tested in groups prior to the experiment on the pretext that they would be matched with congenial partners in the main part of the experiment, said to be a learning study. These Ss were volunteers from introductory psychology classes at the University of Wisconsin. During the group sessions, which lasted approximately 45 minutes to 1 hour, several personality scales, including the Attitude Inventory described below, were administered. The personality scales were not scored until the completion of the experiment.

The Attitude Inventory[3]

The Ss filled out the Attitude Inventory first in terms of their mother's behavior and then filled out another copy for their father. Since Bronfenbrenner (1961) has indicated that a child is likely to receive most discipline from the parent of the same sex, only the maternal discipline scales were scored for the Ss (all females).

The Attitude Inventory is made up of several discipline scales. The scales of interest for the present discussion are reasoning, withdrawal of love, appeals to shame and guilt, verbal criticism, physical punishment, and material deprivation. Each of these discipline techniques was represented by three to five statements describing a specific application of the particular mode of discipline. S rated each statement in terms of the frequency with which her mother had behaved toward her in the manner described. The frequencies ranged from "never," which was

[2]The procedure and apparatus used are described more fully in Rawlings (1969).

[3]The Attitude Inventory is an adaptation of U. Bronfenbrenner's parental discipline scales (Bronfenbrenner, 1961).

scored one, to "always," which was scored five. The scores for the statements making up each scale were summed to give *S's* total score on any particular scale.

Procedure

*S*s from the pretested group who were unacquainted with each other were scheduled to report to the laboratory in groups of four. When the four *S*s arrived, they were met in the waiting room by the experimenter and told that the original plan of matching them with congenial partners had been abandoned as it had proved too difficult. They were also informed that it was necessary to use mild electric shock in some of the tasks and were assured that the shock was safe. At this point, *S*s were given a chance to withdraw from the experiment if they did not wish to continue. No one refused to participate. Each group was assigned to an experimental condition prior to *S*s' arrival by a random procedure. The girls were randomly divided into those serving as *S*s or as their partners. (These latter people are not of concern to us here.) An arrangement of partitions separated the *S*s from each other but allowed each girl to see her own partner.

As *S*s were individually seated at one of the cubicles, the experimenter placed two silver electrodes mounted on a plastic disk on *S*'s left wrist and fitted her with a pair of earphones. The *S*s were instructed to leave the electrodes and earphones on until the experimenter removed them. They were cautioned to be as quiet as possible throughout the experiment and were requested not to communicate with other *S*s except as instructed to do so. When the above procedure was completed, the experimenter made a few introductory remarks concerning the nature of the experiment and then described the first task. The *S*s were told that the purpose of the experiment was to assess the effects of others on an individual's learning and performance in a variety of tasks. This information was included to justify the tasks used and to provide a rationale for having *S*s work in pairs.

The Experimental Manipulations

The Auditory Discrimination Task

Treatment during the initial auditory discrimination task in the experiment constituted the manipulation differentiating the four experimental conditions. All *S*s listened to a number of tonal patterns through their earphones. Each *S* was asked to estimate the number of tones in a pattern and to signal this information to her partner by pressing one of three buttons. These buttons, located at the top of *S*'s display panel, were labeled "2," "3," and "4." The partner, who merely listened to the tones, was informed of S's estimate by means of three small white lights located at the top of her display panel. For example, if S thought a pattern was composed of two tones, she pressed the button labeled "2" on her panel, causing the light labeled "2" to come on in her partner's panel. The instructions for the various experimental conditions are summarized below.

1. Reactive Guilt Group

When S signaled an incorrect estimate to her partner, a red light flashed on S's panel and the partner received an electric shock. Although the term "incorrect" is used, the actual performance of the Ss was ignored. Apparent errors occurred on trials preselected by the experimenter. The auditory discrimination task was sufficiently ambiguous to allow the experimenter to control the number of shocks delivered to the partner.

2. Observation Group (Anticipatory Guilt)

In this condition the red light flash on S's panel and the shock delivered to her partner were said to be (and actually were) randomly administered by the experimenter and were not contingent on S's actual performance. The alleged purpose of this treatment was to assess the effects of irrelevant feedback on learning. This group is assumed to experience anticipatory guilt as a result of the awareness of another's being hurt.

3. Nonshock Control Group

Neither the S nor her partner were shocked during the auditory discrimination task. As a control for effects due to the possible feeling of failure arising from errors in the Reactive Guilt group, the Nonshock group was informed of "mistakes" by having a red light flash on S's panel with the same frequency that occurred in the Guilt groups.

4. Shock Control Group

When S made an "incorrect" estimate, a red light flashed on her panel and both the subject and her partner received a shock.

During the auditory discrimination task, 16 tonal patterns were presented. In all conditions, on ten critical trials selected from a table of random numbers a red light flashed on S's panel and, if appropriate to the experimental condition, an electric shock was administered to her partner. To provide a rationale for the procedure, the partners were presumably to be retested later in the session on a similar task to assess the effectiveness of this "training" period.

At the conclusion of the auditory discrimination task the experimenter explained that Ss were to work on a new task with a different partner. Emphasizing the change of partners, the experimenter inserted a center panel which physically isolated all the Ss. The identity of the new partner was never specified.

Measurement of Altruism

The Concept Formation Task

Hereafter, all Ss were treated alike. The new task was introduced as a concept formation task. Each S was led to believe that she was to be an instructor who would teach a concept to her partner, known as "the student." All Ss were given a booklet which contained the instructions and clues for teaching the student a concept. They were requested to read the instructions in the manual as the experimenter read them over the intercom. In these instructions Ss were told that any word could be described by a unique word profile made up of a select group of adjectives. The "instructor" was to give the "student" a word profile selected from a list of adjectives and the student was to identify the word on the basis of the word profile provided by the instructor. Thus the performance of each pair was determined in part by the instructor's ability to select an appropriate word profile and the student's capacity to match the correct word with the profile.

The trials were numbered in the booklet and five clues were listed for each trial. The clues consisted of five adjective pairs. From each pair the instructor selected the adjective which best described the word and signalled her choice to the student. One of the adjectives in each pair was listed under a column headed A, and the other under a column headed B. The instructor signalled the clue to the student by pressing either the A, B, or 0 button on her display panel. The 0 button was used only when neither adjective seemed appropriate. The Ss were cautioned against too liberal use of the 0 button. The word the instructor was attempting to portray was "serenity."

The exact nature of the student's task was not clarified. The Ss were told only that the student had her own manual which fully explained her task. To make the situation more realistic, after Ss were given the directions for the instructor's task, they were told that there would be a short delay while the experimenter went over the procedure with the students. During the interval in which the experimenter was allegedly giving instructions to students, white noise was fed into Ss' earphones.

On each trial that the student failed to identify the concept, both the instructor and the student received an electric shock. To justify shocking both the instructor and student, Ss were told that the purpose of the shock was to increase motivation and that learning was facilitated when both the instructor and student were motivated. Also, they were informed that there was an inverse relationship between the duration of shock delivered to the student and the duration received by the instructor. Prior to each trial the instructor decided how the shock duration should be divided between herself and the student and set her dial accordingly. If the instructor set the dial so as to deliver a shock of short duration to herself, the student received a shock of long duration. Conversely, if the instructor selected a long duration shock for herself, the student received a short duration shock. The Ss were allowed to set the dial in any position they wished at the beginning of each trial, but were advised to divide the shock in such a way as to maximize the performance of the instructor and student as a team.

Seventeen trials were given in the concept formation task. On the first 16 trials, Ss received shock indicating that the student had not attained the concept. The duration of shock delivered to S was proportional to her dial setting. The duration was recorded by a concealed Esterline-Angus which measured the duration to the nearest 1/100 second. The length of shock S selected for herself was taken as the measure of her altruism.

Throughout the concept formation task white noise was fed into the earphones to eliminate auditory cues about other Ss' activities. On the seventeenth trial, Ss were told that the student had identified the concept, and further, that both pairs had then finished the task. Thus, it was implied but not stated that the other pair had already finished. The experimenter then removed the electrodes and introduced the postexperimental measures.

Postexperimental Measures

The Ss were asked to write two 5-minute stories to TAT-like pictures. These thematic stories will not be further discussed in this paper. In addition, Ss filled out Semantic Differential rating forms for themselves and their partner (P_2) on the concept formation task. The same six adjective pairs were used for each rating.

The Ss were also given three self-report scales on which they were asked to rate to what extent they (a) enjoyed the concept formation task, (b) approved of setting shock duration, and (c) desired to be with the same partner (i.e., the alleged student P_2) in another experiment. Analyses of responses to these scales revealed no significant differences between groups, and no further mention of these scales will be made in this paper.

RESULTS

Measurement of Altruism

A *conditions* X *trials* analysis of variance was performed on the shock duration data. The durations of shock for the 16 trials of the concept formation task were averaged over four trial blocks to minimize the effects of trial variability. No significant trial differences were found.

Table 1 indicates that while there was no overall difference in mean altruism between Reactive Guilt Ss and Observation (Anticipatory Guilt) Ss, Ss in both these conditions behaved significantly more altruistically than Nonshock Control Ss and Shock Control Ss. Thus, as expected, both reactive guilt and the presumed reminder that others should not be hurt apparently served to increase the Ss' subsequent motivation to lessen the punishment a peer would receive.

TABLE 1

Mean Duration of Self-Directed Shock[a]

Experimental condition	Duration
Reactive guilt	5.93[a]
Observation (Anticipatory Guilt)	5.20[a]
Nonshock Control	3.77[b]
Shock Control	3.30[b]

[a]Means with no common subscripts are significantly different (at < .05 level) by Duncan Multiple Range Test. Shock duration was measured in seconds and averaged over 16 trials. Higher scores indicate greater altruism. $N = 40$.

Relationship of Altruism to Child-Rearing Practices

Pearson product-moment correlations were obtained between the score on each of the discipline scales and the average duration of shock selected during the concept formation task. These correlations are given in Table 2. The only group in which signficiant relationships between maternal discipline and altruism were found was the Observation (Anticipatory Guilt) group. For these Ss, high altruism was associated with low verbal criticism, low physical punishment, and infrequent appeals to shame and guilt. Altruism was moderately associated with frequent use of reasoning by the mother. The highest correlations between altruism and maternal discipline scale scores in the Reactive Guilt group were moderate, but nonsignficiant, relationships between altruism and infrequent withdrawal of love and infrequent material deprivation.

TABLE 2

*Correlation between Discipline Scale Scores
and Mean Self-Directed Shock Duration[a]*

| | Experimental condition | | | |
Discipline scale	Reactive Guilt	Observation (Anticipatory Guilt)	Shock Control	Nonshock Control
Reasoning	.245	.527[b]	.192	-.071
Withdrawal of love	-.502	-.710[c]	-.436	-.010
Appeals to shame and guilt	-.066	-.439	-.121	.158
Verbal criticism	-.175	-.674[c]	.288	-.350
Physical punishment	-.146	-.652[c]	.218	.121
Material deprivation	-.422	.227	-.139	.104

[a]Positive correlations indicate that high scores on the discipline scales are associated with longer self-directed shock durations. That is, a negative correlation indicates that altruism tends to be associated with low use of the discipline techniques named.

[b]$p < .10, df = 9.$

[c]$p < .05, df = 9.$

The higher correlations obtained between altruism and type of maternal discipline in the Observation (Anticipatory Guilt) group as contrasted with the Reactive Guilt group were not due to a smaller range of shock duration in the latter group. An F_{max} test for homogeneity of variance between Ss in the Reactive Guilt and Observation (Anticipatory Guilt) conditions was not significant. (An F_{max} of 4.03 is required for significance at the $p = .05$ level for $2/9$ df while the obtained F_{max} was only 1.14.) This indicates that the condition differences in magnitude of correlations is not due to condition differences in the range of scores.

Only three out of 24 correlations between maternal discipline and altruism were significant, with one additional correlation of borderline significance. The finding, however, that all the significant correlations appear in one group and that the directions of the correlations are consistent with the theoretical propositions offered by several investigators make these results meaningful in the context of this investigation. It is unlikely that chance alone would produce the observed pattern.

DISCUSSION

On the basis of the performance of the Reactive Guilt group alone, one might argue that the observed heightened altruism was motivated purely by a desire for guilt reduction, particularly since in the second task the partners were not the same victims harmed in the initial task (Freedman *et al.*, 1967). This type of explanation cannot be advanced for the altruism of the Observation (Anticipatory Guilt) group, however, since these Ss were not responsible for the harm inflicted on the victims in the initial task. While there is no evidence in the present study to suggest that anything more than expiation of guilt motivated the altruistic behavior of the Reactive Guilt Ss, the behavior of those who only witnessed harm inflicted on another indicates that other processes might have been involved in the Observation condition. The finding that only in this latter condition does altruism appear to be related to childhood discipline also suggests that at least partially different processes are at work.

There are at least two possible explanations for the heightened altruism seen in the Observation group. The first is the one discussed above: When the subjects saw their first partner shocked they became very aware of their ideal that people should not hurt each other. They then felt anticipatory guilt at the possibility that they might not adhere to this rule, and thus tried to minimize the harm inflicted on their second partner.

The second possible explanation is one of sympathy. This explanation is related to the first one but does not involve the unparsimonious assumption of Anticipatory Guilt: Sympathy for the first victim might have produced a heightened sensitivity to the possible suffering of others. As a result of having watched their first partner being shocked, subjects might have anticipated the pain that their new partner would feel and thus, out of empathy, tried to minimize her pain. Carlsmith and Gross (1969) also tested the possibility that sympathy rather than guilt was behind the helpfulness of their subjects who had been induced to harm another person. In one of their experimental conditions, Carlsmith and Gross had subjects merely observe the harm done to another and then gave them a chance to help a third person, as in the present study. However, unlike the present study, their help was not minimizing physical harm but involved giving a positive benefit to this third person. The presumed sympathy manipulation in the Carlsmith and Gross study did not lead to any more helping than was displayed by their control group. If sympathy motivates some altruism, it apparently operates only when relief of distress is needed.

Being responsible for injury to another or witnessing injury to another may lead to increased desire to minimize someone's suffering in later situations, but receiving punishment oneself seems to dampen this effect. The girls who had been shocked along with their first-phase partner when they made errors (Shock Control) subsequently displayed only a low level of altruism toward their second partner. The punishment received by these girls may have been regarded as sufficient expiation for injury in the first person. It could also have produced some hostility which lessened the magnitude of the later altruism.

Direct measures of guilt following the initial manipulations might have strengthened the guilt interpretation of the results of this study, but it seemed unwise to try to get such measures because of the danger of communicating to the subjects some idea that they should feel guilty. However, since many authors (e.g., Aronfreed, 1963) contend that guilt leads to self-criticism, it was decided that relatively low self-evaluation would reflect guilt feelings to some extent.

In the conditions in which guilt was likely to have been aroused (Reactive Guilt and Observation), Ss also had an opportunity to expiate their guilt through altruistic behavior toward another person. As the results for self-directed shock duration show (Table 1), Ss tended to take advantage of this chance. Thus, they could think well of themselves for having behaved well, and as Table 3 shows, Ss in these two guilt conditions tended to evaluate themselves favorably in comparison with Ss in the control conditions. However, the correlations between altruism and self-evaluation are not significant in any condition and, in fact, are moderately negative in the Observation (Anticipatory Guilt) condition $(r = -.39)$. This finding suggests that nonaltruistic Ss in these conditions might have defended against guilt by distorted self-evaluation. Miller and Swanson (1960) have suggested that such a process might occur. They contend that even if harsh maternal punishment did lead to strong internalized standards, such discipline could result in a reduced capacity to act in accordance with the internalized standards. Persons who lack the capacity to live up to their moral standards would, according to these authors, be more likely to experience guilt as a result of their transgressions. Consequently, they would be very likely to erect defenses against guilt as a means of reducing anxiety. These defenses involve "... the distortion of a person's self-critical application of his standards to his own actions or impulses. . ." (p. 188).

TABLE 3

Mean Ratings of Self and Other[a]

Experimental condition	Self	Other
Reactive Guilt	50.92$_c$	53.84$_b$
Observation (Anticipatory Guilt)	51.13$_c$	58.97$_a$
Shock Control	46.14$_d$	46.40$_d$
Nonshock Control	46.17$_d$	46.85$_d$

[a]A high score indicates high self-evaluation. N = 36. One S in each condition failed to complete the questionnaire satisfactorily. Means with no subscripts in common are significantly different at the .05 level by Duncan Multiple Range Test.

To assess this notion, an analysis was made of the relationship between maternal discipline and the Self and Other (P_2) ratings taken at the end of the experiment. Presumably, defensive distortion would be reflected in high positive relationships between favorable self-evaluation and harsh maternal discipline. Since the Observation (Anticipatory Guilt) group was the only group showing significant correlations between maternal discipline and altruistic behavior, we expected to find chiefly in that group that positive self-evaluation was strongly related to those discipline techniques which were negatively related to altruism (Table 2). Table 4 confirms this expectation. The correlations between favorableness of the Self ratings by this group and withdrawal of love and appeals to shame and guilt scales were significantly positive at the $p < .05$ level. Borderline significance was found for physical punishment. The only other signficiant relationship occurring in Table 4 was a .80 correlation between ratings of Other and tha material deprivation scale in the Reactive Guilt group. The latter relationship was not anticipated.[4]

[4]One might speculate that high ratings of Other by the Reactive Guilt group represent an attempt at altruism. It seems reasonable that persons who had experienced punishment in the form of material deprivation might be most willing to compensate for prior harm when they are able to do so in some superficial way that involves low costs to themselves.

In summary, the results of this study indicate that both Reactive Guilt and Anticipatory Guilt or sympathy tend to heighten altruism. The phenomenon of altruism resulting from Reactive Guilt is well established in the psychological literature, but the possibility of altruism resulting from enhanced norm salience deserves more attention, particularly as it suggests alternative explanations of the results of Reactive Guilt studies.

Further results indicate that the elicitation of altruism may, in part, depend on the internalization of moral standards as determined by antecedent social learning conditions, i.e., type of parental punishment. The level of altruism was found to be related to reported techniques of punishment used by the Ss' mothers. This relationship was strongly evident only in the Observation condition which presumably involved heightening awareness of social responsibility norms without the complicating awareness of having actually hurt another.

TABLE 4

Correlation between Discipline Scale Scores and Ratings
of Self and Other in the Reactive Guilt and Observation Conditions[a]

Discipline scale	Self		Other	
	Reactive Guilt	Observation (Anticipatory Guilt)	Reactive Guilt	Observation (Anticipatory Guilt)
Reasoning	.019	.074	−.127	.021
Withdrawal of love	.069	.655[b]	.062	.304
Appeals to shame and guilt	−.430	.699[b]	−.281	.019
Verbal criticism	.034	.074	.256	−.021
Physical punishment	.203	.563[c]	.267	.380
Material deprivation	.015	.330	.800[d]	.027

[a]Positive correlations indicate that high scores on the discipline scales are associated with favorable evaluations on the ratings. One S in each condition failed to satisfactorily complete the two ratings. $N = 36$.

[b]$p < .05, df = 8$.

[c]$p < .10, df = 8$.

[d]$p < .01, df = 8$.

REFERENCES

Aronfreed, J. The effects of experimental socialization paradigms upon two moral responses to transgression. *Journal of Abnormal and Social Psychology,* 1963, **66,** 437–448.

Berkowitz, L., & Daniels, L.R. Responsibility and dependency. *Journal of Abnormal and Social Psychology,* 1963, **66,** 429–436.

Bronfenbrenner, U. Some familial antecedents of responsibility and leadership in adolescents. In L. Petrullo & B.M. Bass (Eds.), *Leadership and interpersonal behavior.* New York: Holt, Rinehart & Winston, 1961.

Carlsmith, J.M., & Gross, A.E. Some effects of guilt on compliance. *Journal of Personality and Social Psychology,* 1969, **11,** 232-239.

Charters, W.W., Jr., & Newcomb, T.M. Some attitudinal effects of experimentally increased salience of a membership group. In E.E. Maccoby, T.M. Newcomb, & E.L. Hartley (Eds.). *Readings in social psychology.* (3rd ed.) New York: Holt, 1958, Pp. 276–281.

Daniels, L.R., & Berkowitz, L. Liking and response to dependency relationships. *Human Relations,* 1963, **16,** 141-148.

Darlington, R.B., & Macker, C.P. Displacement of guilt-produced altruistic behavior. *Journal of Personality and Social Psychology,* 1966, **4,** 442–443.

Freedman, J.L., Wallington, S.A., & Bless, E. Compliance without pressure: The effects of guilt. *Journal of Personality and Social Psychology.* 1967, **7,** 117–124.

Goranson, R.E., & Berkowitz, L. Reciprocity and responsibility reactions to prior help. *Journal of Personality and Social Psychology,* 1966, **3,** 227–232.

Miller, D.R., & Swanson, G.E. *Inner conflict and defense.* New York: Holt, 1960.

Mussen, P.H., Conger, J.J., & Kagan, J. *Child development and personality.* (2nd ed.) New York: Harper & Row, 1963.

Rawlings, E.I. Witnessing harm to other: A reassessment of the role of guilt in altruistic behavior. *Journal of Personality and Social Psychology,* 1969, **4,** 377-380.

Schopler, J., & Bateson, N. The power of dependence. *Journal of Personality and Social Psychology,* 1965, **2,** 247–254.

Schopler, J., & Matthews, M.W. The influence of the perceived causal locus of partner's dependence on the use of interpersonal power. *Journal of Personality and Social Psychology,* 1965, **2,** 609–612.

Sears, R.R., Maccoby, E.E., & Levin, H. *Patterns of child rearing.* Evanston, Ill: Row, Peterson, 1957.

THE EXPLOITED: JUSTICE OR JUSTIFICATION?[1]

Elaine Walster, Ellen Berscheid, and G. William Walster

Research has demonstrated that an exploiter may react in several different ways after injuring another: He may attempt to make restitution, he may justify his harm doing, or he may engage in self-punishment. The victim of exploitation and his sympathizer would undoubtedly prefer that the exploiter's reaction consist of restitution rather than justification.

In this paper we will: (*a*) present a theoretical framework and supporting data which will enable one to specify the conditions under which an exploiter will react by providing restitution to the victim and when he will justify his harmful act instead, (*b*) suggest some techniques by which the exploited individual and his sympathizers can increase the probability that the exploiter will compensate the victim for his suffering and decrease the probability that the exploiter will justify the victim's suffering.

THEORETICAL FORMULATION

In this section we will outline a theoretical framework from which predictions can be made as to whether an exploiter will make reparation to the exploited, or will justify his harm doing, or will seek punishment for his act.

[1]Preparation of this paper was financed in part by National Science Foundation grants 1577 to Berscheid and 1897 to E. Walster and in part by the Dean of Students Office, University of Wisconsin.

In attempting to predict how an exploiter will react following the commitment of a harmful act, one should begin by defining what is meant by "harm doing." Previous studies have generally relied on the reader's intuition as to what was meant by this term. In order to provide a usable definition, we will assume that a harm-doing situation is one in which an inequity is produced in the relationship between two individuals. Our discussion, therefore, will draw upon the conceptions of equity in human interaction which have been advanced by Homans (1961) and, most recently, by Adams (1965).

The Equity Formulation

In general terms, an "equitable relationship" has been defined as one in which a person's ratio of outcomes to inputs is equal to the other person's outcome/input ratio (Adams, 1965).[2]

"Inputs," as defined by Adams (1965), are similar to Homan's (1961) investments, and are "what a man perceives as his contributions to the exchange, for which he expects a just return [p. 277]." Inputs, in the employer–employee relationships with which Adams dealt, included such things as skill, financial investments, education, and so on. While these investments often may be "assets" for which the type of "just return" expected are rewards, it would also seem that some inputs could be "liabilities" which the person brings to the interaction and for which the "just return" may be decreased rewards.

---

[2]For purposes of this paper, it was sufficient to adopt Adams' formula O/I (where I stands for a person's inputs and O stands for his outcomes) for determining when equity did or did not exist in a relationship between people. Adams' formula, which has been utilized chiefly in industrial situations, is adequate so long as the inputs of all participants are positive. His formula is not suitable in social situations, where inputs may be negative as well as positive. For example, a relationship would be calculated as "equitable" if Person A had (Outcomes = –.10/Inputs = 5) and Person B (Outcomes = 10/Inputs = –.5). Obviously neither Adams nor we would feel such a relationship was, in fact, equitable. A formula suitable for general use is: $O - I/[I]$, where $[I]$ designates the absolute value of an individual's inputs.

Let us demonstrate how this formula operates. This measure will be zero if one's Outcomes equal his Inputs. It will be positive if $O > I$, and negative if $O < I$. Thus the sign of this measure indicates how "profitable" the relationship has been to each of the participants. The measure is scaled by the magnitude of the input. For example, an individual who has outcomes of 10 and whose inputs are +5 has a $O - I/[I]$ value of 1. If his inputs were –5, his $O - I/[I]$ value would be 3. This formula simply puts the subjects' outcomes in a metric which enables us to compare them.

"Outcomes," as defined by Adams (1965, p. 278), are the individual's "receipts" from a relationship. They may be positive consequences of the individual's relationship with the other person, or they may be negative. We shall, following Homans (1961), refer to positive outcomes as "rewards" and negative outcomes as "costs." The person's total outcome from the relationship we shall define as the rewards he obtains from the relationship minus the costs he incurs.

Given this equity formulation, it is now possible to define the terms we will be using throughout this section.[3] "Harm Doing" shall be defined as the commitment of an act which produces an inequitable relationship between the members, such that the actor's outcome/input (O/I) ratio becomes greater than that of the other member of the relationship. We shall term an act which impairs the equity of a relationship in the above manner as "harmful," the perpetrator of such an act a "harm doer," and the member of the relationship whose O/I ratio has been reduced as a "victim."

We can proceed now from the point at which the harmful act has been committed to a consideration of some of the factors which motivate a harm doer to make some kind of response after doing harm.

Hypothesis I: A harm doer will feel distress upon perceiving that he has committed a harmful act.

Virtually every theorist who has examined the reactions of a harm doer after committing a harmful act has assumed that one feels some kind of distress after injuring another. Various theorists have labeled this distress "guilt," "fear of retaliation," "dissonance," "empathy," "conditioned anxiety," etc. We too propose that a harm doer will experience distress after injuring another. We will emphasize two potential sources for the harm-doer's distress: retaliation distress and self-concept distress.

Because individuals are often punished when they perform harmful acts, we might reasonably expect that to the extent that stimuli in the current harm-doing situation are similar to stimuli previously associated with punishment, the harm doer should feel distress and should anticipate punishment for his behavior. The development of this type of distress has been discussed in great detail by the learning theorists.[4] We shall term "retaliation distress," then, that discomfort which arises from the harm-doer's anticipation that the victim, the victim's

---

[3]For discussion purposes, we shall assume that prior to the time the harm doer commits the harmful act, the relationship between the harm doer and the victim is equitable.

[4]See, for example, Aronfreed (1969).

sympathizers, legal agencies, or even God, will restore equity to the harm-doer-victim relationship through a lowering of the harm-doer's total outcome and/or through an increase of his inputs.

Harm doing may produce another type of discomfort. In this society, there is an almost universally accepted moral code to the effect that one should be fair and equitable in his dealings with others (cf. Fromm, 1956, for an interesting discussion of the pervasiveness of the "fairness" principle). Doing a harmful act, then, should be inconsistent with a normal individual's ethical principles and with his self-expectations. The distress that arises from such unethical or inconsistent acts has been discussed in great detail by guilt theorists and by cognitive dissonance theorists.[5] We shall term discomfort emanating from this source "self-concept distress."

Although we have differentiated between distress arising from these two sources, we do not assume that they are completely independent. Self-concept distress, as well as retaliation distress, is assumed to have its roots in the socialization process in which individuals are punished for the commitment of inequitable acts.

There is a great deal of experimental, as well as clinical, evidence to support the view that individuals do feel distress following the commitment of harmful acts, and we shall present some of this evidence later in the paper. There is even evidence that people are uncomfortable when another commits an inequitable act which produces an inequity in their favor (cf. Jacques, 1961; Adams & Rosenbaum, 1962; Adams, 1963).

Corollary I-A: The more harm the harm doer perceives he has done, the more distress he will feel.

The greater the inequity a harmful act produces, the more probable it should be that the harm doer should anticipate retaliation, and the more retaliation distress he should experience. In addition, as the amount of inequity produced by an act increases, the easier it should become for the harm doer to recognize that the act is a harmful one. Therefore, self-concept distress should increase as harm doing increases.

Corollary I-B: Distress should result whether the harmful act is deliberate or unintentional.

Many harmful acts are committed without premeditation. The framework we have utilized leads us to argue that even unintentional harm doing should

[5] See, for example, Maher (1966) or Arnold (1960a,b) and Bramel (1969) for an elucidation of these two points of view.

produce some distress. In naturalistic situations, contingencies are often unclear. It is always difficult for a person to know the extent to which his own carelessness or lack of foresight may be the cause of an inequity. Thus, self-concept distress may follow even unintentional acts. It is also difficult for others to assess a harm-doer's intentions, and for this reason, retaliation often follows unintentional acts. Past experience with such situations should produce retaliation distress even in the inadvertent harm doer.

That unintentional harm doing will produce distress has been documented in several experiments. Lerner and Simmons (1966) found, for example, that an individual who merely chooses, by chance, a card that assigns him to a pleasant condition and his partner to an unpleasant condition, will feel distress. Whether unintentional harm doing generally produces less distress than does intentional harm doing is open to investigation, however.

Hypothesis II: The harm doer will attempt to reduce his distress through the restoration of equity to his relationship with the victim.

From the discussion of the antecedents of distress, it is clear that to the extent to which the harm doer can restore equity to his relationship with the victim, distress may be reduced. It also follows that:

Corollary II-A: The greater the magnitude of distress, the stronger will be the harm-doer's attempts to reduce it.

There is some indirect evidence to support this notion: Brock and Buss (1962, 1964) found that the stronger the electric shock subjects administered to a victim, the more they denied responsibility for the decision to administer shock; Lerner and Simmons (1966) found that the more the victim suffered, the more subjects derogated him; Lerner and Matthews (1967) found that the more responsible subjects felt for the victim's suffering, the more they derogated him. If we assume that the more the victim suffers or the more responsible the harm doer is for the inequity, the more distressed the harm doer will be, the finding that more self-justification occurs under such conditions is consistent with our hypotheses.

There are a number of ways by which the harm doer may restore equity:

Corollary II-B: The harm doer may reduce his distress through restoration of "psychological equity" to his relationship with the victim or through restoration of "actual equity."

RESTORATION OF PSYCHOLOGICAL EQUITY

One way a harm doer can "restore equity" to his relationship with the victim is simply by distorting reality and convincing himself that the relationship should, in fact, be perceived as equitable. By distorting his own or the victim's outcomes and inputs, a harm doer can make the harmful act appear to be an equitable one. Such distortions, or "justifications," as we shall label them, can include the following.

Derogation of the Victim

An act which harms another is not inequitable if the victim was deserving of the harm. Thus, one can restore equity to an inequitable relationship by derogating the victim's inputs.[6] That harm doers will often derogate their victims has been demonstrated by Sykes and Matza (1957), Davis and Jones (1960), Berkowitz (1962), Davidson (1964), Glass (1964), and Walster and Prestholdt (1966).

Denial of Responsibility for the Act

If the harm doer can perceive that it was not his behavior, but rather the actions of someone else (the experimenter or fate) that caused the victim's suffering, then his relationship with the victim becomes an equitable one. (That person who is unjustly assigned responsibility for reducing the victim's outcomes will now be perceived as the harm doer, and it will be his relationship with the victim, not the actual harm doer's relationship, that is perceived as inequitable.)

That harm doers will often deny their responsibility for harm doing has been documented by Sykes and Matza (1957) and by Brock and Buss (1962, 1964).

Minimization of the Victim's Suffering

To the extent that the harm doer can deny that the victim was harmed, he will be able to perceive his relationship with the victim as equitable. Minimization of the victim's suffering has been found by Sykes and Matza (1957) and Brock and Buss (1962).

[6]If, for example, both the harm doer and victim had an O/I ratio of 50/50 prior to the harmful act, and if following the act the victim's ratio was reduced to 25/50, by cognitively reducing the inputs the victim has brought to the relationship (e.g., his intelligence, his attractiveness, his "deservingness") to 25, the harm doer can restore equity.

RESTORATION OF ACTUAL EQUITY

The harm doer, of course, may restore actual equity to the relationship by increasing the victim's outcome or by decreasing his own outcome, relative to his inputs, so that a state of equality between the two ratios is restored.

Compensation

When an act is designed primarily to increase the victim's O/I ratio, we will speak of compensation. Compensatory acts most often take the form of increasing the victim's total outcome through increasing his rewards and/or reducing his costs. Acts which decrease the victim's inputs are probably rare since one seldom has control over another's inputs.

Despite cynics such as Junius, who commented in his *Letters* that "a death bed repentance seldom reaches to restitution," recent studies have verified the fact that individuals often do make compensation following harm doing. That a harm doer will compensate his victim has been demonstrated by Walster, Walster, Abrahams, and Brown (1966), Walster and Prestholdt (1966), Brock and Becker (1966), Berscheid and Walster (1967), Freedman, Wallington, and Bless (1967), Carlsmith and Gross (1969), and Berscheid, Walster, and Barclay (1969).

Self-Punishment

A harm doer may also restore equity by reducing his O/I ratio to the level of the victim's. He can do this either by reducing the rewards or increasing the costs he incurs as a consequence of the relationship, or by increasing his inputs into the relationship. When the harm doer achieves equity by decreasing his own O/I ratio, we shall speak of self-punishment.[7]

The anecdotal and clinical literature provides support for the notion that individuals sometimes do react to the commitment of harmful acts by administering punishment to themselves or by seeking punishment from others. Indeed, it has been suggested that ". . . punishment is the only kind of response that is sufficient to reduce the tension of guilt [Sarnoff, 1962, p. 351]." Attempts to

---

[7]Although self-punitive acts may restore equity to a relationship, restoring equity in this way has a disadvantage: self-punitive acts decrease the overall O/I ratio in the relationship, and thereby reduce the amount of satisfaction the harm doer and victim obtain from their interaction with each other.

demonstrate self-punishment in the laboratory have been surprisingly unsuccessful.

Several quite different types of behavior have been classified as self-punitive by various theorists.

Self-Abasement and Self-Injury

After injuring another, individuals often apologize for their wrongdoing and ask for forgiveness. These apologies may be accompanied by self-abasement; the harm doer may elaborate on the fact that his cruelty, thoughtlessness, etc., have shown him to be a worthless individual, and that as a result of committing the harmful act, he has himself experienced much suffering and pain. It is difficult to know if such a response should be classified as a self-punitive or as a compensatory response. To the extent that self-abasement is a dramatic presentation, whose aim is to restore the self-esteem of an insulted victim, such self-derogation should probably be classified as compensatory. If self-abasement or self-injury occurs in private, without the expectation that the victim will feel benefited by one's suffering, the response probably should be classified as self-punitive.

The clinical literature also mentions the fact that on occasion, guilty individuals may actually physically injure themselves and sometimes even be driven to suicide if necessary to "even the score" (e.g., Lindemann, 1944).

Altruism

Several theorists have proposed that after injuring another, individuals will be especially willing to endure costs to perform altruistic acts for the benefit of persons other than the victim. For example, Freedman et al. (1967) have hypothesized that:

> Given the opportunity to engage in some extremely unpleasant behavior the guilty person should be more likely to agree than the non-guilty since the former can use this as a form of self-punishment. Similarly, if he is asked to do someone a favor, pleasant or otherwise, the guilty person should be more likely to agree than the non-guilty because the former can view it as his good deed for the day which will make up for the bad deed about which he feels guilty [p. 117].

Freedman et al. (1967) and Darlington and Macker (1966) have demonstrated experimentally that a harm doer may be especially likely to perform unpleasant altruistic acts after injuring another. Such altruistic acts do not restore equity directly to the harm-doer–victim relationship. It is possible, however, that the performance of such altruistic acts may be perceived as restoring equity with the "world in general" and, therefore, with the victim indirectly.

We can see that there are a number of techniques, all experimentally documented, by which a harm doer may restore equity to his relationship with the victim. We shall now present two major hypotheses concerning the conditions under which a harm doer may be expected to use one equity-restoring technique rather than another.

Hypothesis III: Other things being equal, the more adequate a harm doer perceives an available equity-restoring technique to be, the greater the probability that he will choose to restore equity by utilizing this technique.

The "adequacy" of a technique is defined as the extent to which use of that technique will exactly restore equity to the relationship.

Corollary III-A: The more adequate a harm doer perceives available compensations to be, the greater the probability that he will restore equity by utilizing this technique.

Given our definition of "adequacy," it is clear that the "adequacy of a compensation" would be defined as the extent to which the compensation would exactly balance the costs the victim has suffered as a consequence of the relationship. Accordingly, an available compensation may lack adequacy for two reasons: it may be insufficient to balance the harm done, or it may be an excessive compensation for the harm done.

Although a victim may prefer an insufficient compensation to no compensation at all, making a partial compensation is, from the harm doer's point of view, an unsatisfactory way to restore equity. A partial compensation cannot by itself completely restore equity since the victim is still left in a deprived state.

Similarly, a compensation which is inadequate because it is excessive cannot, by itself, eliminate the harm doer's distress. An excessive compensation would eliminate one kind of inequity by producing another. The harm doer who compensates his victim excessively does not restore equity. He simply becomes a victim rather than a harm doer.

There is evidence that individuals experience distress (dissonance) when they overbenefit another without sufficient reason for doing so, as well as when they harm him without justification (Walster & Prestholdt, 1966; Jecker & Landy, 1969).

For these reasons it is proposed that one's tendency to compensate his victim will be an increasing function of the adequacy of available compensations. Berscheid and Walster (1967) found support for this hypothesis in an experiment conducted with women's church groups. In this experiment, women were led to cheat fellow parishioners out of trading stamps in a vain attempt to win additional stamps for themselves. When the women were subsequently given an opportunity to compensate the victim at no cost to themselves, it was found that adequacy of available compensation was crucial in determining whether or not the women would choose to compensate. Women who could compensate with an adequate compensation, exactly restoring the number of books the partner had lost, were much more likely to compensate than were women limited to insufficient compensation (a few stamps) or to excessive compensation (a great many stamp books). This finding was replicated by Berscheid, Walster, and Barclay (1969).

Corollary III-B: The more adequate a harm doer perceives available justifications to be, the greater the probability that he will choose to restore equity by utilizing this technique.

In order for a harm doer to completely restore psychological equity to his relationship with the victim, he must be able to conceive of justifications which he feels are credible and which he feels are sufficient to make his behavior seem entirely equitable. The adequacy of a sufficient justification depends in part, then, on how credible the harm doer judges the justification to be. A great variety of factors necessarily influence how "credible" a given justification will be judged to be by the harm doer himself and how credible he anticipates the same justification will appear to others.

A delightful and extensive account of the factors which determine a justification's credibility is available in Scott and Lyman (1968). We wish to mention specifically only three general points:

1. *Justifications should be more credible (adequate), and thus more readily used, when they require little distortion of reality than when they require a great deal of reality distortion.* The more serious or extensive a distortion of reality which a justification requires, the harder it should be for the harm doer to believe that his justification is a credible one or to believe that others would find it credible, and the less willing the harm doer should be to utilize justifications to restore equity.

Some tangential support for this proposition comes from Rosenberg and Abelson (1960). They provide evidence that individuals prefer to distort reality as little as possible, and demonstrate that even when one does restore cognitive balance by distorting reality, he tries to alter as few cognitions as possible.

2. *The more public a justification must be, the less likely it should be that the harm doer will utilize justifications to restore equity.* If the harm doer has

only himself to please, it should be fairly easy for him to come up with a totally convincing rationalization for almost any behavior: He has only to conceive of some justification that is not contradicted by any other beliefs he has about the victim. However, in many instances, the harm doer will anticipate that his justification must be made publicly, and that as a consequence, its validity may be challenged by unsympathetic and perhaps retaliatory others. When the fact that others will be judging the credibility of one's justifications is salient, the individual would be more critical of the justifications that occur to him and more likely to require that suitable justifications be credible to critical others as well as to himself (cf. Walster *et al.*, 1967). It should, of course, be more difficult for the harm doer to conceive of justifications which are credible to others than to conceive of justifications credible only to himself. For these reasons, a harm doer is probably more likely to restore equity by utilizing justification techniques when his justification must be public than when it can be private.

3. *Justifications which involve distortion of the victim's characteristics should be more credible and thus more readily used, the less contact the harm doer has had (or anticipates having) with the victim.* There are two reasons why distortions of an intimate's characteristics should be less credible than distortions of a stranger's characteristics. First, the more intimate we are with someone, the more likely we are to have realistic information and attitudes concerning him. Thus, distortions of an intimate's characteristics should require more reality distortion and thus should be less credible than are distortions involving a stranger.

Virtually all the cognitive consistency theorists (Cartwright & Harary, 1956; Festinger, 1957; Abelson & Rosenberg, 1958; Rosenberg, 1960; Zajonc, 1960) acknowledge that one is less likely to change a belief which is consistently related to many other cognitions than to change a belief which exists in isolation.

Second, Walster *et al.* (1967) have demonstrated that one is more likely to avoid distortions when future objective evidence could conceivably contradict these distortions than when future evidence will not be forthcoming. Thus, if one expects to continue to associate with the victim, it becomes risky to distort his characteristics. If one engages in a massive distortion of an intimate's character, one must anticipate that it is inevitable that he will soon be embarrassingly confronted with the victim, who may demonstrate that he possesses traits quite different from those one has ascribed to him, and will thus demonstrate that the harm doer's distortions were not credible.

Familiarity with the victim, then, should tend to breed accuracy and to discourage the use of justification as a distress-reducing technique. Data are available to support this hypothesis: Davis and Jones (1960) found that subjects who expected to see their victim after delivering a negative personal evaluation of him did not derogate him as much as did subjects who did not anticipate subsequent interaction with the victim. Davis and Jones assumed that they secured this result because subjects who anticipated future contact expected to "neutralize their harm doing" by explaining that their negative evaluation did not represent their true feelings. However, since the victim had already suffered by the time neutralization could occur, this explanation is not totally satisfactory. An equally plausible interpretation is that distortion becomes more difficult when future interaction is anticipated.

Data from an experiment designed to test another hypothesis is also relevant: Ross (1965) conducted an ingenious experiment in which students were led to choose to consign their partner to electric shock in order to avoid painful shock themselves. In some conditions, subjects believed they would work with their partner only once. In other cases they believed they would work with her on many tasks. Ross' finding—that when the subjects caused the other to be injured, derogation occurred more often when subsequent contact was not anticipated—is satisfactorily explained by the hypothesis that anticipated intimacy makes justification an unpreferred mode of response.

We must add to adequacy a second determinant of choice of technique:

Hypothesis IV: Other things being equal, the harm doer will use that technique which will yield the highest overall O/I ratio in the harm-doer–victim relationship.

In the analyses to follow, we shall assume that after the commitment of a harmful act, the harm doer is not only motivated by a desire for equity restoration, but also that the harm doer will act in such a way as to achieve the highest possible profit and satisfaction from his relationship with the victim (i.e., so that he and his partner can achieve as high O/I ratios as possible).

This hypothesis would appear to be somewhat similar to an assumption made by Adams (1965) that a person ". . . will reduce inequity, insofar as possible, in a manner that will yield him the largest outcomes [p. 284]." Adams presents evidence supporting the validity of his hypothesis (Adams & Rosenbaum, 1962; Adams, 1963). This hypothesis is also supported by the results of an experiment concerning preferences among forms of equity resolution in fictitious work situations recently conducted by Weick and Nesset (1969).

Derivation IV-1: If all three techniques are available and equally adequate, self-punishment will be the least preferred of the three responses.

Since inequitable acts are those which result in the harm-doer's experiencing a higher O/I ratio than the victim's, self-punishment (or decreasing one's own

O/I ratio) may restore equity to the relationship. However, such a response requires the harm doer voluntarily to lower the amount of satisfaction both he and the victim receive from their relationship. It directly follows from Hypothesis IV that there should be resistance to such a step.

There is no direct evidence to support this derivation. However, experiments which have demonstrated that individuals are more willing to engage in unpleasant altruistic acts following commitment of a harmful act (e.g., Darlington & Macker, 1966; Freedman *et al.,* 1967) have consistently blocked compensation routes to the harm doer. In addition, the guilt-inducing procedure used in these experiments was such that justifications—denial of responsibility for the harm, denial that the harm was done, or denial that the act was unjust—were difficult, if not impossible, for the subjects to employ. Thus, evidence of self-punishment following harm doing has been restricted to situations in which compensation and justification techniques were almost totally unavailable to restore equity. The frequency with which use of self-punishment would be found, had one or both of the other techniques been available and perceived as adequate, is unanswered.

At this point we wish to consider the reactions of a harm doer when no single equity-restoring technique is totally adequate. Specifically, we wish to consider when the harm doer will use two or more "partially adequate" techniques to totally restore equity and when he will not use the various techniques in concert.

Hypothesis V: The harm doer will tend not to use the justification technique in concert with compensation and self-punishment techniques.

Corollary V-A: In cases in which both compensation and justification techniques are available, but are inadequate, only one technique will be used; they will not be used in concert to reduce distress.

Why do we propose that a harm doer will use predominantly compensation or predominantly justification, rather than a combination of techniques, to restore equity in a given situation? For logical reasons it appears unlikely that a harm doer can restore equity in a given situation by using the compensation and justification techniques in concert.[8] It should be difficult for a harm doer to

[8]Hypothesis V does not exclude the possibility that the harm doer may use compensation and justification techniques in sequence. I.e., a harm doer may attempt to make compensation, find it impossible, and then resort to justification. Or, justification may be attempted, found challenged, and compensation will follow. Hypothesis V only states that when the harm doer is in the process of attempting to compensate, he will not justify; while attempting to justify he will not simultaneously attempt to compensate the victim.

convince himself that the victim was deserving of harm, that the victim has suffered no inequity, or that he was not responsible for the victim's reduced outcomes, at the same time that he is acknowledging the inequity and is exerting himself in an attempt to compensate the victim.

Evidence that there is a negative relationship between one's tendency to compensate for his harm doing and one's tendency to justify his harm doing can be gleaned from several sources: Walster and Prestholdt (1966) conducted an experiment in which social work "trainees" were led to harm their clients by providing misleading information about them to their psychiatrist. Subsequently, trainees were asked to evaluate their injured clients, and were also asked to volunteer their free time to help one of the clients. In this study, the tendency to derogate the victim was negatively related to the amount of time the trainees volunteered to help him. In addition, Lerner and Simmons (1966) have found that observers only derogate a victim when they are powerless to aid him in any way. When it is clear that compensation will occur, no derogation is detected.

Corollary V-B: If the justification technique is inadequate, the harm doer will not use this technique in concert with self-punishment.

For logical reasons, it should be difficult for the harm doer to convince himself that he did not in fact harm the victim at the same time that he is punishing himself (lowering his O/I ratio) as a consequence of that "harmless" act.

Corollary V-C: Compensation and self-punishment techniques may be used in concert by the harm doer to reduce distress.

Since both compensation and self-punishment require that the harm doer recognize that an act performed by him created an inequity in his relationship with the victim, there is no logical incompatibility in the simultaneous use of both techniques. Indeed, we have previously mentioned that compensatory acts, which have as their focus the conferring of benefit upon the victim, ordinarily involve cost to the harm doer and, thus, involve one element of self-punishment.

The preceding discussion has focused upon the means by which the harm doer himself may restore equity to his relationship with the victim. It is clear, however, that the harm doer is not the only possible agent of equity restoration. At this point we wish to hypothesize that:

Hypothesis VI: To the extent that external events intervene to produce an equitable relationship between the harm doer and victim, the harm-doer's distress should be reduced and he, therefore, should be less likely to voluntarily use any of the three distress-reducing techniques.

Derivation VI-1: If following commitment of the harmful act, the victim produces equity through retaliation, the probability that the harm doer will engage in either self-punishment, compensation, or justification should decrease.

The victim would probably prefer that a harm doer restore equity to their relationship by using compensatory techniques rather than justificatory ones. Frequently, however, it is obvious to the victim that compensation is unlikely to be forthcoming. In such circumstances, he might anticipate the possibility that justification techniques will be used to restore an equitable relationship. However, the exploiter's justification of his harmful act is potentially dangerous for the victim. It is probable that the harm doer who justifies his harm doing will end up with a distorted and unreal assessment of his own actions. If he distorts the extent to which the victim deserved to be hurt, for example, or minimizes the victim's suffering as a consequence of the act, he may commit further acts based on these distortions (Berscheid, Boye, and Darley, 1968a).

The harm-doer's use of the justification technique, then, is likely to leave the victim in rather sad straits. Not only has he been hurt, but as a result of the harm-doer's justification, the probability that the harm doer will hurt him again has been increased. Thus, from the victim's point of view, it is desirable to have equity restored before the harm doer is tempted to justify what he has done. If the harm doer is unable or unwilling to restore equity through compensation, how may the victim prevent justification? In our culture the phrase "getting even" suggests that equity can be restored by the victim's retaliation against the harm doer.

Berscheid, Boye, and Walster (1968b) conducted an experiment designed to assess the effect that a victim's retaliation will have on the exploiter's tendency to justify the victim's suffering by derogating him. The results of this study indicate that a victim can indeed restore equity through retaliation against the exploiter. In this experiment, individuals were hired to administer severe electric shocks to another person. If the victim could not retaliate against the harm doer, the harm doer subsequently derogated the victim. However, when the exploiter expected retaliation for his harmful act, the derogation process was arrested; the harm doer did not derogate the victim.

It is also interesting that the relationship between retaliation and derogation was diametrically opposed for control subjects who merely observed the victim's suffering; those observers who expected to be hurt by the victim in the future liked him less than did those who did not expect to be hurt.

These results have an interesting implication for the use of retaliation by victims: James Baldwin (1964) in a statement concerning the Negroes' struggle for minority rights in this country, argues, "Neither civilized reason or Christian love would cause any of these people to treat you as they presumably wanted to be treated; only fear of your power to retaliate will cause them to do that, or seem to do it, which was (and is) good enough [p. 34] ." Negro militants have taken an even stronger position. They have argued that widespread Negro violence is necessary to restore the Negro to full citizenship. The variables they discuss sound much like those we have considered. They talk of the "white devil," his guilt, his denial of racial injustices, and the equity-establishing effects of violence. If extrapolation from our findings is relevant, we might suggest that retaliation, or the anticipation of retaliation, will be beneficial only if the recipient of the violence feels that he is in some way directly responsible for the Negroes' suffering. Retaliation against those who feel themselves to be innocent observers of injustices would seem to be a disastrous strategy.

Derivation VI-2: If following commitment of the harmful act, an outside agency requires the harm doer to compensate the victim or if the outside agency punishes the harm doer for his act, the probability that the harm doer will voluntarily use any of the three distress-reducing techniques should be decreased.

There is no direct experimental evidence to support this proposition. Penal theorists (e.g., Spencer, 1866; Del Vecchio, 1959; Schafer, 1960) have assumed that requiring a criminal to make restitution to his victim will prevent him from justifying his harm-doing and thus will promote his rehabilitation. Institutional punishment is generally assumed to have the same effect. The anecdotal evidence they provide is at least consistent with our hypothesis.

One would speculate, however, that coerced compensation should not be as equity restoring, nor as distress reducing, as voluntary compensation. For example, voluntary compensation may eliminate the affront to the victim's pride which is often associated with being victimized. Forced compensation does not eliminate such indignities. In addition, even though the harm doer who is forced to make compensation may have less reason to fear retaliation than he had initially, forced compensation may not completely reduce his self-concept distress.

Derivation VI-3: If following commitment of the harmful act, the victim offers "forgiveness" to the harm doer, the probability that the harm doer will engage in any of the three distress-reducing techniques may decrease.

A common way by which the harm-doer's distress may be reduced following a harmful act is through absolution tendered by the victim and others. Such absolution implies that the relationship between the harm doer and victim has regained equity. Such absolution may reduce an individual's distress by strengthening his self-esteem and reducing his fear of retaliation.

Up to this point we have assumed that the harm doer has not been aware that "forgiveness" could conceivably extricate him from his dilemma and, further, that he has no skills which could be used to elicit forgiveness from others. Obviously, this is not always the case. Self-punishment, for example, may easily be "faked"; a harm doer may engage in profuse verbalizations of how much personal suffering he has endured as a consequence of his unjust treatment of the victim. The notion that a description of one's remorse and suffering, if convincing, may in fact attenuate the wrath and retaliatory intentions of the victim and others has been supported by an experiment conducted by Bramel, Taub, and Blum (1968). It is for this reason, perhaps, that a commonly used elicitor of forgiveness is the phrase "I'm sorry."

The common television scenario of the careless driver rushing to the hospital room of his victim to express his anguish and remorse becomes explicable through this reasoning. A person not familiar with the common "I'm sorry"—"You're forgiven" sequence might wonder what benefit is conferred upon a dying victim, or what wrong is righted, by such a demonstration of the harm-doer's personal suffering as a consequence of his act. Perhaps the answer is none. It can be hypothesized that the act is performed not for the victim's benefit, but for the harm-doer's benefit. To say "I'm sorry" is to imply personal suffering and to beg for forgiveness to end one's distress.

When apologies and derogation do not elicit "forgiveness," it is interesting that harm doers often switch with ease to another technique, often the incompatible justification technique.

Additional Comments

1. This theoretical framework has taken the nomothetic approach and has attempted to provide a framework to guide prediction of how the average individual will respond following his commitment of a harmful act. In spite of the fact that we have relied entirely on the nomothetic approach, one cannot assume that personality differences are unimportant. Personality characteristics should affect how much distress a harm doer feels after injuring another, and how he will respond to that distress.

For example, in Hypothesis I, we proposed that a normal harm doer would experience distress from two sources after injuring another. (a) He would experience self-concept distress, since he had performed a harmful act which should be inconsistent both with his own good opinion of himself and with his moral principles. (b) He would experience fear of retaliation distress. One interested in individual differences would be led to the obvious conclusion that harm doers who have high self-esteem and strongly internalized ethical principles should feel more distress after harming another than should individuals with low standards and low self-regard. High self-esteem individuals, then, would be expected to make a greater effort to restore equity after harming another than would low self-esteem individuals. (Review Corollary II-A.)

There is some experimental evidence to support this derivation. In an experiment by Glass (1964), an individual's self-esteem was experimentally raised or lowered by providing him with authoritative information about his own personality. After harming another, high self-esteem subjects justified their harm doing (by derogating their victims) more than did low self-esteem subjects.

Profitable and interesting attempts to identify some of the individual difference variables which will affect a harm-doer's reaction have been made by Aronfreed (1961) and others. Such studies may be expected to considerably sharpen prediction in individual situations.

2. We should point out that the predictive statements we have made rest to some extent upon the assumption that the harm doer will have some time in which to evaluate the various techniques before being forced to respond. Unfortunately, not all situations afford the harm doer such an opportunity. Often, for example, distress-reduction opportunities present themselves immediately after commitment of the harmful act and decisions concerning whether or not to take advantage of the opportunity must be made with little forethought. Under such circumstances, there is evidence that the predictions we have made concerning choice of distress-reduction technique would not be likely to hold. The effects of time are discussed in greater detail in the experiment by Berscheid, Walster, & Barclay (1969).

ELICITING JUSTICE RATHER THAN JUSTIFICATION

From the theory and data reported in the preceding section, one is led to speculate that a person interested in persuading an exploiter to make voluntary restitution should utilize certain persuasive techniques which will be enumerated in this section.

Finding techniques to elicit voluntary restitution might be more important than one would think. Since it is often difficult to conceive of ways to induce an exploiter to make voluntary restitution, injured individuals often first consider court action designed to force the exploiter to make restitution.

In some cases, legal action might be a very profitable strategy. Often, however, the private individual with limited time and resources might better invest his time in attempting to elicit voluntary restitution than in attempting to extract compensation by legal means.

There is much evidence that court action seldom provides a victim with very much in the way of compensation. At least since republican Roman Law, men have been concerned with developing procedures to insure that victims of crime will be justly compensated.[10] Thus far, legal theorists have been unable to devise a completely adequate system. Schafer (1960) conducted a world-wide survey of the legal means various nations have utilized to provide restitution to exploited individuals. A wide variety of techniques to restore equity have been tried. In places (e.g., Germany, Switzerland, and Mexico), a victim may be awarded a Busse (a compensatory fine) in criminal proceedings; the victim may attempt to attach the harm-doer's prison wages (e.g., in France, Canada, Israel), the victim may apply for state compensation to the victims of criminal violence (e.g., Cuba or Switzerland), etc. It is Schafer's dour conclusion concerning all of these procedures that:

> This general situation involves the victim of crime in more or less hopeless position with regard to his claim for restitution. It has been found in practice that the injured party has very little success in recovering damages because of lack of means of the ordinary criminal and the opportunity which the criminal has to hide or transfer his property before attachment. Frequently the victim despairs of turning to civil procedures or wants to save additional costs. Victims know that most offenders tend to be impecunious and a civil action alone or an award having merely a civil character will probably be worthless to them [p. 107].

Even if the victim does secure a judgment against the harm doer, the bulk of his compensation often must go to pay attorney fees or court costs—both of which have been ruled to have priority over the victim's right to compensation.

In recent years legal theorists have so despaired of providing restitution to exploited individuals under currently established legal procedures that a movement has begun to insure that the state will make adequate restitution to unjustly injured individuals (see Fry, 1959). Fry's proposal is not the first time that the idea of community compensation has been proposed. The code of Hammurabi presents an example of claim insurance in ancient law. Under Sections 22 and 23 of this code, dating perhaps as early as 2270 B.C., when a traveler had been robbed on a highway and the perpetrator escaped, the entire community had to contribute to the compensation of the victim. Since 4000 years has elapsed between the "Code" and Margery Fry's proposal, one might anticipate that there will be some delay in implementing her proposal that the state provide restitution to victims of violence.

[10]Digest 42.2. 1.3; Paul .2 .32 .1; Institutes 4.1 .6, 4.1 .3, and 4.4 .7.

Suggestions for Eliciting Voluntary Restitution

1. In Corollary III-A, it was proposed that "The more adequate a harm doer perceives available compensations to be, the greater the probability that he will restore equity by utilizing this technique." Data supported the proposal that an exploiter becomes more likely to make restitution when he perceives that available compensations can completely balance out the harm he has done, than when the compensations available to him are seen as inadequate.

This finding has interesting implications. Exploited minorities often try to impress on those in a position to make restitution how much they have suffered, in the hope of eliciting increased restitution. It is natural to assume that the better case one makes for his claim, the more likely it is that he will be compensated. The preceding research, however, indicates that in some instances, it might be a more effective strategy for a victim to minimize his suffering than to aggrandize it. Increasing the amount of debt claimed might be an effective way to secure increased benefits if the harm doer can conceivably make a restitution adequate to cover the suffering described. If, however, a victim aggrandizes his suffering to such an extent that it exceeds the highest level of compensation available to the exploiter, the victim may decrease his chances of receiving any compensation at all.

The above argument can be illustrated with a practical example. Most Americans probably feel that no matter how hard they tried they could not make adequate restitution to the Negro for his centuries of exploitation. Negro leaders have argued that citizens should at least take some small steps toward restoring equity. However, the idea of making a small step toward restoring equity, making a small compensation, is not very attractive to many citizens. The effort to make a partial compensation mocks their rationalizations that no harm was done or that the exploited deserved their treatment. If one cannot compensate enough to redress another's grievance, he is perhaps happier sticking to his rationalizations. If we can generalize the preceding findings, we might suggest that additional arousal of guilt may only make it more difficult for the exploited to secure compensation. In view of Hypothesis III, a more effective strategy for deprived minorities may be to minimize their description of their suffering, and to make it clear that if available compensations are extended, it will eliminate the debt owed to them. While this may not be true, it might be effective, and would leave the victim in a better situation than if he were not to employ this strategy.

It is possible that exploited individuals might be unwilling to minimize their descriptions of their suffering because they are less interested in receiving material compensation than in the emotional catharsis that comes from punishing those associated with one's suffering.

At the time of Martin Luther King's death, the University of Wisconsin held a series of interracial seminars. Negro students from neighboring high schools talked to overflowing crowds of white students in many of the classrooms in the Social Science Building. Presumably, these seminars were designed to further racial understanding. The pattern of these meetings was strikingly similar. The white students who attended were generally the most liberal students and the most pro Civil Rights students on campus. The Negro high school students who attended were generally very militant. Everyone was upset by Dr. King's death at the time of the meetings. The first question the white students asked their Negro colleagues was "What can we do?" The answer of the Negro student was "Nothing"; they denounced the white liberals as being so steeped in racism that no hope for rehabilitation was possible—they noted that the whites had such a heritage of racism that even if they devoted their lives to civil rights, they could not atone for their own racism.

While such denunciations might provide some degree of emotional satisfaction for Negroes, they probably are unlikely to be effective in eliciting practical restitution for the Negro. Three lines of research would agree that one is very unlikely to induce desired change in an individual by degrading him and telling him he is such a miserable person, his life is beyond repair:

First, commitment research warns us that the more one ties a person publicly to beliefs, the more difficult it is for that person to change his beliefs when faced with new information that these previous beliefs are wrong (see Brehm & Cohen, 1962). Evidence exists that the more committed an individual is to his harm doing, the more likely he is to justify his behavior and the less likely he is to compensate for it. In one experiment (Walster & Prestholdt, 1966), women who were interested in social work were led to misdiagnose their clients' condition, and on the basis of their error, to recommend incorrect therapy for the client. Half of the time the social work trainees' misdiagnoses were public; the other half of the time their errors were private. Trainees then received incontrovertible evidence that their diagnoses were incorrect. Subsequently they were given a chance to compensate for their errors or to justify them. (They could compensate the clients by volunteering free time to help with their therapy or they could justify their misdiagnoses by insisting that the original diagnoses had been correct.) Commitment was found to be an important determinant of whether trainees reacted to their harm doing with justice or with justification. Those individuals publicly committed to their beliefs tended to justify their own errors more and to compensate the victims less than did uncommitted trainees.

Second, attitude change research indicates that a communicator should never identify the recipient of his communication as an opponent, but should, instead, identify him as a sympathizer, regardless of how far apart their views are in fact. It has been found that by identifying the recipient of the communications as a sympathizer, one makes him more receptive to unpleasant advice than he normally would be (Hovland, Lumsdaine, and Sheffield, 1949).

Finally, as mentioned earlier, stressing that available compensations are inadequate should decrease the individual's willingness to attempt to make any compensation at all.

That exploited individuals react to prolonged frustration by verbally attacking those around them is perfectly understandable. The three lines of research that we have cited suggest that condemning the audience is not a very good strategy to adopt if one is interested in producing attitudinal and behavioral changes. If an individual is interested in securing practical benefits, rather than emotional catharsis, he should make an attempt to control his natural inclinations. He should probably select those individuals most interested in Negro equality, and make it clear to them that specified efforts on their part can result in virtually complete restitution for the exploited for which they feel partially responsible.

2. The theory and research reported in the Theoretical Formulation section of this report generates a second set of suggestions as to how an exploited individual should go about persuading a harm doer to make voluntary restitution.

In Corollary III–B, it was proposed that: "The more adequate a harm doer perceives available justifications to be, the greater the probability that he will choose to restore equity by this technique." In elucidating this hypothesis, we noted: "(3) Justifications which involve distortion of the victim's characteristics should be more credible, and thus more readily used, the less contact the harm doer has had (or anticipates having) with the victim."

Distortions of reality can only be effective in making an exploiter feel like a virtuous citizen if he can think of distortions that are credible to himself and to others. An individual can reduce the distress he feels from violating accepted ethical principles (self-concept distress) only if he believes his justifications himself. He can ward off the retaliation of others (and reduce retaliation distress) only if he can persuade others that his justifications are credible.

If one accepts the proposition that the more difficult it is for the exploiter to think of adequate justifications for his behavior the more likely he will be to compensate instead, then it would seem to be a good strategy for an exploited person to do everything he could to make it difficult for the exploiter to justify his exploitation. It should be more difficult for an individual to conceive of credible justifications for his exploitation if the exploited person is a friend, or if the exploiter expects to have to see him again and again, than if the victim is a soon-to-be-forgotten stranger. There is unpublished as well as published data which support this notion. Since we considered the published support for this proposition earlier, let us now discuss the unpublished research results.

In most experiments, pretest groups are run before the actual experimental sessions begin. At various times, Darley and Berscheid (personal communications) and Ross (1965) all ran cognitive consistency experiments in which the extent to which subjects expected to see a confederate again was varied. Quite a surprising result emerged from various pretest groups and experimental groups in their research. These researchers had predicted that individuals in certain experimental conditions would restore cognitive consistency by derogating others. In pretests, however, it was found that the predicted derogation occurred most clearly, and sometimes only, when subjects believed that they would never actually see their partner again. There seemed to be something about the subject's knowing that he would have to face a person again that prevented him from distorting the other's characteristics. This was true even when the other would never know of the subject's derogation. This kind of unpublished data is of course consistent with the data and the theory reported in the Theoretical Formulation section of this paper.

If we accept the hypothesis that the more contact a harm doer has had or anticipates having with the exploited, the more likely he is to restore justice and the less likely he is to justify his harm doing, some techniques for eliciting restitution emerge: (a) A victim interested in securing compensation should make it very clear to the harm doer that they can expect to meet frequently and that the victim, by his presence, will make distortion of the harm-doing situation very difficult. (b) The victim should do everything in his power to make it clear to the harm doer that others are unlikely to believe the exploiter's justifications.

Let us consider a concrete example of this last point. The grape growers of California had paid low wages and provided inadequate housing for the migrant workers who worked in their vineyards for many years. Since the grape growers' associates were mostly other grape growers, who also engaged in the same practices, the farmers probably felt little guilt at their treatment of the migrant workers. If they considered the possibility that their behavior was unjust, they could simply seek out another farmer and assure one another that their behavior was fair and reasonable. Suddenly, however, national attention was focused on the farmers. Reporters came first from educational television and then from national television to interview both the farmers and the striking workers. In the early programs the land owners were quite confident in explaining the justifications underlying their behavior. They explained: "We are not exploiting the migrant workers, actually they are exploiting us. . . . They damage the facilities we provide for them and would not appreciate any improvements that we made. . . . The reason the plumbing doesn't work is that the migrants flush beer cans down the toilets." The reporters quickly provided air time to public health officials and union leaders who disputed the farmers' claims. In broadcasts later in the series, grape growers had moderated the justifications for their behavior to a great extent, possibly in response to their critics. Whether this decrease in justification will eventually result in an increased willingness on the part of farmers to compensate the migrant workers is yet to be seen.

Jane Piliavin (personal communication) has suggested that one function of the "flight to the suburbs" of white majority members is to enable them to avoid acknowledging the suffering which exists in city ghettos. As long as Negroes are geographically and socially segregated, an exploiter can conveniently reduce whatever distress he feels over his exploitation by justifying his behavior. It is very easy for him to maintain that minority members deserve their exploitation ("They are shiftless and lazy and don't want a job") or that they are not really suffering ("A Negro can live better on $1 than a white man can on $5"). Integrated housing and forced association would be expected to make utilization of such rationalizations more difficult. If they were constantly exposed to communications from minority members which belied their justifications of Negro inequality, exploiters would either have to devise some justifications less blatantly opposed by the evidence or would have to be more willing to alter their own behavior.

REFERENCES

Abelson, R.P., & Rosenberg, M.J. Symbolic psychologic: A model of attitudinal cognition. *Behavioral Science,* 1958, 3, 1–13.

Adams, J.S. Toward an understanding of inequity. *Journal of Abnormal and Social Psychology,* 1963, 67, 422–436.

Adams, J.S. Inequity in social exchange. In L. Berkowitz (Ed.), *Advances in experimental social psychology,* Vol. 2. New York: Academic Press, 1965, Pp. 267–299.

Adams, J.S., & Rosenbaum, W.B. The relationship of worker productivity to cognitive dissonance about wage inequities. *Journal of Applied Psychology,* 1962, 46, 161–164.

Arnold, M.B. *Emotion and personality,* Vol. 1, *Psychological aspects.* New York: Columbia University Press, 1960. (a)

Arnold, M.B. *Emotion and Personality.* Vol. 2. *Neurological and physiological aspects.* New York: Columbia University Press, 1960. (b)

Aronfreed, J. The nature, variety and social patterning of moral responses to transgression. *Journal of Abnormal and Social Psychology,* 1961, **63**, 223–240.

Aronfreed, J. Conduct and conscience: The socialization of internalized control over behavior. In Hoffman (Ed.), *Moral character and moral processes: A symposium.* Chicago: Aldine, 1969, in press.

Baldwin, J. *The fire next time.* New York: Dial, 1964.

Berkowitz, L. *Aggression: A social psychological analysis.* New York: McGraw-Hill, 1962.

Berscheid, E., Boye, D., & Darley, J.M. Effects of forced association upon voluntary choice to associate. *Journal of Personality and Social Psychology,* 1968, **8**, 13–19. (a)

Berscheid, E., Boye, D., & Walster, E. Retaliation as a means of restoring equity. *Journal of Personality and Social Psychology,* 1968, **10**, 370-376.(b)

Berscheid, E., & Walster, E. When does a harm-doer compensate a victim? Journal *of Personality and Social Psychology,* 1967, **6**, 435–441.

Berscheid, E., Walster, E., & Barclay, A. The effect of time on the tendency to compensate a victim. *Psychological Reports,* 1969, **25**, 431-436.

Bramel, D. Interpersonal attraction, hostility, and perception. In J. Mills (Ed.), *Experimental social psychology.* New York: MacMillan, 1969. Pp. 1-120.

Bramel, D., Taub, B., & Blum, B. An observer's reaction to the suffering of his enemy. *Journal of Personality and Social Psychology,* 1968, **8**, 384–392.

Brehm, J.W., & Cohen, A.R. *Explorations in cognitive dissonance.* New York: Wiley, 1962.

Brock, T.C., & Becker, L.A. Debriefing and susceptibility to subsequent experimental manipulations. *Journal of Experimental Social Psychology,* 1966, **2**, 314–323.

Brock, T.C., & Buss, A.H. Dissonance, aggression, and evaluation of pain. *Journal of Abnormal and Social Psychology,* 1962, **65**, 192–202.

Brock, T.C., & Buss, A.H. Effects of justification for aggression in communication with the victim on post-aggression dissonance. *Journal of Abnormal and Social Psychology,* 1964, **68**, 403–412.

Carlsmith, J.M., & Gross, A. Some effects of guilt on compliance. *Journal of Personality and Social Psychology,* 1969, **11**, 232-239.

Cartwright, D., & Harary, F. Structural balance: A generalization of Heider's theory. *Psychological Review,* 1956, **63**, 277–281.

Darlington, R.B., & Macker, C.E. Displacement of guilt-produced altruistic behavior. *Journal of Personality and Social Psychology,* 1966, **4**, 442–443.

Davidson, J. Cognitive familiarity and dissonance reduction. In L. Festinger (Ed.), *Conflict, decision and dissonance,* Stanford, Calif: Stanford University Press, 1964.

Davis, K.E., & Jones, E.E. Changes in interpersonal perception as a means of reducing cognitive dissonance. *Journal of Abnormal and Social Psychology,* 1960, **61**, 402–410.

Del Vecchio, G. The problem of penal justice (imprisonment or reparation of damage), *27 Revista Juridica de la Universidad de Puerto Rico,* Silving translation, 1959.

Festinger, L. *A theory of cognitive dissonance.* Evanston, Ill: Row, Peterson, 1957.

Freedman, J.L., Wallington, S.A., & Bless, E. Compliance without pressure: The effect of guilt. *Journal of Personality and Social Psychology,* 1967, **7**, 117–124.

Fromm, E. *The art of loving.* New York: Harper & Row, 1956.

Fry, M. Justice for victims. In M.H. Rubin (Ed.), *Compensation for victims of criminal violence: A round table.* Atlanta, Ga: Emory University Law School, *Journal of Public Law,* 1956, **8**, 155-253.

Glass, D.C. Changes in liking as a means of reducing cognitive discrepancies between self-esteem and aggression. *Journal of Personality,* 1964, **32,** 520–549.

Homans, G.C. *Social behavior: Its elementary forms.* New York: Harcourt, Brace, 1961.

Hovland, C.I., Lumsdaine, A.A., & Sheffield, F.A. *Experiments on mass communication.* Princeton, N.J.: Princeton University Press, 1949.

Jacques, E. An objective approach to pay differentials. *Time Motion Study,* 1961, **10,** 25–28.

Jecker, J., & Landy, D. Liking a person as a function of doing him a favor. *Human Relations,* 1969, in press.

Lerner, M.J., & Matthews, G. Reactions to the suffering of others under conditions of indirect responsibility. *Journal of Personality and Social Psychology,* 1967, **5,** 319–325.

Lerner, M.J., & Simmons, C.H. Observers reaction to the "innocent victim": Compassion or rejection? *Journal of Personality and Social Psychology,* 1966, **4,** 203–210.

Lindemann, E. Symptomatology and management of acute grief. *American Journal of Psychiatry,* 1944, **101,** 141–148.

Maher, B.A. *Principles of psychopathology: An experimental approach.* New York: McGraw-Hill, 1966.

Rosenberg, M.J. An analysis of affective-cognitive consistency. In M.J. Rosenberg, W.J. McGuire, C.I. Hovland, R.P. Abelson, & J. W. Brehm (Eds.), *Attitude organization and change.* New Haven, Conn.: Yale University Press, 1960, Pp. 15–64.

Rosenberg, M.J., & Abelson, R.P. An analysis of cognitive balancing. In M.J. Rosenberg, C.I. Hovland, W.J. McGuire, R.P. Abelson, & J.W. Brehm (Eds.), *Attitude organization and change.* New Haven, Conn.: Yale University Press, 1960.

Ross, A. *Modes of guilt reduction.* Unpublished doctoral dissertation, University of Minnesota, 1965.

Sarnoff, I. *Personality dynamics and development.* New York: Wiley, 1962.

Schafer, S. *Restitution to victims of crime.* London: Stevens, 1960.

Scott, M.B., & Lyman, S.M. Accounts. *American Sociological Review.* 1968, **33,** 46–62.

Spencer, *Essays: moral, political and aesthetic* (new and enlarged edition), 1866.

Sykes, G.M., & Matza, D. Techniques of neutralization: A theory of delinquency. *American Sociological Review,* 1957, **22,** 664–670.

Walster, E., Berscheid, E., & Barclay, A.N. A determinant of preference among modes of dissonance reduction. *Journal of Personality and Social Psychology,* 1967, **7,** 211–216.

Walster, E., & Prestholdt, P. The effect of misjudging another: Overcompensation or dissonance reduction? *Journal of Experimental Social Psychology,* 1966, **2,** 85–97.

Walster, E., Walster, B., Abrahams, D., & Brown, Z. The effect on liking of underrating or overrating another. *Journal of Experimental Social Psychology,* 1966, **2,** 70–84.

Weick, K.E., & Nesset, B. Preferences among forms of equity. *Organizational Behavior and Human Performance,* 1969, in press.

Zajonc, R.B. The concepts of balance, congruity, and dissonance. *Public Opinion Quarterly,* 1960, **24,** 280–286.

THE DESIRE FOR JUSTICE AND REACTIONS TO VICTIMS[1]

Melvin J. Lerner

All of us know that there are great numbers of people in our midst whose lives are filled with suffering—pain, emotional anguish, deprivation of the body and spirit. Many people live under conditions of devastating poverty. Many others spend the greater part of their lives in mental hospitals with budgets barely adequate to provide minimal care, let alone the kind of treatment which could give them back their lives. And many children spend their most vulnerable and formative years in overcrowded and potentially crippling institutions.

The question that plagues the concerned observer is: Why do we allow such suffering to continue? As a nation, we have the money and technology to virtually eliminate poverty and to provide the kind of professional facilities and services which would dramatically enhance the life chances of the parentless child or the emotionally ill person. Yet we allow this suffering and deprivation to continue while we pursue comparatively frivolous, self-interested, and often quite expensive goals—our television sets, automobiles, special clothes for special occasions, liquor, etc. We seem not to care enough; possibly we do not care at all. We are apparently callous, indifferent, and cynical about the suffering of others.

[1]The research presented in this paper was supported by a grant from the National Science Foundation (GS-957).

205

One of the explanations that has been offered for these traits points to traditions arising from our history as a land of frontiers. The early development of our country is, in the main, a story of pioneers, rugged individualists who struggled to carve out a life for themselves and their families in a difficult and often dangerous environment. In order to survive in this kind of world, a man learned to depend upon and to put his trust only in himself and his family. This pattern of individualism persists as a traditional theme in our contemporary life. Now, as in the days of the frontier, each man makes his own way and takes care of his own. We tend to assume that the other man's suffering is probably a result of his own failures; in any case, help offered to him deprives me of what I earned and what I need to take care of my family.

The second kind of explanation looks to our more recent history. The relatively rapid development of our industrial economy brought with it migration of people from stable rural communities to the cities where they have lived as strangers among people who are strangers to one another. This leads to a sense of having no roots—of belonging to no place, group, or tradition—and to a sense of isolation—of being alone in an indifferent world. When one adds the constant exposure to reports of organized crime, acts of violence, and corrupt public officials, it is easy for these feelings of isolation and alienation to turn to extreme cynicism or to "anomie"—the feeling that one lives in a kind of human jungle where no one can or should be trusted. A natural solution to these problems is to confine one's emotional ties and concerns to the immediate family. A man comes to believe that the important thing is to learn the techniques of getting along with "them" out there so that he can make his own way for himself and his family and get some pleasure out of life.

These explanations seem reasonable. They fit well-established facts about our history and changes in our society. On the other hand, is it not possible that the original diagnosis is incorrect? While one cannot really argue about the fact of our tolerance of widespread suffering and deprivation, does this necessarily indicate that we are callous, indifferent, or cynical? We can also find evidence of compassion for our fellow man and concern with social justice. Our society has elaborate, well-supported institutions which attempt to insure that no harm shall come to the innocent and that wrongdoers will be punished. Considerable money and effort are devoted each year to help victims of illness, natural disasters, and economic deprivations. We teach our children to be good and kind—to cause others no harm and to help those in need. The laboratory research of Lazarus, Speisman, Mordkoff, and Davison (1962), Stotland and Dunn (1963), Tannenbaum and Gaer (1965) and others supports what we have often observed in ourselves and others: We are often deeply moved by the suffering of other people and reactions of sympathy and compassion are easily aroused in most of us.

Apparently, then, we are, or can be, both cruelly indifferent and compassionately concerned about the suffering of others. How does one make sense out of this apparent contradiction? The obvious answers do not seem to apply easily. Although there are probably individual differences in the propensity to react with compassion or rejection, it is easy to see that most people exhibit both kinds of reactions from time to time. Identification (in the sense in which it is usually used), or lack of it, does not seem to be the mediating factor. For example, as a parent I have seen many instances of both kinds of reactions between my children and on the part of my wife and me toward the children, and I believe it is safe to assume that we are all highly identified with one another.

The research I am going to describe here was designed to explore the possibility that both rejection of victims and compassionate reactions toward them derive from the same underlying psychological process. One observation of my own reactions and those I could see in others served as the guide for the search for this process: It is extremely upsetting to witness another person's suffering; however, I am much less disturbed if he deserved it—if the victim is a "bad guy" or if he did something to deserve his suffering.

It seems that most people care deeply about justice for themselves and others—not justice in the legal sense, but more basic notions of justice. We want to believe we live in a world where people get what they deserve or, rather, deserve what they get. We want to believe that good things happen to good people and serious suffering comes only to bad people. In the same vein, we want to believe that people who work hard will get what they deserve, what they have earned and worked for. We like to think that people fail or are deprived because of inability or unwillingness to do what was necessary to achieve their goals or avoid suffering.

Unfortunately, we are regularly confronted with incidents which seem to contradict this belief. We learn of an innocent child killed or brutalized, or of a man whose security derived from a lifetime of hard work is wiped out by an illness, a flood, the closing down of a mine, the act of a criminal. Each such incident may be frightening or sickening. We do not want to believe that these things can happen, but they do. At least we do not want to believe they can happen to people like ourselves—good decent people. If these things can happen, what is the use of struggling, planning, and working to build a secure future for one's self and family? No matter how strongly our belief in an essentially just world is threatened by such incidents, most of us must try to maintain it in order to continue facing the irritations and struggles of daily life. This is a belief we cannot afford to give up if we are to continue to function.

What I am postulating here is that for their own security, if for no other reason, people want to believe they live in a just world where people get what they deserve. Any evidence of undeserved suffering threatens this belief. The observer then will attempt to reestablish justice. One way of accomplishing this is by acting to compensate the victim; another is by persuading himself that the victim deserved to suffer, after all. In our culture, and probably many others, suffering is seen as deserved if the person behaved poorly or if he is inherently "bad," or undesirable.[2] It is also reasonable to conjecture that most observers would prefer to attribute suffering to something the victim did rather than to his personal worth. The assumption here is that attaching responsibility to behavior provides us with the greater security—we can do something to avoid such a state.

OBSERVER'S REACTION TO THE "INNOCENT VICTIM"

In order to generate some evidence relevant to these notions, it was necessary to confront observers with an instance of undeserved suffering in a context where we could vary some aspects of the situation. Because we already had some evidence that observers will tend to ascribe behavioral responsibility to a victim for his suffering and that if this is done there may not be any devaluation of the victim (Lerner, 1965b), we wanted to create an "innocent" victim whose suffering was inflicted upon him as he followed the normal routine of his daily activities—the victim had done nothing foolish, stupid, etc., to bring him to his fate.

We reasoned that if the observers were confronted with an innocent victim and were given a legitimate and virtually effortless opportunity to help the victim, they would do so. And if this were successful they would have no need to alter their perceptions of the victim—no need to reject him because justice would have been reestablished. On the other hand, if they were rendered virtually powerless while observing the victim's suffering they would be impelled to reestablish justice in the situation by devaluing the victim. It should also be true that the greater the injustice in terms of degree of undeserved suffering, the more devaluing of the victim when the observer is unable to help.

To approximate these conditions in a laboratory setting, groups of female students who volunteered to participate in an experiment on the perception of cues of emotional arousal found themselves observing another experiment in which a female student (Victim) was receiving extremely painful electric

---

[2]See Adams (1963) for a similar set of assumptions.

shocks.[3] It was established that the victim had signed up to participate in a study of human learning as part of a requirement of an introductory psychology course. It was only after the victim had begun to receive her instructions that she learned that she was taking part in a study of the effect of strong negative reinforcement on pair-associate learning. Also, the observers knew of a potential penalty for failing to complete one's required number of experiments.

The subjects watched the victim suffer for 10 minutes over closed-circuit TV (actually a videotape). They were then asked to describe the personality of the victim by assigning positive or negative attributes to her (bipolar adjectives) and by assessing how others would react to this person (Social Stimulus Value).

The instructions the observers received prior to rating the victim created the differences among conditions. The observers in one condition (Known Reward) were told that they were at the midpoint in the experiment and they had the opportunity to decide what would be most valuable for them: observe the victim in a second session of negative reinforcement, a neutral condition, or a strong positive reinforcement condition where she would not be shocked but given 25 cents for each correct answer. The subjects then voted (anonymously) and were told that the victim would receive positive reinforcement in the next session. A second condition (Uncertain Reward Decision) differed only slightly from this in that the observers were not told the victim's fate before they completed their ratings of her.

Four other conditions were used to gain evidence about the degree of unjust suffering as a determinant of the amount of rejection. There were two conditions of minimal suffering. In one (Past Event), subjects were told they had observed a videotape of an event that had occurred in the past. In the other (Endpoint), the subjects believed they had seen the event as it was happening. The subjects in both of these conditions understood that the victim's suffering was terminated before they made their ratings.

To increase the perceived injustice, the subjects in a third condition (Midpoint), were told before they made their ratings that there was a second session of negative reinforcement awaiting the victim. In this condition injustice was greater than in those described earlier because of the increased duration of the victim's suffering. In another condition (Martyr) the degree of injustice was increased in a different manner. The observers were led to believe that the victim, after expressing fear of the shock and reluctance to participate, had agreed to undergo the shock so that they, the observers, might receive their needed credit

[3]The procedure and findings of this study are described more fully in Lerner and Simmons (1966).

for participating in an experiment (as observers). The intention here was to create the impression not of an "innocent" victim but of someone whose suffering derived from altruistic motives. (When the observers rated this victim they believed she would receive no further shock—her suffering was at an end.)

Results

The main results of this study can be summarized briefly (see Table 1). When the observers were given an opportunity to affect the victim's fate in the Known Reward and Uncertain Reward Decision conditions, almost all of them voted to place the victim in a condition where not only would her suffering be ended but she would be compensated—23 of the 25 subjects voted for positive reinforcement and two voted for the neutral condition. The attributes which the observers ascribed to the victim were reliably affected by the various experimental conditions. The more unjust the suffering, the more negative were the attributes assigned to her. The least negative ratings occurred in the Known Reward condition and the most negative ratings appeared in the Martyr and Midpoint conditions. (These differences are signficiant at .01 levels.) The comparatively negative ratings in the Uncertain Reward Decision condition are of particular importance. In this condition all but one of the observers voted to compensate the victim and yet they devalued her significantly more than in the Known Reward condition ($p < .02$). Apparently acting on a victim's behalf is not sufficient to prevent rejection. Rejection may still occur unless the observer is convinced that justice will actually be reestablished—the victim will be compensated.

TABLE 1

Ratings of the Victim[a]

Rating	Known reward (N=14)	Uncertain reward decision (N=11)	Past event (N=10)	Endpoint (N=14)	Midpoint (N=14)	Martyr (N=9)
Attractiveness	−5.07	−25.18	−11.10	−12.85	−25.78	−34.00
Social stimulus value	19.21	15.27	18.70	17.00	14.71	14.11

[a]Means are of the difference between self and other ratings. The more positive (less negative) the rating, the more attractive the victim. From Lerner and Simmons (1966).

One additional finding provided some interesting support for our theoretical notions. After rating the victim, but prior to learning the true nature of the experiment, the observers wrote descriptions of their reactions to the experiment. Although the great majority reacted positively to the experiment (e.g., "I think it is about the most important experiment I have been able to participate in. I enjoyed it very much."), there were some who reacted quite negatively ("I thought there was no sense in the experiment and it was very cruel."). Those subjects who reacted positively to the experiment gave a mean rating of the victim of –24.35, whereas those who rejected the situation rated the victim significantly nearer their rating of themselves, –5.16 ($p < .001$). Apparently if the subjects were willing to condemn the situation they had no need to devalue the victim.

The findings of this initial study were encouraging for our theoretical notions. Apparently, observers of an innocent victim will act to help and compensate him, if it is a relatively easy act. On the other hand, if they cannot do this then the observers may construe the victim as the kind of undesirable person who "deserves" to suffer. The greater the injustice of the victim's fate the greater the efforts at condemnation and rejection.[4]

REACTIONS TO AN "ALTRUISTIC" VICTIM

The subjects' rejection of the "altruistically" motivated victim in the Martyr condition of the previous study is a provocative finding because of its apparent contradiction of common sense. Everyone knows that in our culture we revere and love martyrs; we don't reject them. This may be true for a number of reasons that do not contradict our findings or theoretical notions. One is that the more comfortable reaction of rejecting martyrs requires an inordinate amount of distortion. Our prior cognitions surrounding the martyrdom are likely to be stable and important to us, so we suffer along with the martyr and the injustice of his fate. Another possible reason for our not rejecting all altruistically motivated victims is that many of us believe these people will be compensated appropriately for all their suffering—either here on earth, as was Job, or in some afterlife. Only if we do not hold such a belief concerning a particular martyr and if our prior cognitions of the event are not stable are we likely to find some way to condemn and reject him.

[4]The subjects in this study were female students at the University of Kentucky. Piliavin, Hardyck, and Vadim (1968) found a similar rejection of the victim in the Midpoint condition with male and female observers who were high school students in California. (Piliavin, I., Hardyck, J., & Vadim, T., 1968).

Although the initial experiment provided some support for this hypothesis, the evidence was not conclusive. One criticism of our interpretation of the Martyr finding is that the rejection was an appropriate response to the character portrayed by the victim. We created the Martyr condition by having the victim express fear and reluctance upon learning that she was to receive electric shocks. One of the experimenters then reminded her that the observers would not be able to obtain "Lab credits" for participating in an experiment if the victim refused to do her part—undergo the shocks. After a few moments of such gentle persuasion the victim agreed to go on with her part "since it is necessary for all of them to get credit. . ." Of course, during all this the observers were never consulted about their wishes in the matter. In fact, the entire scene took place in an anteroom behind the subjects and they merely overheard the event. Although three psychologists observed this scene in rehearsal and agreed unhesitatingly that the victim created the impression of acting generously from altruistic motives, there is no direct evidence that the observers in the experiment actually viewed the victim in this light. It has been suggested that the scene did not create the impression of an altruist but, rather, of someone who submits easily to unreasonable authority or someone who will subject herself to unnecessary humiliation and suffering for the sake of others' approval. These perceptions could easily lead to the kind of devaluation of the victim we found.

The main purpose of the next study[5] was to obtain more direct evidence about the impression created in observers who witness someone in this kind of scene. Our hypothesis was that most people would consider this person relatively admirable or at least not worthy of condemnation or ridicule. It is only when we add awareness of this person's suffering that the observers are impelled to reject and condemn her—because it is so unjust.

Procedure

The strategy employed in this study was to have all subjects first observe another student in a simple digit-span learning situation which was to be followed by a second learning task. This was presented on videotape, but subjects were led to believe it was "live." The observers were told either that the second task would involve strong electric shocks (negative reinforcement) or no shock. Immediately after the first task, but prior to the ratings, half of the observers in each condition saw the model engage in interaction designed to elicit the impression that she would go through with this second task for the sake of the observers although she really wanted to avoid doing it. The rest of the observers

[5]Lerner, M.J. Conditions eliciting acceptance or rejection of a Martyr. Unpublished manuscript, University of Kentucky, 1968 (a).

did not see this Martyr sequence. Following this, subjects made ratings of the model. The observers were female students who, as in the earlier study, believed they were engaging in a study of cues indicating another's state of emotional arousal.

The hypotheses were: (1) When the observers (subjects) believed they would see the student receive a shock, they would describe her as less attractive than when they did not expect her to be shocked.

(2) When the observers believed the student would be shocked, the Martyr would elicit greater rejection than the Nonmartyr.

(3) When the observers believed the student would not be shocked, the Martyr would be described as equally, if not more, attractive than the Non-martyr.

Results

As predicted in Hypothesis 1, the observers described the model as significantly less attractive when they were led to believe she would be shocked than when they were not told she would be shocked ($p < .005$, see Table 2). The Martyr elicited significantly more rejection than the Nonmartyr when the observers expected her to be shocked (Hypothesis 2, $p < .05$, one-tailed). However, in the Nonshock conditions the Martyr is described as being as attractive as the Nonmartyr (Hypothesis 3). Thus, in two separate studies, the Martyr condition increased rejection when observers believed the person would suffer in the future. The findings of the present study indicate that this rejection is not the result of something inherently distasteful or pathetic about the Martyr's decision. When the observers believe the Martyr will not suffer they describe her as no less attractive than the same person who has not made a Martyrlike decision.

We have recently gathered some evidence related to another alternative explanation for the rejection in the Martyr condition. This explanation suggests that the observers are more directly implicated in the victim's suffering in the Martyr condition than in any of the others. In a sense they are "responsible" for her suffering. Although they were not consulted and did nothing to implicate themselves, nevertheless the victim is pressured into complying so that they will be able to receive their needed credit for participating in an experiment. She is doing it for them. It is reasonable then to conjecture that they would feel guilty and to reduce this guilt they reject the victim.

TABLE 2

Ratings of Victim Attractiveness[a]

	Nonmartyr	Martyr
Nonshock	95.64	96.70
	(N = 11)	(N = 10)
Shock	89.63	75.22
	(N = 8)	(N = 9)

[a]Cell means represent ratings summed over 15 bipolar scales. The range is 15–135. The higher the rating the more attractive the victim. For procedural reasons, in this study only the victim was rated. For purposes of comparison with the earlier study (Table 1), where the measure was the subject's score subtracted from the victim's score, the absolute attractiveness mean in the Martyr condition was 65.78. From Lerner.[5]

If this explanation is true then observers who were not so implicated in the victim's suffering would have less guilt and less need to reject her. To test this we recruited students from sociology classes to be observers. These subjects believed that others in the observation room were students from Introductory Psychology for whom the Martyr was to suffer. We found that these observers reacted almost identically to those from the introductory psychology course. The mean rating of the victim in the Martyr–Shock condition was 76.3.

The most reasonable explanation for these findings is the one proposed earlier. The suffering of someone whose fate derives from altruistic motives is more threatening to the observer's belief in a just world than the suffering of less nobly motivated victims. The most comfortable way the observer can maintain the belief in a just world is by rejecting the victim—ascribing sufficiently negative personal qualities to the victim so that the suffering becomes an appropriate fate.

ALTERING THE FATE OF A VICTIM

The first two studies offer some insights into the bystander's reaction to "innocent victims." If the observer is unable to alter the fate of the victim he is likely to be compelled to find some undesirable attributes in the victim which make his suffering appear to be a relatively acceptable, just fate. This personal rejection can become rather extreme if the victim appeared initially to be suffering out of altruistic motives. Most people do not want to believe that suffering can be visited upon decent, good people who did nothing to merit such a fate.

The theory presented here also offers hypotheses about the occurrence of acts intended to benefit a victim. If a person desires justice in his view of social events, it follows that he will be motivated to help someone who has been unjustly deprived. This same desire for justice, however, would also demand that the person limit his efforts on behalf of someone whose rewards apparently exceed what he deserves on the basis of his actions or personal worth.

A more complex derivation from this theory yields some hypotheses about how the person's own experiences will affect his desire to act on someone's behalf. We reasoned that if the person has himself been unjustly victimized by someone on whom he depended, then in addition to experiencing resentment and anger, he should be motivated to find or create additional evidence that a person's fate is not usually so capriciously or unjustly determined. That is, the experience of having been treated unjustly will make a person more likely to help someone who has been treated in a similar unjust fashion and less willing to help (or possibly prone to harm) someone who has been fortuitously benefited than would a person who has not had such an experience. This hypothesis was tested in a study by Simmons and Lerner (1968, Study II).[6]

Procedure

Female undergraduates participated in what they believed to be a study of supervisory ability. Each subject had one of three experiences in the first of two experimental tasks. Some subjects (Rewarded) were supervisors who were paid a large sum of money because of the unusually good efforts of their student "workers." Other subjects (Fail Betrayed) were supervisors who received virtually no money—far less than the average—because their workers refused to produce in spite of the fact that the subjects had done their parts well. A third group of subjects (Control) participated in a solo task for a small reward. The subjects' reactions to their workers supported the effectiveness of the manipulation. They attributed their fate in the first task to their workers' willingness to be of help. In comparison with Rewarded subjects, the Fail-Betrayed subjects described their partner as a significantly less able worker and indicated considerably less desire to work with her again or to have her as a roommate. In the same vein, the betrayed subjects indicated that they enjoyed being a supervisor less than did those who received an unusually high payment.

[6]The procedure and findings of this study are described more fully in Simmons and Lerner (1968).

Our hypotheses were tested by observing the performance of these subjects while they were working on a second task for another student (not the one who had worked for them). All the subjects were led to believe that the other student's chance to win a large reward would depend upon how many envelopes the subject made in a given work period. Some of the subjects were led to believe that the person they were working for had received, as a supervisor in the first task, an unusually large reward (Supervisor, Rewarded). Others learned that their dependent supervisor had been let down by her first worker and had received nothing (Supervisor, Fail Betrayed) and still others believed that their supervisor had worked alone and received a small reward (Supervisor, Control).

Results

The performance of the subjects in the various conditions can be seen in Table 3. Subjects did significantly less work for a supervisor who had previously received an excessively large reward than for a supervisor who had been in a control condition or one who had been betrayed ($p < .001$). As expected, the subjects who appeared most sensitive to the previous fate of their supervisor were those who had been betrayed themselves. These subjects exhibited greater effort for the betrayed supervisor than subjects in any other condition did for their supervisor.

TABLE 3

Number of Envelopes Made for Supervisor[a]

Subject's previous fate	Supervisor's previous fate			
	Rewarded	Fail betrayed	Control	Combined
Rewarded	14.50	14.75	14.75	14.64
Fail betrayed	13.25	21.25	16.66	17.05
Control	9.67	15.43	16.50	13.87
Combined	12.47	17.14	15.94	

[a]Study II, Simmons and Lerner (1968).

The findings of this study indicate that the desire for justice will lead, under appropriate circumstances, to predictable differences in the way they behave toward others. People are most likely to help someone who has been unjustly deprived and least likely to exert themselves for someone who already has more than he deserves. The underlying motivation seems to be a desire to arrange matters so that people have just what they deserve. Of most importance theoretically was the finding that the experience of having been unjustly deprived themselves leads to even greater efforts on behalf of someone who has been treated in a similarly unfair fashion.

It is tempting to use these and other related findings to conjecture about the conditions under which responsible social action is likely to take place. For example, it would be comforting to believe that people who have themselves been deprived will be sensitive to the fate of others and exhibit great efforts on behalf of other victims. There is evidence that this not invariably true. Those communities in our society which contain large pockets of deprived people are not noted for a high incidence of altruistically motivated, beneficient acts. The social conscience of the slum dweller does not appear to be any more developed than that of the inhabitant of more favored sections of the community.[7] In fact, antisocial acts are more numerous in communities containing a high proportion of economic victims than in more favored communities (Chein, Gerard, Lee, & Rosenfeld, 1964; Dohrenwend & Chin-Shong, 1967; Eysenck, 1954; Foster, 1965; Glueck & Glueck, 1950; Lewis, 1959.) Perhaps some essential factor present in this experimental situation is lacking in most slums.

If the desire for justice is to be translated into action designed to help a victim, one essential factor is that the deprived person clearly should not appear to have earned his fate. Studies done by Lerner (1965b) and Walster (1966) show that people tend to persuade themselves that a victim really did earn his fate. Similarly, in an earlier version of this last study (Simmons & Lerner, 1968, Study I) it was found that the subjects viewed the previously betrayed supervisor in the second task as significantly less attractive than the Control or Rewarded supervisor ($p < .025$). As Table 4 shows, this rejection tended to appear even among those subjects who had themselves been betrayed. In the earlier study not only did the similarly betrayed subjects reject the betrayed supervisor but as Table 5 shows, they, as well as subjects in the control condition, worked least hard for the betrayed supervisor and exerted most effort on behalf of someone who had been highly rewarded in the first task. However, when the subjects were prevented from deciding that their supervisors had deserved their fate on the first task—by presenting objective evidence of the merits of the supervisor's efforts (as in Study II)—then we found them translating their desire for justice

[7] Some studies (Mizruchi, 1960; Roberts & Rokeach, 1956; Srole, 1956) have shown people in the lower socioeconomic statuses are most likely to agree with "anomic" descriptions of their environment. The implication is that these people do not believe they live in a just world. Most important for our purposes, however, would be the demonstration that they have less desire for justice or to believe that they live in a just world.

TABLE 4

Willingness to Have Supervisor-Partner as a Roommate[a]

Subject's previous fate	Supervisor's previous fate			
	Rewarded	Fail betrayed	Control	Combined
Rewarded	7.50	6.77	7.88	7.38
Fail betrayed	8.20	7.66	8.00	7.94
Control	8.11	6.33	8.63	7.69
Combined	7.94	6.92	8.17	

[a]A high score indicates high willingness. From Study I, Simmons and Lerner (1968).

TABLE 5

Number of Envelopes Made for Supervisor[a]

Subject's previous fate	Supervisor's previous fate			
	Rewarded	Fail betrayed	Control	Combined
Rewarded	15.75	19.88	18.50	18.04
Fail betrayed	19.60	14.25	17.50	17.12
Control	19.33	14.88	16.00	16.74
Combined	18.23	16.34	17.33	

[a]Study I, Simmons and Lerner (1968).

into social acts. It appears that without this evidence, the subjects persuaded themselves that justice had been done, that the supervisors had deserved their fate and so they worked hard for the "desirable winner" and exerted little effort on behalf of the person they persuaded themselves had deserved to be a "loser."

THE EFFECT OF A SERIOUS OUTCOME ON ATTRIBUTION
OF RESPONSIBILITY

In the research discussed to this point, the subject has always entered the scene after the victim's fate has been determined. In some instances the subject was given the opportunity to intervene or alter the victim's fate, but in no way was he involved in the events which initially singled out the victim. Even in those conditions in which the victim supposedly agreed to receive the electric shocks so that the subjects could observe her, the situation was arranged so that the subjects were never consulted about their wishes in the matter; in fact, it would have been quite out of order for them to attempt to intervene on the victim's behalf. The last study to be reported here will focus on situations in which the person is involved in the process which leads to someone's suffering.

In our society there are usually limited amounts of desired resources available and the success of one person implies the relative failure of others. Unlike direct competition, however, this competition for the desired and sometimes essential resources usually occurs without acknowledgment of specific competitors, although everyone knows that there are others in the race. Each competitor typically does not act directly to impede the progress of others; he devotes his skills and energy to the promotion of his own interests with the awareness that others are doing likewise.

If these assumptions about the nature of most important goal-directed activities in our society are correct, then this raises questions about reactions to deprived people—victims—in our society. One question is: "How do winners—those who get the promotion or the job—feel about losers?" There is already considerable evidence available showing that under certain conditions the awareness of responsibility for another person's suffering can lead to rejection of the victim (Davis & Jones, 1960; Glass, 1964; Lerner, 1965a). Apparently the persecutor justifies his action by persuading himself that the victim deserves his fate. Inflicting harm on an undesirable, unworthy person may sometimes be considered an acceptable, if not legitimate, act. Thus, it becomes important in a competitive situation to know when the winner is likely to feel a sense of responsibility for the fate of those who are deprived through his actions.

No matter what role external events (chance or luck) may have actually played, the theory presented here suggests that people are highly motivated to believe that they are responsible for the outcome of important events in their lives. If people want to believe they are responsible for achieving their own goals, they may be forced to feel responsible for depriving those who fail, even though their acts were not primarily intended to harm the other. One key to understanding some of the observed rejection of victims of social and economic suffering is determination of the effect of feeling involved in another person's suffering. The following studies tested the limits of the required connection between a person's act and another's suffering in order for the sense of responsibility to be elicited.

Study I[8]

Procedure

Pairs of female students who had volunteered to participate in a study of human learning discovered upon arriving at the laboratory that one of them would have to be in a "negative reinforcement" condition, i.e., learn under conditions of electric shock, while the other would be in a control (or positive reinforcement) condition. The decision as to which of them would receive negative reinforcement and which would be the control was to be determined entirely by which of two slips of paper in a bowl the first subject selected. One slip designated the shock condition and the other control. It was made clear that the fate of both subjects depended upon which slip of paper was selected by the subject choosing first.

The subject's reaction to the other person and the situation were compared under three conditions. The subject always had the desirable condition and the other student always was to receive a shock. What was varied was how this appeared to come about. In one condition the subject picked first and got the desirable slip. In a second condition the subject learned that the other person had picked first and received the slip designating the shock condition and therefore the subject would be in the desirable condition. The third situation was altered slightly so that there were many slips in the bowl rather than two—half containing the designation of shock and the other half a nonshock condition. In this situation where fates were determined independently, the subjects selected nonshock slips and were told that the other subject had picked one indicating shock.[9]

---

[8]From Lerner and Matthews (1967).

[9]The design of these studies also included a Control–Control condition in which both subjects were assigned to a neutral condition. This was to assess the effect of the awareness that the other person was to suffer on the subject's evaluation of her. Also included in the design was a variation of the fate available to the fortunate, nonsuffering subject. In half the experimental conditions, the subject believed she was to be in a positive reinforcement condition where she would earn a considerable amount of money (Shock–Money). In the other half, the desirable condition was merely a neutral condition where she would receive feedback about her responses (Shock–Control). This variation did not lead to any significant differences.

Results

As can be seen in Table 6, subjects, when questioned later, tended to attribute responsibility for their own and the other subject's fate to whomever picked the determining slip. When the subject made the first selection, she attributed primary responsibility to herself and when the other subject picked first, responsibility was ascribed to her. In the condition in which there were many slips available the subject allotted responsibility to the other subject for her fate and to herself for her own fate.

TABLE 6

*Attribution of Primary Responsibility
for Self and Other's Fate[a]*

Subject's perception of responsibility	Experimental conditions		
	Fate independent	Subject picks first	Other picks first
For subject's fate[b]			
Experimmenter	3	2	1
Other	0	0	12
Self	12	13	5
For other's fate[c]			
Experimenter	5	2	2
Other	9	6	15
Self	1	7	1

[a]Cell entries are number of subjects making choice indicated. From Lerner and Matthews (1967).

[b]Comparing Subject Picks First with Other Picks First, eliminating Experimenter's choices. $x^2 = 12.50$, $df = 1$, $p < .001$.

[c]Comparing Subject Picks First with Other Picks First, eliminating Experimenter's choices, $x^2 = 5.91$, $df = 1$, $p < .02$.

As Table 7 shows, the subjects' reactions toward the other person who was to receive unpleasant shock indicate that this sense of responsibility was not superficial but was strong enough to influence their general perception of her. In the condition in which the subject picked the first slip, thereby causing the other to suffer, the other subject was described as an undesirable person relative to the attractiveness of "an average college student." In contrast, when the other person was considered to be responsible for her own suffering (Fates Independent and Other Pick First) the subject showed significantly less rejection ($p < .005$).

TABLE 7

Ratings of Other's Attractiveness[a]

	Experimental conditions		
Situation	Shock–Control	Shock–Money	Control–Control
Fates independent	–5.25 (N = 8)	–3.57 (N = 7)	–6.30 (N = 10)
Other picks first	6.55 (N = 11)	3.14 (N = 7)	
Self picks first	–11.22 (N = 9)	–19.33 (N = 6)	

[a]Cell entries are mean differences between ratings of the other subject and an "average college student." A negative rating indicates a relatively unfavorable rating of the other subject. From Lerner and Matthews (1967).

This is what one would have expected on the basis of the theory presented here. Unlike the other person in the "innocent victim" studies reported earlier, this one was considered responsible for her own suffering. The subjects could see an appropriate connection between what the victim had done and her suffering. There was no need, then, for the subjects to devalue the victim in order to believe she deserved her fate.

The positive reaction to the other subject when she not only brought about her own suffering but at the same time saved the subject from suffering (Other Picks First Condition) was unexpected but understandable. Apparently the subjects felt somewhat grateful to the other person for their satisfactory outcome.

Another unexpected finding was the willingness of the subjects in both conditions in which their fate had been tied to the victim's to return to comfort the victim prior to her undergoing the shocks. All subjects, after overhearing a plea from the other subject for someone to wait with her, were given the opportunity to await the beginning of their own task in various places. The choices subjects made are shown in Table 8.

Study II[10]

The subjects' willingness to return to the victim suggested the possibility of conducting a further test of an important hypothesis from an earlier study. Apparently the observers in the Lerner and Simmon study who had voluntarily chosen to aid an innocent victim but did not know if they were successful

[10]From Lerner (1968b).

TABLE 8

*Choice of Place to Await Onset
of Experiment[a]*

	Experimental conditions		
Subject's choice	Fate independent	Subject picks first	Other picks first
With other	4	11	12
No preference	10	3	4
With books	1	1	2

[a]Comparing Fates Independent with Fates not Independent (Subject Picks First and Other Picks First combined): $x^2 = 9.49$, $df = 2$, $p < .01$. From Lerner and Matthews (1967).

continued to ascribe undesirable characteristics to her. It was only when and if they learned that the victim's fate had been actually altered to end her suffering and compensate her that this form of rejection was given up by the observers.

It would seem only reasonable to expect that the personal act of attempting to aid a victim should be accompanied by at least neutral, if not positive, feeling for her. A similar prediction would also be required by dissonance or a balance-type theory. However, the data clearly supported the alternative hypothesis that the observers would reject the victim unless they learned that "justice" had been reestablished in the situation by the victim being compensated for her unmerited suffering.

These alternative hypotheses (balance *vs.* just world) were tested in the situation of indirect responsibility by allowing the subjects the opportunity to choose the return to the frightened victim before committing themselves to a devaluation of her. If the balance hypothesis is correct the subjects should not reject someone they have just chosen to help.

In addition to the condition in which the subject picks first, a condition was included in which the experimenter picked the slips designating each subject's fate. As in the earlier study, the subject was always placed in the desirable condition and the other was always to receive shock. For purposes of comparison some subjects participated with the expectation that neither they nor the other subject would receive electric shocks (Control — Control).

Results

As Table 9 shows, the subjects again tended to attribute responsibility to the person picking the slip of paper. Also, as in Study I, the majority of subjects in all conditions chose the opportunity to return to comfort the victim (Table 10). However, as Table 11 shows, contrary to the balance theory prediction, although most subjects offered to wait with the victim, they found her significantly less attractive when they felt responsible for her fate than when they felt the experimenter was responsible ($p < .05$). The mean rating of the victim's attractiveness given by the 19 subjects in the Subject-Picks Condition who chose to return to the victim was close to the mean rating by the seven who elected not to comfort the victim. (Return $\overline{X} = -7.74$, Not Return $\overline{X} = -10.00$.) In fact, of these same 26 subjects, 11 spontaneously offered to take the victim's place. (For purposes of the experiment these subjects were told that this was probably not possible since the specific arrangements were already in effect.) In spite of these attempts to act on the victim's behalf, it nevertheless appears that the determining factor in the subject's reaction to the victim was the fact that the victim would undergo electric shocks. It was sufficient, however, for the subjects to attribute responsibility to the experimenter for the victim's suffering in order for them to have no need to reject her. As in the "innocent victim" study, if the observers can bring themselves to "blame" the experimenter they do not need to devalue the person who is suffering.

TABLE 9

Attribution of Primary Responsibility
for Self and Other's Fate[a]

Subject's perception of responsibility	Experimental conditions	
	Experimenter picks first	Subject picks first
For subject's fate[b]		
Experimenter	17	1
Other	2	0
Self	4	23
Fate	1	2
For other's fate[c]		
Experimenter	17	1
Other	4	6
Self	2	17
Fate	1	2

[a] From Lerner (1968b).
[b] $\chi^2 = 29.58$, $df = 2$, $p < .001$. (Subjects answering "fate" dropped from analysis.)
[c] $\chi^2 = 26.45$, $df = 2$, $p < .001$. (Subjects answering "fate" dropped from analysis.)

TABLE 10

*Choice of Place to Await Onset
of Experiment[a]*

Subject's choice	Experimenter picks first	Subject picks first
With other	22	19
No preference	2	4
With magazines	0	3

[a]From Lerner (1968b).

TABLE 11

Ratings of Other's Attractiveness[a]

	Shock–Control	Shock–Money	Control–Control
Experimenter picks	-2.75 ($N = 12$)	+1.17 ($N = 12$)	+4.91 ($N = 11$)
Subject picks	-4.92 ($N = 13$)	-11.77 ($N = 13$)	

[a]From Lerner (1968b).

In the course of collecting data with male students for a somewhat different study, additional confirmation of the effect of this indirect level of responsibility was found. Although the males showed a slightly greater tendency to attribute responsibility to the experimenter, their reactions in general were quite similar to those of the females. When they picked first, 16 out of 24 subjects attributed primary responsibility to themselves for their own fate and 12 of 24 took responsibility for the other subject's fate. In addition the male subjects' ratings of the victim's attractiveness in this condition showed virtually the same amount of rejection as the females in the previous studies (Males: $\overline{X}$ = -9.01; Females: Study I, $\overline{X}$ = -8.16; Females: Study II, $\overline{X}$ = -13.26).

SUMMARY AND CONCLUSIONS

This program of research began with the assumption that people prefer to believe they live in a world where they can obtain those things they desire and avoid those they fear. This goal becomes translated into an attempt to believe that people in general deserve their fate either by virtue of their actions or because of their intrinsic personal worth. The research presented here points to what people may do to maintain this belief.

Some of the findings create an optimistic picture. For example, when given the opportunity, almost all bystanders voted to end the suffering of an innocent victim and provide her with some compensation. They could have voted to allow the suffering to continue, or merely to end the suffering, but instead they chose to balance out the victim's undeserved suffering with a substantial reward. Similarly, students were sufficiently motivated by a sense of what is just and fair to work hard to help someone who had been unjustly deprived of a reward while exhibiting little effort on behalf of someone who already had more than he deserved. It was also understandable to find that people who have themselves been unjustly harmed tend to be most concerned with seeing that others obtain the fate they deserve—they are most likely to help someone who has also been deprived and to deny help to another who has been overly favored. Apparently, receiving unmerited harm threatens the belief in a just world and the person will attempt by his own acts to create evidence to support this belief.

Unfortunately this optimistic picture shows only part of the effort people make to maintain the belief they live in a just world. In some circumstances when people are confronted with an innocent victim, they will derogate the victim in order to maintain this belief. For example, one group of studies reported here illustrates the strength of the person's desire to assign responsibility to someone for a victim's suffering. For most subjects the seemingly chance picking of a slip of paper out of a bowl seemed to serve as a basis for assigning responsibility for the victim's fate. When it was the victim who had picked the slip and brought about his own suffering, the subjects assigned responsibility for his fate to him and did not devalue him. However, when the subject picked the deciding slip of paper and thus assigned responsibility to himself for the victim's suffering, he then tended to find fault with the victim apparently in order to reduce this sense of guilt.

Apparently a similar rejection of the victim may occur for another reason—not out of an attempt to reduce guilt, but because of an inability to see any way in which the victim brought about his own suffering. When the person becomes aware of a victim who is clearly innocent of any act which might have brought about the suffering, he is confronted with a conflict. He can decide he lives in a cruel, unjust world where innocent people can suffer or that the only people who suffer in this world are those who deserve such a fate. The evidence supported the hypothesis that most people will persuade themselves that "innocent" victims are sufficiently undesirable people—that their suffering may be an appropriate fate. Even the apparently altruistically motivated victim tends to be seen as possessing undesirable attribute.[11]

It was also important, theoretically, to find that a factor which usually leads to attraction toward someone operates somewhat differently when that person is a victim. Choosing to act on someone's behalf should lead to increased attraction toward that person, or at least be accompanied by some neutral feelings. However, it was found that unless the benefactor is convinced that the victim's suffering is ended he will maintain negative attitudes toward the victim. Apparently in this way the person can preserve his belief that people deserve their fate.

The findings reported here seem to present fairly consistent and compelling support for the initial assumptions that people have a need to believe in a just world. One serious limitation of this approach to the understanding of reactions to victims is that it does not take into account social norms relevant to deciding who is a worthy or unworthy victim and what sanctions should be given for helping the unworthy or failing to help the worthy. In certain contexts the norms appear to be virtually irrelevant to the person's reaction to the victim. Most people would agree in principle that martyrs are to be admired, that innocent victims are to be approached with compassion, and that those who harm themselves are considered pitiful figures. However, the studies just reported indicate that when the person is confronted with an actual victim this order of liking or respect for various victims may be reversed.

In other contexts, norms appear to be employed only as a justification for certain behavior. For example, the norm which dictates that people should not allow themselves to be easily persuaded to accept harm in order to please

[11]There are two sets of findings reported here which seem contradictory. (a) Observers rejected the martyr victim. (b) Subjects reacted positively to the other person who saved them at her own expense from suffering. The essential difference, however, is that in the second set of findings there is no threat to the observer's desire for justice. The victim was seen as having brought her fate on herself—having caused her own suffering. Is this not true also of our Martyr-Victim? Probably not. Martyrs typically are not perceived as the direct agent or "cause" of their own suffering. Their good motives make them vulnerable to others who inflict the suffering on them. Thus, there is clearly an injustice involved.

others ("Don't be a sucker") was not the basis for the rejection of the Martyr-Victim in our study but rather appeared to offer an excuse for the rejection determined by the psychological process. The rejection came first—the norm provided the excuse and the label.

Other findings indicate a more subtle interplay of the psychological and normative factors in reactions to victims. For example, in one of the studies reported here, the subjects ascribed good performance to someone fortuitously rewarded and poor performance to someone who was deprived. This appears to be identification with the rewarded and rejection of the deprived. I would propose that the impetus for these reactions is the desire to assign responsibility. If the behavior in question is relatively neutral in its effects on the actor or on others, the assignmenr of responsibility may not have much effect on the perception of the actor; but if norms indicate that certain acts are thought to be in themselves good or bad, then judgment of the actor will parallel judgment of the acts themselves.

There is other evidence available which indicates that in some situations norms which are made salient may be the major determinant of what the person does in relation to a victim. For example, when someone is clearly dependent upon a more powerful person for the attainment of an important goal, there seems to be a general expectation that the powerful person should act on behalf of the dependent one—a potential victim (Berkowitz & Daniels, 1964; Schopler & Bateson, 1965). In contrast, there also seem to be norms in our society which allow people to pursue their own interests even when this leads to suffering for others (Lerner & Lichtman, 1968). The task of integrating the evidence available concerning the desire for justice and the various and often contradictory norms in society which define what is "just" must be the goal of future research and theory.

REFERENCES

Adams, J.S. Towards and understanding of inequity. *Journal of Abnormal and Social Psychology,* 1963, 67, 422–436.

Berkowitz, L., & Daniels, L. Affecting the salience of the social responsibility norm. *Journal of Abnormal and Social Psychology,* 1964, 68, 275–281.

Chein, I., Gerard, D.L., Lee, R.S., & Rosenfeld, E. *The road to H: Narcotics, delinquency, and social policy.* New York: Basic Books, 1964.

Davis, K.E., & Jones, E.E. Changes in interpersonal perception as a means of reducing cognitive dissonance. *Journal of Abnormal and Social Psychology.* 1960, 61, 402–410.

Dohrenwend, B.P., & Chin-Shong, E. Social status and attitudes toward psychological disorder: The problem of tolerance of deviation. *American Sociological Review,* 1967, 32, 427–433.

Eysenck, H.J. *The psychology of politics.* London: Routledge & Kegan Paul, 1954.

Foster, G.M. Peasant society and the image of limited good. *American Anthorpologist,* 1965, **67,** 293-315.

Glass, D.C. Changes in liking as a means of reducing cognitive discrepancies between self-esteem and aggression. *Journal of Personality,* 1964, **32,** 531-549.

Glueck, S., & Glueck, E. *Unraveling juvenile delinquency.* New York: Commonwealth Foundation, 1950.

Lazarus, R.S., Speisman, J.C., Mordkoff, A.M., & Davison, L.A. A laboratory study of psychological stress produced by a motion picture film. *Psychological Monographs,* 1962, **76** (34, Whole No. 553).

Lerner, M.J. The effect of responsibility and choice on a partner's attractiveness following failure. *Journal of Personality,* 1965, **33,** 178-187. (a)

Lerner, M.J. Evaluation of performance as a function of performer's reward and attractiveness. *Journal of Personality and Social Psychology,* 1965, **1,** 355-360. (b)

Lerner, M.J. Conditions eliciting acceptance or rejection of a martyr. Unpublished manuscript, University of Kentucky, 1968. (a)

Lerner, M.J. The effect of a negative outcome on cognitions of responsibility and attraction. Unpublished manuscript, University of Kentucky, 1968.(b)

Lerner, M.J., & Lichtman, R.R. Effects of perceived norms on attitudes and altruistic behavior toward a dependent other. *Journal of Personality and Social Psychology,* 1968, **9,** 226-232.

Lerner, M.J., & Matthews, G. Reactions to suffering of others under conditions of indirect responsibility. *Journal of Personality and Social Psychology,* 1967, **5,** 319-325.

Lerner, M.J., & Simmons, C.H. Observer's reaction to the "innocent victim": Compassion or rejection? *Journal of Personality and Social Psychology,* 1966, **4,** 203-210.

Lewis, O. Five families. New York: Basic Books, 1959.

Mizruchi, E.H. Social structure and anomia in a small city. *American Sociological Review,* 1960, **25,** 645-655.

Piliavin, I., Hardyck, J., & Vadim, T. *Reactions to a Victim in A Just or Non-Just World.* Unpublished paper, University of California, Berkeley, California, 1968.

Roberts, A.H., & Rokeach, M. Anomie, authoritarianism, and prejudice: A replication. *American Journal of Sociology,* 1956, **61,** 355-359.

Schopler, J., & Bateson, N. The power of dependence. *Journal of Personality and Social Psychology,* 1965, **2,** 247-254.

Simmons, C.H., & Lerner, M.J. Altruism as a search for justice. *Journal of Personality and Social Psychology,* 1968, **9,** 216-225.

Srole. L, Social integration and certain corollaries: An exploratory study; *American Sociological Review,* 1956, **21,** 709-717.

Stotland, E., & Dunn, R. Empathy, self-esteem and birth order. *Journal of Abnormal and Social Psychology,* 1963, **66,** 532-540.

Tannenbaum, P.H., & Gaer, E.P. Mood changes as a function of stress of protagonist and degree of identification in a film-viewing situation. *Journal of Personality and Social Psychology,* 1965, **2,** 612-616.

Walster, E. Assignment of responsibility for an accident. *Journal of Personality and Social Psychology,* 1966, **3,** 73-79.

AN ATTRIBUTION ANALYSIS OF SOME DETERMINANTS
OF RECIPROCATING A BENEFIT

John Schopler

Heider's (1958) comprehensive analysis of phenomenological causality has recently been systematized and extended by Kelley (1967). In Kelley's incisive analysis, attribution processes are relevant not only to the traditional sphere of person perception, but also to such apparently disparate topics as source credibility and labeling of emotions. I will, however, use the more conventional application of attribution concepts to the kinds of inferences a perceiver makes about another person's intentions as a way of understanding some of the determinants of reciprocating a benefit.

When one person receives a favor or a benefit from another, the recipient will feel some pressure to return the favor. Gouldner (1960) has suggested that the source of such pressure stems from the existence of a universal norm of reciprocity which prescribes an obligation to bestow benefits for past favors received. Common experience is often in accord with Gouldner's formulation as, for example, in the usual turn taking involved in such things as dinner invitations or corresponding with friends. Indeed, a tribute to the strength of the reciprocity norm can be seen in a Canadian effort to curb drunkenness by prohibiting anyone in a bar from buying a "round." Some recent experimental studies have also shown how a prior benefit will instigate reciprocation. It has been shown that someone who has received prior help, compared to someone who has been refused prior help, when given the opportunity will provide more help for his benefactor (Goranson & Berkowitz, 1966) or even for a new partner (Berkowitz

& Daniels, 1964). In addition, it has been shown that more reward was reciprocated to a donor the more he had given in the past (Pruitt, 1968).

Gouldner contended that reciprocity is a universal norm but also maintained that it is not unconditional. The purpose of this paper is to understand the conditional aspects of reciprocity by making an attribution analysis of the determinants effecting amount of reciprocation. The basic contention, mentioned peripherally by Gouldner, is that a recipient's reaction to a benefit depends upon the kind of attribution he makes with respect to the donor's intentions. The primary task of the recipient is to differentiate the extent to which the donor is acting out of self interest from the extent to which his motives are solely confined to helping the recipient. When the proximal cause of the donor's act is attributed solely to the recipient's needs or wishes, it will be expected to produce maximum reciprocation because the donor's costs were incurred on behalf of the recipient, who is then uniquely responsible for compensation. The donor will be seen as "generous," or "altruistic." In the limiting case, the donor will be seen as attaining only those rewards he generates for himself from the knowledge of having conformed to the social responsibility norm. On the other hand, it is not only of Greeks bearing gifts we beware. When the cause of any donor's act is attributed to needs or wishes of the donor himself opposite effects should occur because the donor is acting on behalf of his own interests. The donor will be seen as "selfish," "manipulative," etc., and reciprocation will be minimal. Reciprocation may not even be an issue because the potential recipient may merely refuse to accept the proffered benefit. For convenience the former attribution processes will be called "recipient instigated" and the latter will be termed "donor instigated."

The recipient's task of assessing the donor's motive appears to be particularly relevant to the reciprocity sequence, which involves, as Heider (1958) has pointed out, a degree of cooperation between donor and recipient. In distinction to situations involving infliction of harm, in which unilateral decisions are usually implemented, the potential recipient must ordinarily decide whether or not to accept a proffered benefit. Furthermore, a benefit in this context must result from an act which is not part of the explicit role requirements linking the actors. Situations involving reciprocity may be distinguished from ordinary social exchange in this respect.

PREVIOUS RESEARCH

Before discussing the implications of an attribution analysis, it may be well to summarize briefly the results of three studies which have shown some conditions placed on the extent to which a benefit is reciprocated. The previously cited Goranson and Berkowitz study is relevant. In their study help was given signficiantly more to a partner whose prior help had been portrayed as "voluntary" than to a partner whose help was "compulsory." Other restrictions on an unconditional reciprocity principle have also been demonstrated. Kiesler (1966) has suggested that the amount of attraction a recipient feels for the donor depends upon the appropriateness of the favor to the role requirements linking the participants. In her study, subjects worked on a task with a partner who was actually an accomplice and who won most of the money during the experiment. Those subjects who were led to believe that they were working cooperatively with the accomplice were more attracted to him when he "shared" his winnings than when he did not. A slight trend in the opposite direction was demonstrated for those subjects who thought they were competing with the accomplice. Another restriction on the conditions arousing the norm of reciprocity is suggested by Brehm and Cole (1966). They argue that if a favor constrains the recipient's feeling of freedom, the recipient will experience "reactance" and will be motivated to reduce the reactance by engaging in behaviors which will restore his freedom. In their experiment subjects were led to believe they were participating in a first-impression experiment the importance of which was heightened for half the subjects and lowered for the other half. In each importance condition, half of the subjects received a favor (an unsolicited soft drink) from their partner prior to rating him. Reactance was presumably greatest for subjects who thought they were in an important experiment and who received a favor from someone they were about to rate. Brehm and Cole found no differences in ratings of the partner; however, subsequent to the ratings, there was a striking difference in the help offered the donor who had been assigned the task of stacking sheets of paper by the experimenter. For subjects who had been bestowed a favor, almost all in the low importance condition did reciprocate. Of the subjects who had received no favor, roughly half "reciprocated" in both the high and low importance conditions.[1]

---

[1]Subjects who have not received a prior favor can hardly be viewed as "reciprocating." The magnitude of their responses establishes a base against which to compare the effects of the favor.

I will now turn to the attribution analysis and attempt to fit the results of these three studies into a general framework. If an attribution about the donor's intention is a central mediating process determining amount of reciprocation, then it will be necessary to specify the conditions which determine the direction of the recipient's attributions. There are three classes of variables I believe to be particularly critical in determining this direction. Each of them will be discussed in turn.

THE EXISTENCE OF EXTRANEOUS REWARDS

FOR THE DONOR

One compelling circumstance producing an attribution of donor instigation is the presence of rewards, other than those directly related to enacting the favor, which the donor might be attaining. For example, if the recipient possesses resources he believes to be valuable to the donor, the donor's favor is likely to be seen as caused by his desire to obtain future benefits from the recipient. The recipient is not the only source of potential reward for the donor. In some circumstances donors provide benefits because of such factors as conformity pressures. The lower reciprocation in the Goranson and Berkowitz "compulsory" condition may, in part, have been mediated by the recipient's perceiving the donor as obtaining the rewards attendant on conforming to the experimenter's dictates.

In some instances the donor may make a choice which clearly specifies both the rewards he is gaining and the amount of benefit he is giving to the recipient. Pruitt's (1967) decomposed prisoner's dilemma games fit such a requirement. He has shown how separate but algebraically equal game formats produce very different levels of cooperation. Although Pruitt provides no explanation for the occurrence of high cooperation with some games and low cooperation with others, an attribution analysis suggests one possibility. Those decomposed formats in which the cooperative choice necessitates simultaneously gaining nothing (or incurring costs) to provide the partner with substantial gains are most likely to be attributed by the partner to recipient instigation. The occurrence of a cooperative choice should then be reciprocated by subsequent cooperation. Pruitt's results are in keeping with this formulation. His decomposed game II showed less cooperation than the standard game, while decomposed games III and IV showed significantly more cooperation than the standard game. The cooperative choice in game II was, "6 for me, 6 for him," while the cooperative choices in games III and IV were, respectively, "0 for me, 12 for him" and

"-6 for me, 18 for him." Those alterations in the structure of the game which give the illusion that one player has eschewed any rewards, or has incurred costs, in order to provide gains for the second player will be most likely to be attributed to recipient instigation and therefore to increase reciprocation.

SYNCHRONIZATION OF BENEFIT WITH THE
RECIPIENT'S NEEDS

If a benefit uniquely fits the recipient's needs or desires, it will be attributed to recipient instigation, while if it does not, it will be attributed to donor instigation. Of particular relevance in this connection is whether or not the donor could have knowledge about the recipient's needs. In interactions involving unacquainted participants the critical feature is whether the recipient's overt circumstances are such that his needs may be inferred unambiguously. The openness of the recipient's need state will make a benefit appear as if it is uniquely inspired by his needs. A woman who is stranded with a flat tire will gratefully accept offers of help. I believe this to be the case even though factually such an attribution may not always be warranted. Bryan and Test (1967) noted that among the people (virtually all males) who stopped to help the confederate with her flat tire, a large portion made "pick-up" attempts. Nevertheless, without additional evidence the recipient whose needs are publicly evident is likely to make an attribution of personal sacrifice to those offering help.

Inferring needs from overt cues is sometimes a hazardous task. The chief difficulty confronting a potential donor is that his inferences about the recipient's needs cannot merely be accurate, in an absolute sense, but must correspond with the recipient's own phenomenology. This difficulty is accentuated by the fact that the donor's assessment of the recipient's needs are clearly expressed by the content of the offered benefit. He runs the risk, however, of having misjudged the recipient's view of himself and of having his offer attributed to donor instigation. The dilemma of how to react to the physically handicapped comes to mind. For example, I have from time to time offered to help a blind person cross a busy street. The number of times I have been seen as a good Samaritan are roughly equal to the frequency with which I have been viewed as a meddlesome fool.

Benefits differ on a variety of attributes. One dimension, which is usually positively correlated with the openness of the recipient's needs, is whether the favor is universally rewarding (i.e., over many situations) or only rewarding under specific circumstances. Obviously a universal favor is more likely to be seen as donor instigated than a particularistic favor. Money, soft drinks, etc., are likely to be more suspect than offers of such things as iodine for a cut. Second, favors vary on the magnitude of the reward value they contain. The principle of reciprocity implies that the greater the reward value received the greater will be the amount reciprocated. The general statement does not specify the weights to be assigned to the donor's costs and to the recipient's benefit. The question of amount of reciprocation becomes especially poignant when these two factors are not correlated as, for example, when one is invited to a dinner in which the hostess has burned the chateaubriand. In any event, there is undoubtedly a limit to the linear relation between reciprocation and increasing benefits. That limit is set by the recipient's circumstances. Magnitudes which exceed those warranted by the need will suggest a donor source of motivation and should then show an inverse relation with amount of reciprocation. It would probably be difficult to give away $1 bills to strangers whereas the senior Rockefeller is said to have had little trouble dispensing dimes. Similarly, if it is assumed that a subject's ratings of positive feelings toward an experiment, when he is promised a reward for participation, can represent reciprocation by the subject, another possible interpretation can be added to the growing list of explanations for the results reported by Festinger and Carlsmith (1959). Subjects who were promised excessive amounts of money for publicly stating how much fun an objectively dull experiment had been, rated the dull task as less enjoyable than subjects who had been promised a small reward. That is, the excessive reward may have instigated a donor attribution and resulted in less reciprocation. Such an interpretation is consistent with Nuttin's (1966) findings that excessive rewards, compared to small rewards, produced less favorable task ratings even when the public advocacy was in a consonant direction.

CONTEXT OF THE RELATIONSHIP

Any interaction occurs in some social context in which a particular set of normative prescriptions is salient. Among other things such norms prescribe the limits of acceptable behavior. Favors that represent out of role behavior, or, in Kiesler's terms, inappropriate acts, will be more likely to be attributed to donor instigations than acts which are role relevant. The single exception to this generalization may occur when all of the variables discussed above are at values which induce a recipient instigated attribution. In that case, an inappropriate act may still be attributed to the donor, but may then merely heighten the perception of the strength of his desire to help. Kiesler's concept of appropriateness can be seen as a violation of specific relationship norms. Her results, for liking of the partner, can be viewed as a function of the subject attributing donor motives when the experimenter's definition of the situation is violated. In fact, a direct attribution of self-interest is probably the major determinant of the liking ratings, because her results depend primarily on the very low increased liking scores of the accomplice who was supposed to share, but did not. The Brehm and Cole data could also be seen in these terms. In an important experiment involving mutual ratings, the favor was beyond the bounds of expected behavior and was therefore attributed to donor instigation. Vaida Thompson and I have completed an experiment in which we predicted, and found, that a favor would be reciprocated more than no favor when it was in keeping with the definition of the situation, but would be reciprocated less than no favor when it was beyond the definition of the situation (Schopler & Thompson, 1968).

The attribution analysis detailed above suggests that reciprocation will be maximal when the recipient attributes recipient instigated motives to the donor. Attributions in this direction will occur when no extraneous sources of rewards (from the recipient's point of view) exist for the donor, when the benefit is synchronized with the recipient's needs and when the donor's act is in keeping with the context of the relationship. To the extent to which these conditions do not apply, the donor is likely to be seen as instrumentally motivated and reciprocation will be lowered.

In closing I would like to point out one paradoxical implication of this analysis when it is extended to the conditions under which help will be offered. Although reciprocation may be highest when donors are seen to be motivated by no other rewards than the satisfaction involved in complying to the social responsibility norm, these are scarcely the conditions most likely to induce someone to offer help. The chances of a potential donor actually providing help increases as donor rewards increase. The research evidence for this point is quite strong. For example, increased help has been shown for recipients who possess valuable resources (Pruitt, 1968), for recipients who are liked (Daniels & Berkowitz, 1963), and for lower levels of cost of the donor (Schopler & Bateson, 1965). Studies focusing on the social responsibility norm have been specifically designed to eliminate, or hold constant, extraneous sources of rewards. Yet, in considering the wider context of conditions which will induce help, the donor's reward potential is probably a much more potent variable than is conformity to the social responsibility norm. In naturally occurring relationships, some accommodation must take place between the opposing conditions likely to instigate help and reciprocation. Situations fraught with costs and bare of rewards are likely to elicit helping responses from only the hard core conformers to the social responsibility norm. It may be that one calculation made by the potential donor is to participate in situations where his motives will not be suspect and where he can covertly rely on gaining rewards because of the reciprocity norm.

REFERENCES

Berkowitz, L., & Daniels, L.R. Affecting the salience of the social responsibility norm: Effects of past help on the response to dependency relationships. *Journal of Abnormal and Social Psychology,* 1964, 68, 275–281.

Brehm, J.W., & Cole, A.H. Effect of a favor which reduces freedom. *Journal of Personality and Social Psychology,* 1966, 3, 420–426.

Bryan, J.H., & Test, M.A. Models and helping: Naturalistic studies in aiding behavior. *Journal of Personality and Social Psychology,* 1967, 6, 400–407.

Daniels, L.R., & Berkowitz, L. Liking and response to dependency relationships. *Human Relations,* 1963, 16, 141–148.

Festinger, L., & Carlsmith, J.M. Cognitive consequences of forced compliance. *Journal of Abnormal and Social Psychology,* 1959, 58, 203–210.

Goranson, R.E., & Berkowitz, L. Reciprocity and responsibility reactions to prior help. *Journal of Personality and Social Psychology,* 1966, 3, 227–232.

Gouldner, A.W. The norm reciprocity: A preliminary statement. *American Sociological Review,* 1960, 25, 161–178.

Heider, F. *The psychology of interpersonal relations.* New York: Wiley, 1958.

Kelley, H.H. Attribution theory in social psychology. In D. Levine (Ed.), *Nebraska symposium on motivation.* Lincoln, Neb.: University of Nebraska Press, 1967, Pp. 192–238.

Kiesler, S.B. The effect of perceived role requirements on reactions to favor-doing. *Journal of Experimental Social Psychology,* 1966, 2, 198–210.

Nuttin, J. Attitude change after rewarded dissonant and consonant "forced compliance." *International Journal of Psychology,* 1966, 1, 39–57.

Pruitt, D.G. Reward structure and cooperation: The decomposed prisoner's dilemma game. *Journal of Personality and Social Psychology,* 1967, 7, 21–27.

Pruitt, D.G. Reciprocity and credit building in a laboratory dyad. *Journal of Personality and Social Psychology,* 1968, 8, 143–147.

Schopler, J., & Bateson, N. The power of dependence. *Journal of Personality and Social Psychology,* 1965, 2, 247–254.

Schopler, J., & Thompson, V. Role of attribution processes in mediating amount of reciprocity for a favor. *Journal of Personality and Social Psychology,* 1968, 10, 243–250.

NATURALISTIC STUDIES OF ALTRUISM

THE RESCUERS: MOTIVATIONAL HYPOTHESES ABOUT CHRISTIANS WHO SAVED JEWS FROM THE NAZIS

Perry London[1]

The study I am going to describe was never completed, and since the sample involved was small and specialized and the data obtained from it were broad and complex, they were never formally analyzed. Even so, the history of the study, its problems, its potentials, and the hypotheses to which it led, all seemed so provocative and germane to understanding altruism that we felt it would be worth reporting despite its anecdotal limitations. Essentially a personality research project, its aim was to find out if there are stable traits of character connected with the extremely altruistic acts such as those in which the Christians in Nazi-occupied Europe risked their lives trying to save Jews. The study was engendered by the Eichmann trial, conceived and promoted by a Rabbi, publicized by a famous television reporter and by a best-selling novelist, and sponsored by a museum. It was funded (directly or indirectly) by an anthropological foundation, an educational business, a federal agency, and private contributions, as well as by the museum. The study, furthermore, was conducted by three psychologists and a social worker with much help from history documentation institutes in the United States, Europe, and Israel and the consultation services of some outstand-

[1]Part of this investigation and the preparation of this report was supported by a Public Health Service Research Scientist Development Award Number K3-MH-31, 209 from the National Institute of Mental Health, and by the generous provision of facilities by Dr. Seymour Fox, Dean of the School of Education, Hebrew University, Jerusalem, Israel.

ing social and behavioral scientists, and, most importantly, with the cooperation of often embarrassed, shy, and modest subjects. Despite this estimable help, the project never got entirely off the ground and came to a grinding halt after 4 years of sporadic functioning, basically for lack of funds. Since the primary data sources were people, the youngest of whom had reached adulthood before the end of World War II, the attrition rate of potential subjects is both high and accelerating; by now, the study could perhaps no longer be finished.even if it were to be funded.

The idea for the study originated in the mind of Rabbi Harold Schulweis of Oakland, California. In the horrors revealed by the Eichmann trial, he was struck by the lone testimony given about a Christian who had rescued Jews from a concentration camp. Rabbi Schulweis saw in this "a glimmer of redemption" from the "horrendous image of man" which the trial seemed to reveal. A magazine article of his, urging that these people be identified and honored, attracted widespread attention, and on Christmas Day, 1962, NBC commentator Chet Huntley presented a network television documentary in which some rescuers were interviewed and their stories told. The program was produced by Gerald Green (better known to the public as the author of *The Last Angry Man* and *His Majesty O'Keefe)*, who later wrote a novel, *The Legion of Noble Christians,* revolving around the study of the rescuers.

Rabbi Schulweis gradually got the idea that in the long run mankind would be better served by studying the rescuers than by honoring them, so he organized The Institute for Righteous Acts, Study and Documentation Center, which was incorporated by Oakland's J.L. Magnes Memorial Museum, and began to seek funds and scholars to study the personality traits of rescuers. He found a modicum of both. In addition to private donations to the museum, small grants from the Wenner-Gren Foundation for Anthropological Research and from the Educational Testing Service helped complete a pilot study. James H. Bryan of Northwestern University, Robert Kurtzman of the Jerusalem Municipality, David Rosenhan of Swarthmore College, and I did the study collaboratively.

Our initial goal was to identify Christians who had, to one degree or another, risked their lives in an effort to rescue Jews from the Nazis all over Europe. We then wanted to see if we could, in the course of interviewing them, identify some stable personality traits or characteristics which might be related to altruism. If we succeeded in isolating such traits, we hoped to undertake a number of systematic studies to compare different kinds of altruistic behavior in different social contexts, to compare altruistic with other kinds of interpersonal behavior, and eventually to sneak up on a general understanding of the personal and situational dynamics of social deviance. The study of the rescuers seemed ideally suited to launch all of this, not so much because of its inherent drama and historical interest as because of its inherent complexity and the demands it placed on us for confronting important problems of theory and method. As it happened, the problems of theory and method were soluble, but those of funding were insuperable, and while many of the ideas and experiences born of this project continue to flourish, especially in the social deviance studies and laboratory experiments on altruism by James Bryan and David Rosenhan, the initial project only completed some pilot work before it languished.

Our strategy for the pilot study was quite straightforward. We developed a standardized interview schedule, and began seeking out rescuers and rescued people who had moved to the United States. We did a number of interviews in this country, but Kurtzman did most of them in Israel. Although many of those we contacted were reluctant to grant us an interview at first, all of them finally agreed to talk to us and, once they started talking, willingly gave us the information we sought. We ended up with tape-recorded interviews of 27 rescuers and 42 rescued people, all of whom had emigrated from Europe since 1945. These people may be consistently different in important characteristics from rescuers who stayed in Europe. Thus, we cannot generalize from this sample to the majority of those who aided Jews during World War II. The following discussion, then, concerns a limited, albeit interesting, population of rescuers.

Our interview schedules were constructed in a way that allowed them to be used across several different samples, to be coded for quantitative analysis, and to yield a maximum of biographical information, as well as to tap attitudes and values. With only minor variations, we were able to use the same schedules for interviewing rescuers and rescued people in the present study, call girls in social deviance studies (which Bryan has subsequently published), and freedom riders in Rosenhan's work (this volume). The general pattern of the interviews, in all cases, was to begin by asking the subject to tell, in his own words, what the relevant incidents were, then to inquire about the background events that led to them, and only parenthetically to ask about personal details, attitudes, and seemingly incidental aspects of the individual's experience which would fill in the information we were seeking about personality characteristics. The interviewer worked with a detailed checklist of subject areas, all of which had to be completed before he could terminate the session (or series), and none of which had to be taken in any special order. From the subject's own point of view, therefore, much of the personal information he communicated was spontaneous, and the setting, despite checklists and tape recorders, was friendly and informal. From the interviewer's point of view, he was able to approach sensitive material obliquely and tactfully, without being secretive or deceptive and without sacrificing questions that he needed to ask, or making the subject feel uncomfortable or "like a guinea pig." Since all the rescuers available to us for the pilot study had already experienced some publicity, they were understandably sensitive on these scores.

The limited extent of the study prevented us from drawing "conclusions," but it did not stop us from gaining "impressions," two sets of which deserve communication. The first, derived from the variety of material revealed in our interviews, concerns the enormous complexity of defining altruism and studying it meaningfully. The second, deduced from apparent consistencies in the material, suggests to us some hypotheses about personality traits that may predispose people to altruistic acts.

Almost from the beginning it was clear that no easy criterion existed for deciding what kind of rescues to consider altruistic actions. In some cases, an individual's rescue effort was a small part of an underground organization's activity which involved little personal risk to the rescuer. In others, rescue efforts involved life-or-death risks, sometimes so often that they became almost routine for the rescuer. In still a third type of case the rescuer began helping someone in a relatively safe or minor way and, as circumstances changed, found himself embroiled in major ways because there was no longer a safe or easy alternative.

We often think of altruism in terms of relatively simple motives and acts, defining an altruist as one who confers a benefit on someone else without profit to himself, or without intention of profiting from his act, or with positive motives to be helpful. The behavior of rescuers cannot easily be classified by any simplistic definition, however. Some were paid a great deal of money for their efforts, usually in connection with essential parts of their operations, such as buying forged papers, food, or arms, or bribing officials. Some spent fortunes and were left destitute as a result. Some who had almost nothing to begin with shared it with good grace—or without.

In all of the behavioral categories indicated, motives were still less easily classified than were activities—because motives change, because they were conflicting, or because they were obscure. Some rescuers undertook the work deliberately and with benevolence aforethought, in utter secrecy sometimes, and with no possibility of outside help; others began it as an incidental part of other work, responding essentially to social pressure to participate and to social reinforcement for doing so; still others "fell in" to the rescue business thoughtlessly, mistakenly, or for irrelevant or selfish reasons. Some rescuers were fanatically religious, others were devout atheists. Some were deeply affiliated with Jews, others were anti-Semitic. And on and on.

It is difficult to estimate how often initial involvement with rescue work was confounded with a misunderstanding of the risks involved or of how long it might be necessary to continue taking them, but it was not a rare event in our sample. The most famous rescuer we interviewed, a German who devoted himself for almost 4 years to this work at fantastic personal cost and saved about 200 people, reported his initiation into the business with retrospective good humor, as follows: "I was believing in 1942 that the war will be another year. It cannot be any longer. It's impossible. I was then a rich man. I had about 300,000 or 400,000 marks, and I started with one person, then six people, from there to 50, then 100. . . . People came to me—maybe they like my looks—I don't know what it was—asking me very bluntly and very frankly, 'Will you save me?' " It began, for him, when his secretary came to him, said that the Germans were going to kill her Jewish husband, and asked for help. He thought at first that she was crazy, and told her, "Germans don't do things like that!" But she was convinced that they were going to kill all the Jews in town so, although he felt it was not true, he agreed to let her husband stay in his office over the weekend. Through this act of compassion he found himself in the business of rescue. Once he found that the Jews' fears were justified, he was pulled in deeper and deeper. He had access to resources that few others had, he had compassion for his hapless clients, and he had the personal resources of wit, tenacity, and courage to remain with it for years. There were several such cases on a small scale, where a rescuer had taken someone for a few nights until some underground organization could transport them over the border or they could otherwise escape. The pickup or the opportunity to leave never came and the rescuer's choice was turning the people over to the Nazis, which meant death, or keeping them—hiding the adult, passing the child off as his own.

Even though starting to do rescue work may have been a function of situational variables or miscalculations, sticking with it for long periods of time usually was not. In the course of our interviews, we formulated three hypotheses about structural personality traits which would seem to be related to altruistic behavior. These characteristics were: (a) A spirit of adventurousness, (b) an intense identification with a parental model of moral conduct, and (c) a sense of being socially marginal.

Almost all the rescuers interviewed, regardless of where they came from and of what they did to fall into our sample, seemed to possess a fondness for adventure. They had not only a desire to help, but also a desire to participate in what were inherently exciting activities. For example, we interviewed a man from the Netherlands who responded to a question about his recreational preferences by describing what had been his favorite adolescent hobby—racing motorcycles, especially over narrow boards on top of deep ditches. His work as a rescuer in the Dutch underground was a fairly tame job, but he and his friends had a sort of extracurricular hobby of putting sugar in the gas tanks of German army trucks. This was not part of any organized sabotage, just something they did for fun. His daughter was present during the interview, and he asked her if she remembered the underground jobs that she had done, Since she had been about 5 years old at the time she did not remember much, so he described for us how she had carried papers hidden under loaves of bread on her bicycle from one part of town to another. They assumed, apparently correctly, that the Germans would not stop a little girl on a bicycle. Had they discovered the nature of her errand, they might have killed her and her family. In telling about these episodes, the father did not dwell much on the danger involved; he described them as great adventures. If thoughts about the danger occurred to him, as they surely must have, then either they did not faze him or he had long since forgotten that aspect of the events.

A number of people described in varying degrees their general adventurousness. One East European rescuer spontaneously described a sort of private anti-Fascist campaign he conducted in several places after World War II, evidently blowing up the property of assorted extreme right-wing organizations and apparently becoming much sought after by the police. The German rescuer mentioned earlier had been a Nazi party member in 1934, was thrown out for denouncing a local party leader (not for ideological reasons but because he didn't like him and "had something on him" he could make public), and successfully avoided the draft—something quite rare in Germany in World War II. His civilian skills were important to the German war effort, and this put him in a position where he was able to develop an elaborate rescue operation which involved an underground railroad 1000 kilometers long and included many phony branch offices of his railroad engineering business. Most of this was accomplished after he had a severe heart attack from which he never completely recovered. Along with the efficiency and genius of this man went a wild adventurous streak, perhaps best illustrated, in a story well documented by the Polish government, by his colorful rescue of a Polish underground leader from jail. He did this by walking into the place and telling the jailers that he had secret verbal orders to take the man; they were too secret to be written and from too high a source to be questioned, implying that the orders came from Hitler. The jailers let him take the man out. Asked how he worked up the nerve for this scheme, he gleefully told the interviewers, "You have to understand the German mentality! I know, I'm a German, and you have to know how to talk to Germans. You have to be authoritative and you have to bluff them, and that's what I did! "

Two other personal characteristics that our subjects seemed to share gave rise to a single hypothesis. We observed, first of all, that almost all the rescuers tended to have very strong identifications with parents, usually more with one parent than with the other, but not necessarily with the same-sex parent. Second, the parent with whom they had the strong identification tended to be a very strong moralist—not necessarily religious, but holding very firm opinions on moral issues and serving as a model of moral conduct.

The strong identification with a moralizing parent is clear in the interview with the German rescuer. "I come from a poor family. My mother came from Hesse which was mainly small farmers. ... I believe that is part of my personality. You inherit something from your parents, from the grandparents. My mother said to me when we were small, and even when we were bigger, she said to me—she ran the family, my mother, and my father was number two; he could not speak so much in front of people—'Regardless of what you do with your life, be honest. When it comes the day you have to make a decision, make the right one. It could be a hard one. But even the hard ones should be the right ones.' I didn't know what it means . . ." He went on to talk about his mother in glowing terms, about how she had told him how to live; how she had taught him morals, and how she had exemplified morality for him. Asked if she was a member of a church, "Sure, we had to be," he said. "Protestant?" we asked. "Lutheran Protestant—that is another thing. Protest is Protestant. I protest. Maybe I inherit it from way back . . . my mother . . . always in life she gave me so much philosophy. She didn't go to high school, only elementary school, but so smart a woman, wisdom, you know. It is born in you . . . ." When he later described his father at greater length, he said his father was weak and incapable of raising the children, that his father did not set the moral standards for the family, and that his father's moral posture was not significant for the family, only his mother's.

The final characteristic we noted often among our rescuers was social marginality. The German, for example, grew up in Prussia, but his mother was from Hesse and spoke a different German dialect than that common in Prussia. He said that he always felt friendless. His family was nominally Lutheran, but his mother refused to go to church, although his father went—probably the reverse of a typical German family's religious habits. His mother had no political affiliation, but was a fierce anti-Nazi. He himself grew up stuttering (a habit of which he successfully cured himself). Apparently these experiences in marginality served him well when he had to work in isolation for 4 years. His rescue work was originally in Russia, and his underground network eventually spread into Western Europe, involving hundreds of people without his ever revealing his activities to more than two people other than those he actually rescued.

Social marginality and intense identification with one parent were not always obviously related to each other. A Belgian woman who spent years in Nos Petits, the Belgian underground, came from a family that lived for generations in the same house in the same town, characteristics we found among many in our sample. This woman so strongly identified with her father and in describing her family talking so glowingly and at such length about him that the interviewer had the impression her mother was dead. At some point he asked outright if her mother "was also living at home." She answered, "Yes. My father was in business before the great depression, he was sort of a self-made man, very bright man. He had a lot of social confidence. That was the atmosphere at home." She made no other reference to her mother. Her social marginality did not involve her relationship with her parents, however, but her intense personal involvement with Jews.

The strong parental identification does not seem to have been related to any gender link. Another rescuer we interviewed was a Seventh Day Adventist minister who very strongly identified with his father, also an Adventist minister from the Netherlands, a country where almost everyone is either Calvinist or Catholic. Seventh Day Adventists were very marginal socially and not always treated kindly in Holland; his father spent considerable time in jail. Although this minister described himself as mildly anti-Semitic, like his father, during the war he organized a very effective and large-scale operation for rescuing Dutch Jews. The reason he gave for doing so was simply that it was a Christian's duty.

Some kind of active moralism seemed characteristic of all the rescuers and usually was related to parental morality rather than to a specific kind of ideology. The Dutch minister saw himself as motivated by a transcendental religious doctrine, the German and Belgian rescuers by clearly social kinds of morality, but all were acting out roles which their moral parental models would have lauded on the same grounds.

The same general attributes seem to pertain to other rescuers, even when described only briefly. There was a Polish woman who hid two girls from the Nazis throughout the war. During the war she picked up a Russian prisoner and hid him too. She was of peasant origin, self-educated, a devout, informed Roman Catholic, extremely honest and exacting of herself and others. She was a schoolteacher, rather unpopular because she set high standards, was critical of others, intolerant of the slightest hypocrisy, and an independent thinker. In history classes, for example, she eschewed false patriotism and was even critical of Polish national unity—a very unusual stand in Poland. In Communist Poland, therefore, she preferred teaching at the elementary level to avoid voicing her views. She is against the communist regime, and, although she was appreciative of the universal education available, she complained that students in postwar Poland lacked interest and discipline and were indifferent to values. Her husband, like his father and sister, was an Anthropopathist. She told us she was a practicing religionist because this expressed her nonconformity and gave her a challenge. Although in many opinions quite liberal, she was a person of puritanical and Spartan habits, with low tolerance for physical weakness and pampering.

A final example is a woman whose father was a miner; he foresaw the massacre of the Jews and became involved in helping save some. He was supposedly killed in a mine accident, but was possibly murdered. His daughter and wife carried on this man's work after his death. The daughter, whom we interviewed, had been in bad health, but with the great responsibilities she assumed— including an increasing risk to her life—her health improved. She even replaced her father in the mines. When we talked to her, she told us that she believed the holocaust happened because the Jews did not keep the laws of the Bible, and that the destruction visited upon them would soon engulf other people. She had a fanatical belief in a God of rewards and punishments, and felt that her reward for helping the Jews was improved health. Later she suffered a mental breakdown, during which she quoted passages from the Old Testament to prove that man suffers for his own misdeeds.

In summary, it seemed to us that a zest for adventure and the workings of chance both were important in the initiation of rescue behavior, but that, in all of those we interviewed, strong identification with a very moralistic parental model and the experience of social marginality gave people the impetus and endurance to continue their rescue activities. This identification did not seem to be related to extraordinary warmth or closeness in family relationships, to general adequacy of parental models, or to the rescuer's social competence; it seemed, in fact, to be more often positively related to social marginality. I should point out again that all of the people we interviewed were a long way from their native country at the time we talked to them, and perhaps rescuers who did not emigrate were not marginal people. Not all of our sample, moreover, expressed feelings of marginality, though circumstances often were such that the interviewer could not help but infer it. What was expressed directly most often was the admiration for a parent or adherence to his strong moralistic opinions.

The lacunae in our data are so great that we cannot even conjecture about the generality of our hypotheses. The situations which favored or inhibited rescue work in different countries of Europe and at different times should have been separately considered. Differences in Nazi policy or ability to implement it, the sentiments of the civilian population toward the Jews, the effectiveness of resistance movements, even the physical terrain were all interacting factors in the survival or destruction of the Jews and, to some extent, in the initiation or success of rescue work. We lacked means to sample separately by these categories, or to learn who died, or where, in rescue work, or to probe who perhaps did not persist in it and finally betrayed their clients. The original design of the study was to compare among people still living in each country representative samples of rescuers, nonparticipants, and known collaborators. Our initial thought was that, in terms of personality characteristics, we might find the same general traits among collaborationists and rescuers; that is, we would find similarities among people whose behavior was deviant in either direction from general social re- actions to Nazi occupation. None of this was possible for us to do, though a number of excellent documentation centers in Europe, Israel, and America make the work of identification and location quite feasible.

One must not forget, however, how small the total population of rescuers was to begin with. The complete survey we had hoped to do could only have emphasized the gruesome truth that while most people in Nazi-occupied Europe did not collaborate with the Germans in the massacre of the Jews, neither did they take active steps to prevent or interfere with it. This very fact gives the tiny "saving remnant" an importance entirely disproportionate to their numbers. Their capacity for individual action on behalf of fellow men and in the face of social isolation or of lethal peril is a hopeful augur for preserving human dignity and decency in a steadily more complex and imperiled world.

THE NATURAL SOCIALIZATION
OF ALTRUISTIC AUTONOMY[1]

David Rosenhan

This paper describes a study of people who were engaged in activities that reflected concern for others in the context of the civil rights movement. This altruism was either of the normative or socially autonomous sort, which is to say that the behavior was either supported by local conditions of reward and punishment, or it seemed stimulated by internalized altruistic concerns. While the original intent of this study was to examine both normative and autonomous altruistic behavior, and while data for both categories are offered, our focal examination will center on two types of autonomous altruism.

Altruism, in its widest sense, describes a great variety of behaviors which range from doing small favors to saving lives in crises, from "doing good" to inordinate selflessness. We feel intuitively that the small acts of altruism which we encounter in our daily lives and in which we are all participants to a great extent are not identical with the dramatic acts of altruism which often make newspaper headlines and which, for the majority of us, do not exist in experience but only in our fantasy lives. We shall mainly be concerned with the latter kind of altruism but will need to understand something of the former kind before we begin.

[1]Supported in part by grants from NICHHD (1 PO 1 HD 01762) to the Educational Testing Service and NIMH (MH-HD 13893 and MH-16462) to the writer. Gratitude is expressed to Anita F. Thompson and Irene Kostin who assisted in the conduct of the study, to Mollie Rosenhan for her theoretical and literary observations, and to Alice Isen and Dean Peabody who commented on an earlier version of this paper.

NORMATIVE AND AUTONOMOUS ALTRUISM

Let us call the daily helpfulness in which we engage "normative altruism," by which it is implied that the concern for others is supported and elicited by a vast social network of tacit and explicit rewards and punishments. Such altruism, while generally taken for granted, is probably as necessary for social cohesion as it is for the maintenance of a variety of social institutions.

Normative altruism is generally (though not always) characterized by low personal risk and cost to the actor. Giving a few dollars to the Heart Fund, offering a lady a seat on the bus, giving a stranger directions or a hitch, helping someone with a flat tire, and returning a lost wallet are all generally painless. Not contributing to the solicitor's charity leaves me open to his silent contempt and to the risk of being similarly treated when I appeal for my own charity. This is not to say that there are not individuals for whom these acts of giving derive mainly from inner commitments to particular causes, and from a deep concern for other people. It is to say, however, that by and large and for most people, there is a widely accepted and well-understood matrix of reward and punishment governing these acts.

The critical issue for normative altruism, then, is the application of social rewards and punishments. It is well known, for example, that personal solicitations for charity are more effective than mail solicitations, that drivers are less likely to pick up a hiker on the road than at a toll booth, and people more likely to offer a seat to a neighbor than a stranger.

There are altruistic acts that appear to differ from a normative altruism in that no apparent system of reward and punishment exists to legitimatize them and thus their impetus appears to derive mainly from the self. Let us call these acts of "autonomous altruism." Exemplars of autonomous altruism include those who were links in the southern part of the Underground Railroad or who were generally active in the abolition of slavery (cf. Tomkins, 1965, in this regard), those who rescued Jews in German-occupied territories during World War II (cf. London, this volume), or who worked in a leper colony during the time when it was believed that leprosy was a highly communicable disease.

Much as it is possible for normative altruism to be motivated by inner concerns, it is also possible for autonomously altruistic actors to achieve social rewards if the acts are successful. But commonly, no such reward can be anticipated: the very opposite is more likely. The southerner risked being a social pariah, the rescuer risked being killed or imprisoned. Indeed, in many instances, autonomously altruistic actors tend to be relatively anonymous, safeguarding themselves against obvious dangers on the one hand, but guaranteeing themselves few social rewards for success on the other.

It is already clear that autonomous altruism is not only unsupported by the social matrix of reward and punishment, but often flies in the face of it. Being a rescuer during World War II, or a link in the Underground Railroad, or a civil rights worker in the 1950's, exposed the actor to ridicule at the very least and extreme personal danger quite commonly.

Notice that our examples of autonomous altruism, apart from indicating that they seem not to be governed by immediate reward and punishment, also involve great risk and sustained action, while the common examples of normative altruism do not. It can therefore be held that there is more than one dimension involved in this analysis and in the data we shall present shortly. Such an argument may be true, in fact. Conceivably there can be low-risk, brief-contact, autonomous altruism much as there can be high-risk and sustained normative altruism. But a priori logical considerations dictated an initial study which employed a single dichotomy only, since the very fact that there were risks and that the behavior was sustained in the face of danger strengthened the inference that it was autonomous. By the same token, the behavior that was not personally costly and not sustained strengthened the inference that it was determined by the social matrix. As we shall soon see, such a priori considerations availed us little in the long run. The central matter of this paper distinguishes two kinds of ostensibly autonomous altruists, but let us hold this issue for the moment.

Theoretical Considerations

While normative altruism is presumably maintained by a matrix of relatively immediate rewards and punishments, autonomous altruism is more difficult to understand. This is particularly true for those psychological theories that are predicated on tension reduction and justify any behavioral act according to the degree to which it directly gratifies the actor. Learning theories, while they can account quite well for normative altruism, are hard pressed to find the reinforcers that maintain autonomous ones, since these are defined in part by the apparent absence of reinforcement. Similarly, psychoanalytic theories which look to personal gratification as the single determinant of behavior have difficulty accounting for behaviors which are so directly addressed to the gratification of others. Both kinds of theory, learning and psychoanalytic, have reacted rather dramatically to the issue of altruistic autonomy. They have *decreed* on the basis of little concrete evidence, that there must be "something in it" for the actor, even when nothing is apparent.

Needless to say, it is possible to rationalize altruistic behaviors into current theoretical frameworks. Mowrer (1960, p. 435), for example, raises the possibility that what we call courage may simply be the absence of fear where fear is ordinarily to be expected while Glover (1925), Freud (1937), and Fenichel (1945), in the psychoanalytic tradition, suggest that the dynamics of guilt and self-destruction, or conflicts about masculinity may variously be called upon to account for altruistic behavior. Rationalization to theoretical compatibility is not a substitute for evidence, however, and we need to begin to assemble hard data to determine whether altruistic phenomena support or injure current psychological conceptions.

At the same time, it is worth conjecturing that the phenomena of altruistic social autonomy may alert us to dimensions of personality theory and function that have not been fully incorporated into the current popular view. There may, in fact, be dimensions of concern for, and commitment to, others that are functionally autonomous from direct reward and punishment, however much they were initially founded on them.[2]

[2]Maimonides (1135-1204), in his *Golden Ladder of Charity,* attempted to describe a continuum of charitability which ranged from that which was totally dominated by social and egocentric concerns to that which was autonomous in the sense described here. His scheme is worth examining. The first and lowest level of charity, said Maimonides, is to give:

but with reluctance of regret. This is the gift of the hand, but not of the heart.

The second is to give cheerfully, but not proportionately to the distress of the sufferer.

The third is to give cheerfully and proportionately but not until we are solicited.

The fourth is to give cheerfully, proportionately and even unsolicited; but to put it in the poor man's hand, thereby exciting in him the painful emotion of shame.

The fifth is to give charity in such a way that the distressed may receive the bounty and know their benefactor, without being known to him.

The sixth, which rises still higher, is to know the objects of our bounty, but remain unknown to them.

The seventh is still more meritorious, namely, to bestow charity in such a way that the benefactor may not know the relieved persons, nor they the name of their benefactor.

Lastly, the eighth and most meritorious of all, is to anticipate charity by preventing poverty; namely, to assist a reduced brother...so that he may earn an honest livelihood and not be forced to the dreadful alternative of holding up his hand for charity....

The Altruism of Civil Rights Workers

The present study sought to examine the antecedents and correlates of acts of altruistic autonomy, acts which seemed relatively remote from the matrix of immediate reward and punishment. The focal samples for the study consisted of people who had been active in the civil rights movement prior to 1961. Activity on the behalf of civil rights can, like other altruistic acts, be determined by a variety of considerations. Membership in civil rights organizations and contributions to such organizations may be determined by convictions about civil rights, by pressure from one's liberal friends, and by the passing fashion of the moment. It was felt, however, that activism, and particularly activism which involved considerable personal inconvenience and sacrifice, would more likely be determined by considerations that were relatively remote from the immediate presses of reward and punishment. Consequently, the sample that will be described here was divided according to whether or not the respondents had been activists on behalf of civil rights; activism was evident in either participation in freedom rides or in extensive commitments to education and organization of the black people, mainly in the South.

Our concern was to determine whether there were differences between those people whose concern and commitment seemed profound and enduring and those whose commitments seemed more ephemeral, and to delineate these differences theoretically. We were concerned with conditions that sustained such altruistic behavior and the antecedent experience that might have promoted it. Were all these people neurotic, as psychodynamic theories would commonly argue? Were they in any detectible way, self-seeking? Since psychological and social determinants of behavior are complex, not to speak of the general hazards of interview studies, such a study cannot fully explain the many issues associated with altruism. It can, however, yield hypotheses that are amenable to more refined examination, while sustaining their relevance to altruism as it occurs in society.

METHOD

Setting

Interviewing for this study was initiated late in 1963 and continued through the spring of 1965. It was concerned with the people who had been active in, or had financially contributed to the civil rights movement up to and including the summer of 1961. Times have changes greatly, and it will be well to remind ourselves what the civil rights movement was like in that period. Action for civil rights was not widely supported during the late 1950's and early 1960's, and activists on behalf of civil rights were often stigmatized as radicals and "kooks." Such activity as there was was overwhelmingly characterized by pacifism and moral suasion. Although some black militant groups were being formed, most black leaders disavowed separatism and the use of violence as vehemently as they did white supremacy. The dream was of a society moving together, an integrated society in which all men had equal rights to equal things without reference to color. Black leaders understood the potency of confrontation techniques, but those confrontations, manifested in freedom rides, boycotts, and marches, were intended to be peaceful. Although they did not end always peacefully, disorder was not intentionally provoked by the civil rights activists. Rather, they followed closely the Ghandian model and nonviolence was their cardinal principle. The central concerns of these workers were equal rights and integration. Equality of education was the signal issue, but nor far behind were voting rights, poverty, rights to employment, and rights to freedom of transport. The battlefield was still almost entirely in the South. It was then difficult to anticipate that it would spread to the North, to its cities and its slums, and to the universities.

Subjects

With the cooperation of the Student Nonviolent Coordinating Committee (SNCC) and the Congress of Racial Equality (CORE), we located 92 people who had contributed financially to or participated in civil rights activities. Nearly 80% of these respondents were either from urban and suburban centers of the Northeast (mainly, New York, New Jersey, Connecticut, and Massachusetts) or had spent significant amounts of time there. Clearly there is a geographical bias in our sample, but we cannot evaluate its significance as a determinant of these kinds of activities.

Of these 92 respondents, 68 provided usable interviews for this study. Of the remaining 24 subjects, 18 participated in pilot studies which were necessary to organize and structure the interview schedule, to determine which of the many directions that such an interview might take would be most profitable, to pretest the structured interview, and to train the interviewers. Two additional subjects refused to participate, and the remaining four respondents were unable to complete the interview, three because of other pressing commitments, and one because the interview proved too distressing personally.

We explained that the project was housed at an eastern university, and that its purpose was to establish an oral history of this phase of the civil rights movement by examining these events through the eyes of the participants. Since the interviews lasted for as long as 12 hours, mainly in blocks of 2 hour sessions, this entailed no small degree of cooperation on the part of our respondents. Needless to say, we are grateful to them for their efforts.

In order to facilitate the interviews and to minimize the difficulties in perspective and response (cf. Pettigrew, 1964), two experienced interviewers were used, a black one for black respondents, and a white one for whites. However, the black interviewer was female, while the white one was male, contributing some confounding of unknown magnitude to the study. Black interviews tended to run somewhat longer than white ones, but beyond this tendency, no further differences were observed.

Table 1 shows some of the characteristics of the respondents grouped by their color and the nature of their contributions.

TABLE 1

Characteristics of the Respondents

Characteristics	Activists		Financial supporters	
	Black	White	Black	White
Males	6	23	4	14
Females	2	5	3	11
Age in 1961 (years)				
Range	17–48	19–58	21–42	19–56
Mean	26:4	27:1	26:1	29:1
Years of education				
Range	5–16	10–19	10–18	11–19
Mean	11.9	13.2	11.5	14.6
Average annual income($)				
1961	2750	3800	4200	9100
1962	3100	4250	5100	9725
Number of married respondents	1	13	7	20

The Interview

Generally speaking, the interview was conic in structure, beginning with fairly general questions, and ending with quite specific ones. The interview schedule probed the following three areas.

The Facts of Involvement

How did the respondents become involved in the movement (precipitating circumstances) and what, in detail, was the course and nature of their involvement? We asked about dates, people worked with, perceived and actual risks, degree to which missions were accomplished, and material and psychological gains and losses. In this section we "shaped" the respondents to give us as much detailed information as was possible, communicating to them that everything they had to say was of interest to us.

Personal History

This section dealt with such matters as vocational and educational history, relationships with parents, siblings, peers, teachers, and authorities, family and social history, perceived and actual social class, health and appearance, psychological difficulties, and associations with and feelings about deprived groups, minorities, and "underdogs" throughout the course of their development. By and large, the goal for this section of the interview was to obtain a detailed personal history that might be suitable for clinical evaluation.

Perception of Own and Other's Motivations for Participation

In this section we elicited their views on their own behaviors, their philosophies and ideologies, their views of behaviors of others who were like them or different from them, and their views of the "opposition."

SIMILARITIES AND DIFFERENCES BETWEEN PASSIVE AND ACTIVE SUPPORTERS OF CIVIL RIGHTS

In this section we summarize the difference between passive and active supporters of civil rights activity. It will be a brief summary because there is little more to say here than is obvious from the data in Table 1. Except for income and education, which was lower for blacks in both categories, there were only small differences between black and white respondents. Consequently, our analysis combined black and white respondents for each of the two categories: personal participation and financial support. Financial supporters had larger incomes than those who were personally active, which is precisely what should have been anticipated. They were more likely to be married, and as a group tended to be better educated and older, though not significantly so.

Although there were disappointingly few differences that we could locate between these groups, I will pinpoint what they were, as well as describe the similarities between the groups. By and large, both groups came from liberal backgrounds, which is to say that their families were at least attitudinally predisposed toward the human, rather then the institutional side of issues. Where their families were conservative, they seemed to be principled conservatives. Overwhelmingly, they described themselves and their parents as Democrats who had supported Roosevelt and Truman and who endorsed the then current administrations of John F. Kennedy and Lyndon B. Johnson. The parents of the financial contributors, regardless of their liberal or conservative interests, devoted most of their energies to their businesses or professions and to their children (the respondents). As with their parents, the financial contributors themselves tended to limit their membership and activity mainly to church and professional organizations. Indeed, despite the articulation of strong integrationist attitudes, most financial contributors were strikingly inactive. Their strong expressions of faith in the integrationist ethic appeared not to provoke additional engagement of any kind for the organizations to which they belonged. They were neither organizational busyworkers who faithfully attend meetings, stuff envelopes, and make posters nor those who plan policy or solicit support from the public. Although their financial support in many cases seemed quite generous, it appeared to cost them little relative to their financial resources. Moreover, as a group they tended not to value money highly and so their contributions could hardly be seen as a large subjective personal sacrifice. Finally, their contributions were commonly elicited by the appeals of others, usually friends, or by newspaper stories of very moving or tragic, but essentially transient, events.

Consistent with these observations was an interesting finding regarding the potential role of conformity pressures and of attitudinal homogeneity in the financial support for civil rights. To a larger extent than the activists, the financial supporters tended to have friends and associates who were themselves supporters of civil rights. Perhaps because there were fewer civil rights activists or because many of them had been away from old friends for some time, the current friends and associates of the activists tended to come from a broad spectrum of opinion and activity vis-a-vis civil rights.

THE PARTIALLY COMMITTED AND THE FULLY
COMMITTED

In the course of rereading and recoding these interviews (to be frank: in the hope of finding further differences between the above groups that might justify the effort that went into the project) we discovered quite by accident (though it does not seem that way now) that among the physically active respondents we actually had two subsamples. The first had been involved in civil rights only to the extent of having participated in one or two freedom rides. The second had been continuously active for at least a year, commonly longer, mainly in the South with such diverse projects as voter registration and education of the under-privileged. We have yet to find nonevaluative labels for these two groups. Convenience rather than descriptiveness allows us to call the first group—those who went on one or two freedom rides—the Partially Committed, while those who remained physically active in the South for a year or longer are labeled the Fully Committed.

We now had two groups of subjects whose behavior vis-a-vis civil rights was identical in all apparent aspects except the duration of the activity. Duration of commitment, however, particularly under the stressed conditions that marked such commitment, might very well be a signal criterion for differentiating altru-istic behavior which is autonomous from that which merely seems to be auton-omous. Thus, it might very well be one thing to go on a freedom ride with one's friends, and with one's courage bolstered by the cameraderie and intense feeling of the occasion, and quite another to engage in such behaviors over long periods of time where there may be little cameraderie and large cumulative personal risks. We therefore abandoned our analysis of financial contributors which had proved so disappointing in any event, and concentrated instead on the two subsamples of activists: the Partially Committed and the Fully Committed. Table 2 summarizes their descriptive characteristics.

By and large, no significant demographic differences were evident between these two groups except for income where, as might be expected, the Fully Committed earned considerably less than the Partially Committed. There were, however, two striking differences between the Fully and Partially Committed which emerged from the depth interviews, differences which I will elaborate here. The first difference concerned the affective relationship to the socializing agents during the respondents' formative years, and the second dealt with the kind of socializers to which they were exposed.

TABLE 2

Characteristics of the Partially and Fully Committed Altruists

Characteristics	Partially Committed		Fully Committed	
	Black	White	Black	White
Males	4	12	3	10
Females	1	4	0	12
Age in 1961 (years)				
Range	20–48	20–58	17–29	19–51
Mean	29:8	28:4	24:1	25:5
Years of education	5–16	11–19	8–13	10–19
Mean	12.7	12.5	11.0	14.1
Average annual income ($)				
1961	3170	5100	2050	2066
1962	3700	6200	2100	1650
Number of married respondents	0	8	1	5

The Role and Function of the Altruistic Socializer

It was not difficult to obtain reliable reports from the respondents regarding whom they felt was the main socializing parent during their formative years. The primary socializer, invariably, was referred to more often during the course of the interview than adults said to be less influential by the respondent. Table 3 summarizes our judgment regarding the quality of the relationship between the primary socializer and the respondent during the formative years of the latter. Furthermore, the quality of the relationship established then persisted to the time of the interview with little change.

Fully committed respondents seemed to have formed and maintained a positive, cordial, warm, and respecting relationship with their parent (and often with both parents). Indeed, while general discord in familial relationships proved hard to code reliably, the Fully Committed seem to have come from families which had been and still are in good psychological health. True, there were disagreements between parent and child. True, also, these disagreements often extended to matters of considerable importance to both the respondent and his parent, including the matter of whether the respondent should be active in the civil rights movement. Despite this, one easily sensed considerable fondness between parent and child. Even where there was serious cause for disagreement, they seemed to be able to tolerate and respect each other's view.

TABLE 3

Affective Valence toward the Primary Socializer [a]

Valence	Fully Committed	Partially Committed
Positive	12	3
Negative or distinctly ambivalent	3	18

[a] $\chi^2 = 15.55; df = 1; p < .001$

In contrast, the Partially Committed tended to describe their parent (or parents) in negative or ambivalent terms. Many described their relations with the socializing parent as downright hostile during their formative years and at best, cool and avoidant during the time they were interviewed. One sensed discomfort, often anxiety and hostility, sometimes guilt of an unspecified nature flowing from child to parent and perhaps vice versa. There were some instances of fairly brutal handling by parents, and several cases of respondents who had run away from home. By comparison, the problems that the Fully Committed had with their parent seemed trivial indeed.

More striking than the quality of relationship, however, was the cognitive substance, if you will, of the relationship. Both sets of socializers were concerned with moral issues; indeed, during the first coding when we examined merely "moral concerns in the socializing agent," we could locate no differences. But one or both of the parents of the Fully Committed were themselves fully committed to an altruistic cause during some extended period of the respondents' formative years, while the parents of the Partially Committed reportedly evidenced considerable ambivalence and confusion on the nature of particular moralities. At least it seemed so to the respondents, so much so that we had occasion to call their moral confrontations with their parent a "crisis of hypocrisy." Table 4 summarizes the coarse grain of these findings.

Some of the respondents' actual remarks may be illuminating in this regard. One of the Fully Committed reported that "my father carried me on his shoulders during the Sacco–Vanzetti parades"; another described how his father fought on the side of the Loyalists in the Spanish Civil War; a third described how his mother "felt close to Jesus and warmed by His teachings. She devoted her entire life to Christian education." Finally, another respondent's father was outraged by the Nazi atrocities and, though overage and apparently disqualified on grounds of health, was finally accepted into the military during the Second

TABLE 4

*Evidence for Discrepancy between Teaching and Practice
by a Socializer[a]*

Discrepancy	Fully Committed	Partially Committed
Present	2	13
Absent	11	3
Evidence unclear or absent	2	5

[a] $\chi^2 = 13.29; df = 2; p < .01$

World War. In short, we seem to have found the presence of altruistic models in the backgrounds of Fully Committed altruists, models whose very behavior apparently influenced the course of their offspring's activities. The matter may not have been so simple as our laboratory studies of altruistic behavior have indicated (Rosenhan, 1969; Rosenhan & White, 1967; White, 1967), but this was our hypothesis after we analyzed the interview data from this project.

The parents of the Partially Committed were also concerned with moral issues but there was evidence of discrepancy between what they preached and actually practiced. Quite a number of the respondents indicated that they had been told one thing, but observed their parents practice another. Often these discrepancies reflected inconsistencies in culturally prescribed principles of conduct, but regardless of source, it was clear that the respondents had noted these discrepancies and had responded angrily to them. Theirs was a crisis of hypocrisy. Thus, one respondent went into a lengthy tirade against his father who had preached a stern honesty but vigorously condoned dishonesty towards members of a cultural outgroup.

In short, while the Fully Committed had positive training for prosocial action, the Partially Committed had mixed or negative training. Financial contributors, it might be added, had little or no training at all for prosocial action.

Further Observations

Two further differences between the Fully and Partially Committed are of interest, one dealing with the length of the interviews and the other with experience in psychotherapy.

Length of Interviews

The average length of interview was 1 hour longer for the Partially Committed (5 hours and 20 minutes) than for the Fully Committed (4 hours and 15 minutes; $t = 2.11$, $p < .05$, two-tailed). That difference was totally unexpected, indeed, quite surprising, since the nature of the interview gave the Partially Committed less to say. Consider the entire first section of the interview, which dealt with the blow by blow description of the involvement. Those who had been on one or two freedom rides surely had less to tell than those whose involvement had extended over a considerable period. And indeed, this was true. But the Partially Committed more than made up for it in the third section of the interview, which dealt with self-perception and perception of others and which rapidly drifted into a discussion of the philosophy of civil rights. Here, the Partially Committed were brilliant and compelling, offering up insight after insight in inexhaustible profusion. The Fully Committed, on the other hand, had considerably less to say. It was not that they were not as bright: On the dimensions of education and verbal intelligence (the latter assessed from the interview) there were no significant differences between the groups. Rather, they came to the point directly and simply. Perhaps the Fully Committed had exhausted themselves during the earlier parts of the interview. But it is just possible that for the Partially Committed, amplified and reverberated cognition may serve as a substitute for total behavioral involvement, perhaps in the manner described by the sensory tonic theory of Werner and Wapner (1952). On the other hand, having acted, the Fully Committed had less need to speak.

Experience in Psychotherapy

As Table 5 indicates, nearly half of the Partially Committed had spent some period of their lives in psychotherapy, and four of these respondents had been psychoanalyzed for 2 years or more. Only one of the Fully Committed had been in therapy, and then only for two sessions.[3] While it is possible to argue that the Partially Committed had more "insight" into their problems and tended to deny them less than the Fully Committed, our interview data lead to a more simple and direct interpretation: the Partially Committed had more and severer problems than the Fully Committed.

This finding is germane to the theories of altruism cited earlier, and to the evidence presented in psychiatric literature (cf. Coles, 1963; Solomon & Fishman, 1964; Fishman & Solomon, 1964). It would appear that the altruist in that

---

[3]In an earlier publication (Rosenhan, 1969) we overlooked these data and erroneously asserted that none of the Fully Committed had been in psychotherapy.

TABLE 5

*Evidence of Psychotherapy Experience among the
Fully and Partially Committed[a]*

Psychotherapy	Fully Committed	Partially Committed
Yes	1	10
No	14	11

[a] $\chi^2 = 5.12; df = 1; p < .05$

literature who is often depressed and beset by conflicts over aggression, dependency, and identity is likely to be the Partially Committed. And while these conflicts may or may not be relevant to partial commitment, they seem not to be present at all in the genesis of fully committed altruistic autonomy.

TWO VIEWS OF ALTRUISTIC SOCIALIZATION

These data suggest two views of the origins of partial and full commitment. The first stresses the nature of the affective relationship between parent and child. The second leans heavily on the presence or absence of consistency in altruistic socialization.

Affect as Selector

From a child's eye, it can be argued, all parents are indictable on grounds of inconsistency. Children know nothing of the relationship between age and privilege, little of the impact of necessity and impulse on moral judgment and behavior. The younger the child, the less he knows of these matters (cf. Piaget, 1926; Flavell, 1968), but even older ones may have difficulty understanding the factors that lead adults to abandon narrow consistency for a complex hierarchy of moral judgments.

Since all adults are indictable for inconsistency, the central question becomes: What is it that leads one child to select, remember, and model a parent's consistency and to overlook apparent hypocrisy while another attends to and is angered and upset by inconsistency, while overlooking consistency? To some extent, sensitivity to consistency and inconsistency may be a matter of the child's age. Our retrospective data could not shed reliable light on this matter. To a large extent, however, what a child sees in his parents may be a function of his relationship to his parents. Respondents who experienced a positive relationship with their parent were inclined to select, remember, and model those aspects of parental behavior which were socially useful and which the parent was anxious to inculcate. They were less sensitive to the ordinary inconsistencies and examples of hypocrisy that might also have characterized the parent's behavior. Conversely, those who experienced a negative relationship might very well have had a parent who was, in some regard, quite altruistic, but because they came to dislike the parent, they selected and remembered mainly the distasteful and hypocritical aspects of the parent's behavior.

The Crisis of Hypocrisy

A second interpretation of these data, not entirely different from the first, places central emphasis on the crises of hypocrisy. It suggests that the child who is morally polarized by his socializers and is angered thereby will be severe in his judgment of his elder if and only if he is able to see himself as "good" and the elder as "bad" or "hypocritical" on the particular moral dimension or dimensions in question. Avowed sinners, as we know, are quite gentle in their judgments of others; only those who believe themselves without sin can afford to throw stones. But the child, and subsequently the adult, has little basis for internalizing or believing in his moral purity, since he has been exposed to moral models who, insofar as their deeds are concerned, are ambiguous at best and rejected at worst. In order to retain his judgment of bad others, he needs to reassure himself that he is morally good. Going on a freedom ride is sufficient to that need, and having gone on one, there is no real need to engage in another. The actor is already convinced of its worthiness.

Those who grew up in an altruistic environment, on the other hand, respond to the social need for civil rights work from an entirely different matrix. They have learned, by loving precept and percept, to respond easily to the needs of others. Such a response is called forth, as it were, by the structure of the perceptions of the environment. This is, in fact, the meaning of identification: An intense emotional experience, rich in behavioral and cognitive contents, that stamps in a relatively enduring attitudinal and behavior matrix, one that proves relatively resistant to the pressures and temptations of the immediate surroundings.

SUMMARY

All social behavior is the product of an interaction between the impacts of current events and those of prior learning, but some behaviors seem more dominated by the one than the other. Financial contributors to the civil rights movement seemed mainly governed by the press of current events in that they were responding to the immediacies of social reward and censure. Apart from having grown up in a "liberal" home, which might have predisposed them to responding to civil rights causes, their support for these causes seemed to be precipitated by their present social relationships and limited mainly to painless financial contributions. In the hierarchy of their activities and interests, civil rights did not have a dominant or mobilizing status. Theirs clearly seemed to be normative altruism.

Our Fully Committed, on the other hand, seemed very much influenced by identificatory learnings from the past. These learnings consisted not merely of moral precepts, but also of percepts. They were taught not only to believe but to do. Such doing often severely stigmatized them, and was costly in terms of personal risk and effort. Their sustained ability to tolerate high costs and low payoffs, all on behalf of others, leads us to believe that theirs was an autonomous altruism.

And what of the Partially Committed, those whose engagement in the civil rights movement was limited to one or two freedom rides? That they seemed to be conflicted people, at least as indexed by their relationship to their parents and by incidence of psychotherapeutic treatment, is clear. While their activity may very well have been triggered by immediate pressures, their commitment seemed also governed by internal factors, however different these factors were from those that governed the Fully Committed. The latter were certain of their values, while the Partially Committed were still searching. Indeed, at times it seemed to us that the entire involvement of the Partially Committed was inextricably bound to their search for value and their desire to define themselves as valuing people.

REFERENCES

Coles, R. Serpents and doves: Non-violent youth in the South. In E. Erikson (Ed.), *The challenge of youth.* New York: Basic Books, 1963.

Fenichel, O. *The psychoanalytic theory of neurosis.* New York: Norton, 1945.

Fishman, J.R., & Solomon, F. Youth and social action. *The Journal of Social Issues,* 1964, 20, 1–28.

Flavell, J.H. *The development of role-taking and communication skills in children.* New York: Wiley, 1968.

Freud, A. *The ego and the mechanisms of defense.* London: Hogarth, 1937.

Glover, E. Notes on oral character formation. *International Journal of Psycho-analysis,* 1925, **6**, 131–154.

Mowrer, O.H. *Learning theory and behavior.* New York: Wiley, 1960.

Pettigrew, T.F. *A profile of the Negro American.* Princeton, Van Nostrand, 1964.

Piaget, J. *The language and thought of the child.* New York: Harcourt, Brace, 1926.

Rosenhan, D.L. Some origins of concern for others. In P. Mussen, M. Covington, & J. Langer (Eds.), *Trends and issues in developmental psychology.* New York: Holt, Rinehart & Winston, 1969, pp. 134-153.

Rosenhan, D. L., & White, G.M. Observation and rehearsal as determinants of prosocial behavior. *Journal of Personality and Social Psychology,* 1967, **5**, 423-431.

Solomon, F., & Fishman, J.R. Youth and peace: A psycho-social study of student peace demonstrators in Washington, D.C. *The Journal of Social Issues,* 1964, **20,** 54–73.

Tomkins, S.S. The psychology of commitment. I. The constructive role of violence and suffering for the individual and for his society. In S.S. Tomkins & C.E. Izard (Eds.), *Affect, cognition and personality.* New York: Springer, 1965.

Werner, H., & Wapner, S. Toward a general theory of perception. *Psychological Review,* 1952, **59**, 324-338.

White, G.M. The elicitation and durability of altruistic behavior in children. Unpublished doctoral dissertation, Princeton University, 1967.

KIDNEY DONORS

Carl H. Fellner and John R. Marshall

The first renal homotransplantation was performed in 1936, but only the last few years have we ceased to think of it as a clearly experimental procedure, and by now more than a thousand human kidney transplants have been performed (60% from living donors, Murray & Barnes, 1967). The spectacular progress in human organ transplantation in general has spurred public debate of the moral and ethical aspects of human donorship. (See Woodruff, 1964; Nolan, 1966; Starzl, 1964; Beecher, 1968.) Aside from donor physical considerations or those having to do with donor–recipient suitability, it is also the physician's responsibility to protect the donor's right and welfare. The donor must be made fully aware of the many risks he is accepting and of the possibility that his sacrifice may be of little benefit to the recipient ("informed consent"). The donation must be entirely voluntary, free from undue pressure, and must come from a "genuine volunteer." Presently, some renal transplantation teams are insisting on obligatory psychiatric interviews and psychological testing of every potential donor in order to avoid undesirable emotional sequels and to screen out those donors who might be motivated by psychopathological needs (Cramond, Court, Higgins, Knight, & Lawrence, 1967).

In the spirit of this concern for the safeguarding of the donor's rights and welfare, we were approached by the renal transplantation team of our hospital to participate in a routine psychiatric screening of all possible donors. Before acceding to such an extensive obligation, however, we undertook to study all available previous donors to find out how they had become involved, how they had made their decisions, what surgery had meant to them, and how they have fared since.

METHOD

We interviewed the donors, usually in connection with their routine follow-up renal studies. It was made clear at the beginning of each interview that all information was confidential and only general conclusions would ultimately be discussed with the renal team. The interview was conducted in an open-ended fashion with a prearranged questionnaire, and was tape-recorded for future references. The advantage of this technique is that it permits coding of the answers and gives the subject full freedom of expression. The sessions usually lasted 2½ to 3½ hours. A few selected psychological tests, the results of which are noncontributory here, were later administered independently by a psychologist. Of the 20 donors interviewed, 14 were seen at 5 weeks to 24 months after surgery, with a mean of 11 months, and 6 were seen before surgery only. In addition, a number of potential donors who were subsequently rejected as medically unsuitable were interviewed. Another five potential donors who have been interviewed are currently awaiting surgery. In a number of instances, the donor's spouse or parent was also seen and as much supplementary information as possible was obtained from the physicians and nurses of the renal transplant team and from a review of medical charts. There were four mothers and one father among the donors. The rest were siblings. Two of the potential donors awaiting surgery are also mothers.

The medical selection procedure adopted by the renal transplantation team is as follows: When a transplant situation arises, all possible donor relatives are. asked to come to the clinic for blood tests (ABO typing). Great care is taken at this point by the medical staff to inform the volunteer subjects that this is an exceedingly preliminary procedure, and that no commitment whatsoever is involved by their appearing at this clinic, or elsewhere, to have blood samples drawn. Those potential donors who are not ruled out on the basis of blood grouping are then asked to come to the renal clinic for a brief history taking and complete physical examination, including routine laboratory studies. Somewhat later, those possible donors who still remain are asked to return to the clinic for histocompatibility tests. The results of the mixed leukocyte culture tests (MLCT) are not known until several weeks later, and might have to be repeated before they can be read conclusively. Only after this stage does it become possible for the renal transplant team to select from among the available possible donors the most suitable one. This person is then asked to come to the special studies unit at the hospital for a complete workup, careful evaluation of the renal status, etc. During this brief hospitalization he is evaluated independently by at least three of the team physicians. Only at the end of this evaluation and after intensive, repeated briefing on the risks involved and of the chances for success, is the potential donor asked to make a decision, and permitted, if he so desires, to give his informed consent. A final chance to refuse in a dignified and comfortable manner is offered in the team's expressed willingness to supply a plausible medical excuse to the recipient and family.

FINDINGS

In our interviews with the donors we tried to follow events and reactions chronologically from the moment of first communication about renal transplant, through the selection process, decision making, surgery, postsurgical phase, to the interview with us.

Communication

Only one donor had first heard of the transplant possibility from a member of the renal transplant team. Three had heard directly from the recipient, nine from the recipient's spouse, five from their mother, and two had been told by the family physician prior to the transfer of the patient to our hospital. Usually, communication was by telephone call in which the future donor was told about the seriousness of the future recipient's illness, that the doctors were considering a kidney transplantation, and that all close relatives would be invited in the near future to come to the clinic for some blood tests. Usually, the informant followed this up with a brief discussion of who from among the other family members should be asked to participate, and who should not, and for what reasons. The same route of communication was subsequently used to transmit the results of tests and make further appointments.

Decision Making

We wondered, then, at what point in the long drawn out process that followed this first phone call did the donor actually make his decision? Did he hold off, seek information, consider the facts, and make an informed decision at the end, when all studies were completed and he was asked by the doctors to give his informed consent?

Actually, most of the members of the renal transplant team were aware that most donors were ready to make a commitment earlier than that and had to be held off until the team had made its selection. It was thought that the point of commitment to the procedure was reached about halfway through the medical evaluation process.

Our findings were, therefore, surprising. It appeared that not one of the donors weighed the alternatives and decided rationally. Fourteen of the donors and five of the prospective donors waiting for surgery stated that they made their decision immediately when the subject of the kidney transplant was first mentioned over the telephone "in a split second," "instantaneously," "right away." Five said they just went along with the tests hoping it would be someone else. They could not recall ever really having made a clear decision, yet they never considered refusing to go along either, and as it became clear toward the end of the selection process that they were going to be the person most suited to be the donor, they finally committed themselves to the act. However, this decision, too, still occurred before the session with the team doctors in which all the relevant information and statistics were put before them and they were finally asked to decide.

There was one donor who had a good deal of trouble in arriving at a decision. This was a 48-year-old lady, mother of four, a very frightened person whose defenses were organized along strict obsessive–compulsive lines, and who said: "I get worked up over every little thing, and I have never had surgery before." The immediate family consisted of the father, a diabetic who was therefore disqualified right away, the mother, and four children of whom two were under 18 years old. The oldest, a daughter who could have been a potential donor, immediately refused to participate in any way and would not come even for the preliminary blood tests. The second child was the recipient. The first communication that a renal transplant would be necessary came from the doctor who had treated this son. The mother, now the only potential donor, said that "I was thinking all along, should I do it, or not." She went to see her family physician who advised her not to do it. Her daughter was against it. Her husband told her "You make your own decision; don't listen to relatives." She continued with all the preliminary testing, very ambivalent about it, "hoping the test would be good, then hoping the test would be bad."

All her tests were just fine and finally there came the day when the team doctors asked the fateful question. At that point, she decided that she wanted to go home first and talk it over with her family again. She then returned, having made up her mind that she was going to donate her kidney to her son and saying by way of explanation, "I guess I had some encouragement from my husband now."

It appears that of all the people asked to come for the preliminary blood tests, there were perhaps eight who did not show up. Of all those who participated in the initial screening tests, there was only one subject who later refused further participation; actually, she wanted to continue but her husband objected to her becoming the donor after raising the question why her sisters had refused to participate in the first place. None of the final potential donors availed themselves of the "last out" opportunity, although there were one or two subjects who seemed glad when they were rejected for medical reasons after the last of the tests (renal arteriogram). This leads us to believe that for all but one of the participants, and by the same token, for all those who refused to participate from the beginning, decision making is an early event preceding all information gathering and clarification offered by the renal team. Supportive evidence for the instantaneous character of the decision making came from a rather unexpected quarter. We spoke to a resident physician whose blood had been used for a control in the MLC test and by the merest chance he had proved compatible with the potential kidney recipient patient. When he was informed of this finding he immediately refused without even having been asked to be a donor and subsequently was able to tell us that this had been an immediate decision and that he had later spent much time marshalling reasons in support of this decision.

Postdecision Period

The next finding that clearly emerged from our investigation was that once the decision had been made by the prospective donor, he carefully refrained from considering further data and engaged in several maneuvers which permitted him never to vary in his decision or even to question it. For example, nine of the donors felt immediately convinced that in the end, after all of the tests had been done, they would be the ones to be chosen and they never wavered in this conviction. Two were less convinced but hoped very strongly to become the chosen ones. Three had initially equally strong convictions that it would be someone else and not they (these were the three donors who had not made an initial decision but had gone along with the tests until the other possible donors had been eliminated). Of the 19 subjects who, as mentioned earlier, made their decision on the telephone on first hearing of the possibility of the kidney transplant, none had consulted his spouse. When questioned about this particular circumstance they all explained that the spouse later on had either been neutral or reinforced their decision. To the hypothetical question of: "What would you have done if your spouse had said no?" they all answered: "I would have gone ahead and done it anyway." Several of the donors volunteered the information that friends and acquaintances had tried to dissuade them but, as one of them put it, "They might as well have been talking to a brick wall."

Another way in which the original decision was being maintained could be seen in the viewing of the rigorous medical examinations as an achievement test which, if passed, entitled the prospective donor to contribute his kidney. Some comments were "Those were tough tests, but I passed," or "It's good to know you are the healthiest of the bunch," or "The doctors would never let me do it unless I were in perfect condition."

For some of the chosen donors, the time of the initial testing and gradual elimination of the other potential donors was quite stressful and they reported feeling greatly relieved and, in some cases, even elated when they were told of the final decision: "I was glad they told me; the suspense is over." "I was relieved when I was told it was me; I feel good that someone could for sure." "When informed I felt elated that it would be me; it was just a good feeling."

With regard to the instructions and explanations offered repeatedly by the doctors of the renal transplant team in an attempt to provide the basis for an informed consent, the donors all reported that they had not really been very curious or interested in what the doctors were telling them. Almost uniformly, this information was used in exactly the opposite way to that which was intended. The prospective donors reasoned in the following manner: All of the doctors are making an effort to tell me the bad possibilities, which means that they must be honest and therefore capable and I can place my life in their hands without any danger. One donor said: "The doctors were straight with me; I trusted them completely." Another said: "All the doctors said the same thing. They had nothing to hide. They were good." One female donor said: "What the doctors said went in one ear and out the other." She was content to leave the details to the doctors: "They know what they're doing."

A number of prospective donors reported that they had found it very helpful to be able to talk to patients who had previously undergone kidney transplants, as well as to their respective donors. According to their statements, only positive feelings and reassurances were expressed by these informants.

Several of the donors interviewed stated that the most difficult time for them came after the other would-be donors had been eliminated and they were now waiting for the surgery. They "wanted to get it over with." The ambivalance of one of the three donors who had passively gone along without making a decision showed when he expressed his feelings about that difficult time by saying: "It was like a death sentence hanging over me."

The Family System of Donor Selection

In addition to the medical selection system and the donor self-selection described, we believe that there is a third, or family, system of selection in operation. This is rather difficult to demonstrate but, in retrospect, it seems possible that the difficulty arises from the general expectation, which we initially shared, that the family would tend to select a likely donor in the sense of a sacrifice or scapegoat under threat of family ostracism. We could never demonstrate this in our sample, except perhaps in one rather questionable case. What we finally came to see was that a family would *exclude* certain members from participation. This was done most commonly at the time of the initial contact. In one family, the father successfully dissuaded his two sons from even coming for the preliminary blood tests, and his wife from participating beyond the halfway point, and ended up as the triumphant donor himself. In another family, the mother tried very hard to beat out her son in competition for donorship, but lost. One woman, who became the donor for her son, had never mentioned that the father of the recipient, from whom she had been divorced years earlier, was alive and well. One donor who gave up a kidney for his brother explained afterwards that the family decided not to call upon the grown son of the recipient since there was bad blood between father and son over the divorce of the father and mother.

Actually, once the different potential donors are known to the renal team, the power of the family system to influence the medical selection process diminishes greatly. The renal team has learned to be somewhat distrustful of family communication and to be alert to its potential misuses.

The Postoperative Period

Kemph (1966, 1967) has described a period of depression beginning 3–5 days after surgery and lasting for varying lengths of time. Brief supportive psychotherapy was clearly required in every case. According to Kemph,

> They were usually seen every day for two weeks after surgery for supportive psychotherapeutic interviews of 15 to 60 minutes duration, the time varying with the need of the individual patient.

As far as the dynamics of such depressive reactions went, it was Kemph's interpretation that the donors felt depressed and unrewarded for a maximal sacrifice, and resentful of the much greater amount of attention shown to the recipient.

Our own findings, based on the self-report by the donors plus a review of the hospital charts and discussion with the renal team who followed these patients, did not reveal any evidence of the depressive reactions observed by Kemph. None of our subjects had feelings of being neglected or treated less well than the recipient. Of the 14 subjects we interviewed, one female donor reported a period of nausea and mild depression several days postoperatively, which lasted 1 week. Another female donor experienced a period of crying and mild depression and homesickness during the first 3 days postoperatively. One male donor experienced an acute panic reaction which lasted only a few hours on the third night after the operation. He said he woke up and suddenly realized that he had been in a situation of great danger and "it dawned on me that so many things could have gone wrong."

The comment is often made that donors "give up something and get nothing in return." This is a frequent theme in discussions on the ethics of organ transplants in general. The postoperative depression is related to this by some authors, but usually the general unfairness of this exchange is quoted without further substantiation. By contrast, all of our donors reported that this had been a very meaningful experience in their lives, of substantial impact on them, and that it had brought about changes in them which they felt were beneficial. There appeared to be two overlapping phases to this experience. The first began just prior to and continued through the immediate postoperative period, usually a month or two. During this phase they received a good deal of attention from their families and friends and also from strangers who had heard about their sacrifice either by word of mouth or read about it in the local newspapers.

Our subjects were rather hesitant to talk about this attention out of a sense of modesty but seemed relieved when we gave them the opportunity to verbalize their feelings and share them with us.

They related how this attention made them feel "good," "noble," "bigger," "happier," and generally increased their self-esteem. They all added, some with disappointment, that this attention rapidly diminished and they soon ceased to be celebrities. It was at this point, later, that they noted certain changes in their attitudes or ideas of themselves which they considered more lasting. The following are representative quotations:

> (A 30-year-old female donor, 12 months postoperatively.) I have much more confidence; before, I was more afraid of what people would say. . . . . I feel I am a better person, much happier than before . . . . The whole of my life is different. I've done something with my life.

(A 25-year-old female donor, 3 months postoperatively.) I am a better church goer, we think of it as a miracle .... I take things more seriously now. I am careful to lead a good life, perhaps I'll be rewarded later. I was a real snot; I feel I was chosen, to teach me. Now I think of others more. My marriage is better, closer now. I was lucky for the opportunity.

(A 40-year-old male donor, 4 weeks postoperatively.) I feel better, kind of noble. I am changed. I have passed a milestone in my life, more confidence, self-esteem .... In every way I am better. For realizing how far I could go for others, I am up a notch in life .... I value things more, big and small things .... I come in contact with others a bit more. My pleasures are bigger and have more meaning.

(A 31-year-old female donor, 15 months postoperatively.) I have done a lot of growing up as a result of this. I am much more responsible. People say I act older .... It gives me inner satisfaction. When I have moments of depression, I think of my sister. I am happy.

(A 38-year-old female donor, 8 months postoperatively.) I keep thinking how fast it all was and I plan for now rather than the future. We are taking a trip this summer I have been putting off .... I changed, things are more trivial now. I do feel good but more mortal now.

(A 59-year-old female donor, 18 months postoperatively.) I feel I am a better person for having done it, more understanidng, not nearly as critical. I have improved in many ways, even am more respectful of myself as a person. I feel, if I can do this, I can do anything.

One 31-year-old male donor who had undergone considerable life-saving surgery in his childhood said: "I had always wondered whether God had been saving me for something. I knew from the beginning that this was it; it balances things out. I feel bigger now, a better person. It's time I got something out of it. I'm not going to work as hard or be as compulsive. I'm going to enjoy life more now. I'm aged and wiser now. Somehow more considerate and tolerant." One donor who had been on leave from the service for the purpose of donating his kidney said: "I had never done anything like it before. I have always been drifting along with the tide and this is the first time I did something worthwhile. I felt good whilst I was up here; felt more optimistic towards life at first and about my own potential but when I got back to base I got into a rut again; all seemed to stop. The service has done something to me."

When the subjects were asked to compare the act of having donated a kidney to any other act in their lives of equal importance or consequence, most of them could not do so. One of the subjects did compare it to volunteering for a dangerous mission during the Korean War: disarming an unexploded bomb to save the lives of his comrades. A female donor compared it to giving birth to a child. Another female donor compared it to having once saved a child from drowning when she was 16 or 17, but quickly added that it did not really compare in intensity and effect. None of the others could come up with comparable events or actions in their own previous lives and likened their action to a feat of heroism that "ordinary life just doesn't give a person a chance for." There were two exceptions to this particular feeling: two mothers who had donated their kidneys to a son seemed to feel, as one of them put it, "Something had to be done and mothers do more for their children ordinarily anyway. It was not such a big thing."

In addition to describing their own personal gain in terms of increased self-esteem, etc., several of the donors also remarked that the whole family had somehow changed for the better, had become closer, was drawn more together and emerged with a new and positive feeling of unity as a result of the kidney transplantation.

COMMENT

We would like to comment on two points: (a) The immediate decision making and subsequent strategies to adhere to that decision and avoid modifications thereof and (b) the impressive increase in self-esteem and self-perceived changes in life style as a long-term result.

When a person is faced with a decision between two alternatives, his behavior is expected to be oriented toward making an objective and impartial evaluation of the merits of the alternatives. This usually takes the form of information seeking which probably continues until sufficient confidence is acquired that the preference will not be upset and reversed by subsequent information. At this level of confidence the rational person then will make a decision (predecision process).

Contrary to this expectation, we found that our donors made an immediate major decision, before even inquiring into the possible consequences for themselves, or seeking reassurance as to the eventual benefits for the recipient.

A brief review of the literature on decision making did not prove very helpful in our attempt at understanding this particular behavior. It appears that the decisions which a person makes in an experimental situation mostly come about by a very sane and rational process, yet casual observation and personal experience outside the experimental situation show that occasionally decisions are made on a rather impulsive basis or based on some minor or trivial aspects, even in important matters. More helpful were the discussions of the postdecision process, and we found consensus on the view that once a decision is made and the person is committed to a given course of action, the psychological situation changes decisively (Lewin, 1951; Festinger, 1957, 1964). After a decision has been made, there remain a number of things the person knows that are inconsistent with that decision, which create what Festinger has termed a state of cognitive dissonance. Reduction of that dissonance may then begin in several ways (increasing the attractiveness of the chosen alternative and decreasing the attractiveness of the rejected alternative), and the subject's main tendency to justify the decision is manifested.

The cognitive dissonance theory is interesting because it postulates the conflicts before and after decision making to be dynamically different, and offers experimental support of this theory. In our study, there was a marked difference from the usually described triphasic process (from predecision conflict to decision to dissonance). The donors avoided the predecision conflict either by making a split-second decision (yes or no) or by pretending not to decide and to go along passively and let the selection process decide for them. The postdecision dissonance was handled rather as predicted by theory, and in all our cases the decision was upheld and the subjects remained committed to their course of action, even in instances when the final action had to be postponed for long periods of time. The longer the time span between decision and action, the greater was the dissonance.

The second major point concerns the impressive increase in self-esteem and certain reported changes in life style by the donors. It is possible that this might be a temporary feeling which will diminish as time passes but we think not since we interviewed several of these donors more than a year after surgery. If this finding is as extensive as our small sample would indicate, then the prevalent idea that the donor "gives something but receives nothing in return" should be reexamined.

We felt a plausible explanation might be derived from crisis theory (Caplan, 1964):

> Crisis involves a relatively short period of psychological disequilibrium in a person who confronts a hazardous circumstance that for him constitutes an important problem which he can for the time being neither escape nor solve with his customary problem-solving resources. During the upset, the individual works out a novel way of handling the problem through new sources of strength in himself and his environment. The upset then abates, and he returns to psychological equilibrium and consistent behavior [p. 53].

The new pattern may differ from the previous one and become stable, since it is then maintained as the new equilibrium.

This kind of phenomenon may have occurred in our donors. A postcrisis equilibrium can move in a positive or in a negative direction (in other words, beneficial or harmful life-style changes), and Caplan further points out how the direction of resolution may be influenced by the resources present either internally or externally. We saw no indication of detrimental feelings or attitudes related to the surgery. The forces on the donors in a positive direction came from several sources: (a) their belief in the "good" they were doing for the recipient, saving a life, (b) their positive relationship with their physician, both actual and symbolically, (c) the positive emotional reinforcement from the recipient and family, and (d) the considerable attention paid to them by friends, acquaintances, news media, etc.

Actually, we should not be surprised that an act of altruism such as this can and does have far-reaching positive effects in the life of a person. After all, it is in keeping with the highest ideals of our society, in a time and age which does not offer much opportunity for public acts of courage and devotion in which one can transcend oneself. We found that for our group of donors, their action had provided them with a peak experience, or as Maslow (1962) says, an experience in which "the IS and OUGHT merge with each other instead of being different and contradictory," and which "can be considered to be truly a religious experience in the best and most profound, most universal, and most humanistic sense of the word."

It seems to us that the two points discussed here are related. Regardless of theoretical considerations, the fact remains that as far as we could ascertain from our sample, the concept of "informed consent" is just another myth. We would interpret this to mean that the physician's responsibility to safeguard the rights and interests of the donor go even further than heretofore conceptualized. However, in weighing the "pros and cons" for a potential donor, we must also be very much aware that to give a kidney is not solely a liability but can become a turning point, a peak experience of considerable positive impact on the overall life development of the donor.

REFERENCES

Beecher, H.K. Ethical problems created by the hopelessly unconscious patient. *New England Journal of Medicine,* 1968, **278,** 1245–1430.

Caplan, G. *Principles of preventive psychiatry.* New York: Basic Books, 1964.

Cramond, W.A., Court, J.H., Higgins, B.A., Knight, P.R., & Lawrence, J.R. Psychological screening of potential donors in a renal homo-transplantation programme. *British Journal of Psychiatry,* 1967, **113,** 1213-1221.

Festinger, L. *A theory of cognitive dissonance.* Stanford, Calif.: Stanford University Press, 1957.

Festinger, L. *Conflict, decision and dissonance.* Stanford, Calif.: Stanford University Press, 1964.

Kemph, J.P. Renal failure, artificial kidney and kidney transplant. *American Journal of Psychiatry,* 1966, **122,** 1270–1274.

Kemph, J.P. Psychotherapy with patients receiving kidney transplant. *American Journal of Psychiatry,* 1967, **124,** 623–629.

Lewin, K. In D. Cartwright (Ed.), *Field theory in social science: Selected theoretical papers.* New York: Harper, 1951.

Maslow, A.H. Lessons from the peak-experiences. *Journal of Humanistic Psychology,* 1962, **2,** 9–18.

Murray, J.E., & Barnes, B.A. The kidney: Introductory remarks on kidney transplantation with observations on kidney transplant registry. *Transplantation,* 1967, **5,** 824–830.

Nolan, B. Ethical problems in renal homotransplantation. *British Journal of Urology,* 1966, **38,** 680–684.

Starzl, T.F. *Experience in renal transplantation.* Philadelphia: Saunders, 1964.

Woodruff, M.F.A. Ethical problems in organ transplantation. *British Medical Journal,* 1964, **1,** 1457–1460.

AUTHOR INDEX

Numbers in italics refer to the pages on which the complete references are listed.

SUBJECT INDEX

A

Adventurousness, 245, 246
Alienation, 9, 13, 14, 26, 247-249, *see also*
    Anomie, Apathy
Animal altruism, 106, 108-110
Anomie, 206, 207, 217, 217f., *see also*
    Alienation, Apathy
Apathy, 14, 18, 20, 24-26, *see also* Alien-
    ation, Anomie
    contagion of, 15, 18
Apology, 185, 194, 195
Approval, desire for others', 43, 44, 59, 70,
    149, 150, *see also* Self-esteem
Attribution, *see also* Responsibility
    of motives for helpfulness, 30, 31, 35-37,
        39, 40, 231-238
    of responsibility to self, 219-226
    to victims, 207, 208, 213, 214,
        217-228
Awareness of consequences, 6, 122, 128-139,
    see also Norms, salience of

C

Children, altruism in, 4, 61-71, 103-123, *see
    also* Developmental factors in altruism
Choice, freedom of, 129, 130, *see also*
    Attribution of responsibility, Reac-
    tance
Class differences, 92, 93, 148, 257, 259-261

Compensation, 7, 8, 100, 155-160, 185-188,
    191-194, 196-201, 210, 215-218,
    221, *see also* Guilt, expiation of, by
    benefiting third person
Confession, 7, 158, 185, 186, *see also* Self-
    punishment, Apology
Consistency, *see* Hypocrisy

D

Definition of altruism, 2, 3, 84, 103-106,
    108-111, 244, 251-254
Dependency, 129, 130, 147, *see also*
    Responsibility, norm of
Developmental factors in altruism, 5-9, 13,
    61-63, 71, 103-123, 137, 165,
    172-176, 247-249, 261-267
Distortion, *see* Responsibility, denial of;
    Victims, evaluation of

E

Emergencies, help in, 3, 4, 13-26, 80, 81,
    92-96, 100, 132, 245, 272-273
Empathy, 2, 3, 5, 8, 61, 83, 105-123, 144,
    248, 249
Equity, 6-8, 105, 145, 174, 180-202,
    215-218, *see also* Compensation;
    Guilt, expiation of, by benefiting
    third person; Reciprocity

288